SHADOWRUN:
HELL ON WATER

JASON M. HARDY

SHADOWRUN: HELL ON WATER
Cover art by Victor Manuel Leza Moreno
Design by Matt Heerdt

Published by Catalyst Game Labs,
an imprint of InMediaRes Productions, LLC
PMB 202 • 303 91st Ave NE • E502 • Lake Stevens, WA 98258

FOR AISLYNN,
WHO WAS WORTH WAITING FOR

CHAPTER ONE

Listen to me. I am going to tell you this story because I am the one who knows it.

How do I know it? What kind of question is that? When you go to market, do you ask the merchant where he got his breadfruit? No! You just buy it and are happy that you have it! So do not wonder how I know what I know—I just know it. It is my job to know. And I am not even asking you to pay me to tell you what I know. All you have to do is listen.

It starts with Akuchi, which is a good thing. Many, many good stories start with Akuchi. Do you know any of them? Should I tell some of them to you?

All right, all right, you want to hear this one. Perhaps, along the way, we will have time to hear some others, *abi*?

So Akuchi is here, he is in Lagos, and he is charging through the streets like a rhino set to fast forward. And no, you may not ask me how a rhino is to be set on fast forward, because that is not important. When I said that, an image came to your head, didn't it? The image of the rhino, moving very fast? That is enough, then. That is all you need, is the picture. The other thing, the mechanics of it, are unimportant.

Akuchi is moving through a city where most of the people are on foot and he is on wheels. Two wheels, one for each person sitting on the machine, for Akuchi has a passenger. Akuchi sits on the front of the bike, leaning forward, looking through the red dust that is everywhere, making moves in anticipation of obstacles that are far ahead of him. He drives the bike like a chess grandmaster, while the people around him in the street are novices who wouldn't know a rook from their own asses. There are hundreds of them, thousands of them, tens of thousands, the people of Lagos who are in the street during the day because they know how many things there are in the night that can kill them, so they must do all their living while the sun remains in the sky. They make it difficult for people on vehicles to move, but Akuchi has known for a long time how to make his way through such a crowd, and he does it.

It is with some regret that he occasionally hits someone. How is it to be avoided when he is moving so fast among people who are so slow? He is gentle, they are only glancing blows, but a glancing blow from a speeding bike is enough to send people stumbling and staggering away, falling into other people or merchant stalls, hitting the ground and then pivoting and shaking a helpless fist at the bike that is already far past them. Sometimes Agbele Oku looks back at these people who are on the ground, but her face shows no regret. No anything, really.

Yes, yes I *did* mention her. I said that two people were on the bike. Agbele Oku is the other. She sits on the back. Her fingers tingle, because she knows of many ways she could help push people out of the way without having to touch any of them, but Akuchi has told her no, that is not yet necessary. Save your strength, he has told her. I can get through this on my own. We may need what you have later. Soon but not now.

They are in Kosofe, and there is a long trail of dust behind them. Most of it is the slowly settling dust left in Akuchi's wake, but some of it is the dust raised from the sad, tired tramping of the Lagosians through the streets, and some of it is from the sudden collapse of an old abandoned building that, many years ago, was first stripped of its wiring, and then was stripped of all metal that could be taken from it, and then was stripped of the pieces of solid wood that could be used to light fires, and then there was enough stolen that there was little besides dust holding it up, and so it collapsed not long after Akuchi passed it by.

He makes a maneuver then, on the way to the docks, that is a thing to behold. He presses the throttle, darting forward and left, then hits the brakes just as he is about to run into a broad wagon packed with melons, raises the bike on its front wheel, nearly throwing Agbele Oku off over his head, pivots, then makes that front wheel accelerate again, running forward before he can fall on top of it, outracing the momentum of his own inertia as he executes a pinpoint pivot and dashes through a small opening in the crowd that was not there a fraction of a second before.

It is none of my concern if you are not familiar with bikes equipped with front-wheel drive. I am telling you what happened as I know it happened. You, you can go back to your equipment manuals and catalogs and what have you and figure out what model he had purchased or what adjustments he made in order to make that maneuver. All that matters is the fact that he did it.

He is moving close to the docks now, and he feels himself relaxing. The docks will make everything easier. There are pirates and ammits in the water, of course, but there are far fewer of them than there are people on the streets. He will have room to maneuver on the water, and that is all he wants. He will be able to outrace anything, he believes, and if he can't, he will have Halim. Halim, as I am sure you must know, is a most valuable insurance policy to have.

In fact, there are moments when the crowd shifts and Akuchi sees Halim. Halim is standing there, tall and broad, arms crossed, sword visible over his shoulder, which is a stern warning in a city that is very hard on people who carry weapons without knowing how to use them. People in Lagos quickly learn that any statement you make about your own capabilities is likely to be challenged by someone in short order. And so you do not make such a statement unless you are always prepared to back it up.

Halim is always prepared to back it up.

When Akuchi sees Halim, he also looks for the tiny woman that should be near the ork, but does not see her. He does not worry about her, though. Groovetooth is a dwarf and easy to overlook, just like the mouse after which she is named. She would be especially small next to Halim's orky bulk. Halim looks calm and ready, and Akuchi believes that must mean Groovetooth is either there or nearby.

So Groovetooth and Halim are accounted for, and Akuchi, of course, knows where he is and knows where Agbele Oku is, for they are both right there. That only leaves the matter of the two *oyibos*, the people Halim brought in. Hopefully they are there or close by. Hopefully they are alive. Hopefully the wind and the sun did not conspire to tear away their fragile, pale skin and grind them into the dust that is everywhere.

Akuchi does not know this, but the two *oyibos* are not far away. They are hampered by the fact that they are on foot, but the one in front is large and wears his dark, armored vest like a skin, and his white T-shirt underneath gives clear indications that he is sweating heavily, but it does not seem to bother him in the least. He strides with heavy purpose, and he glares at everyone in front of him and his glare has a simple meaning and that is this: *If you do not get out of my way,* the glare says, *bad things will happen to you, and possibly to your ancestors.*

People on the street in Lagos have a certain experience with people. They know who they should be wary of and who poses no threat. They know which threats can be carried out and which ones are empty. And when they see the threat conveyed by this man's glare, they move out of his way.

No one would move out of the way of the second man if he were on his own. He has a deceptively casual stride, a walk that looks effortless until you realize he is keeping exact pace with the bigger man in front of him. He has a hand in his pocket and a light smile on his face, and he seems to take great enjoyment from the fact that people move out of his companion's way so easily. He looks at these people with laughter in his eyes, and those that see this are not sure if he is laughing at them or laughing at some larger, cosmic joke that they are not privy to, but they do not much care. For as long as the smaller man is with his larger companion, there are many things he will be able to laugh at without concern of consequence.

The larger man barks orders at the few people who do not see his glare or try to withstand it, and the low rasp of his voice finishes the work that his eyes started. He cannot move as fast as Akuchi, of course, because he is on foot, but he has a clear path whenever he wants it. He does not need to nudge anyone out of his way. There are even some area boys who are drawn to this man's path, who see the way he is clearing for himself, and think that perhaps this is someone they should challenge and humble, but then they see him, and they slink into that pose that attempts to say, "I'll let you go by this once," but really says, "I know how this would end for me, and it is not good."

The second man, walking through the path cleared by the first, speaks.

"Just shoot a few of them," he says. "You're armed, you know. That would get them out of the way faster."

The first man, who is called Cayman, turns to the second man, who bears the somewhat unlikely moniker of X-Prime, but also answers to Alex. "When did you get so bloodthirsty? I'm not killing people just because they're in my way."

X-Prime shrugs. "That's fine," he says. "But really, most of them are going to be dead pretty soon anyway. Gangs'll get them, or they'll get sick and die of this catchy new VITAS III.V thing that's all the rage these days, or they'll just finally get tired of living in this hellhole, and they'll drop dead where they're standing. Nine out of ten people here, you kill them, it's a mercy killing."

Cayman, he grunts while continuing to move through the crowd without drawing a weapon.

The timing of this group, as it turns out, is quite good. Just as Cayman catches sight of Halim, standing like a firm rock in the swarming sea of people around him, he hears the sharp whine of Akuchi's approaching cycle. He doesn't bother to look for the rigger—he has full confidence that Akuchi will get where he is supposed to be. He just quickens his pace, and lets X-Prime jog behind him to keep up.

Cayman and X-Prime arrive at Halim's side just as Akuchi brakes his cycle to a stop. Agbele Oku is off the bike quickly, ready to move, and Akuchi is beside her.

Cayman looks quickly at the members of the team. "Where's the mouse?"

Groovetooth steps from behind Halim, frowning at being overlooked. But she is difficult to see, small and wiry, or at least wiry for a dwarf, dressed in casual clothing that would be at home in hundreds of countries across the globe. Her hair is tied in several pointy, spiral knots, which she hoped would make her look tough, but her large brown eyes and narrow chin mitigate whatever aggressive effect her hair might have had. She would look sweet and gentle no matter how she did her hair, and perhaps someday she will realize that her appearance is a strength, because it leads people to underestimate her, and not be prepared for her to be as ruthless as she is.

"Everyone got everything?" Cayman says, without any words of greeting or questions about the others' well-being. The others nod, except for Akuchi, who says "Yup" in a way that seems to take five seconds.

"Let's get out of here, then," Cayman says, and the six of them travel toward the docks.

They are in the eastern section of Kosofe, near the entrance to the Third Mainland Bridge, but they are not going to take the bridge. They are busy people, and they are not going to waste time with all the nonsense that a trip on that bridge entails. No, they have a boat tied up near the bridge, and they will get on the boat and cross the lagoon in safety to get where they need to go.

They jog, moving together, and the crowds thin because these people are not the only people who do not want to deal with the bridge. If you have common sense and enough resources to travel some other way, the bridge is to be avoided, but it is fortunate for the toll-takers and other bridge dwellers that there are enough people in Lagos who have neither, which means traffic on the bridge is regular, if not crowded.

But there will be more time, plenty more time, to talk about the bridge. Right now we are concerned with the boat the six people are running toward. The boat is a simple affair, but it has a big engine. The six people may not be extremely comfortable on the wooden bench seats of the boat as they ride it south, but they will not be on it long because it has an engine that will start with a roar and continue with a putter and will take them quickly where they need to go, and then all will be well.

Akuchi does not normally use boats, as he has plenty of ways to get around the city without having to deal with the occasional frustrations of the lagoon, but with conditions on land being as they are, a boat seemed like the best alternative, so Akuchi used some of the generous pay he received for this mission to buy the boat. When the mission is over, he plans to keep the big, wonderful engine on the boat and repurpose it somehow. The rest of the boat he will sell to scavengers, who will likely chop it up and make it into the wall of a house.

This is the boat to which they are running, this is the end they have in mind, but their plans are changed dramatically when that engine, that wonderful, precious engine, develops a problem once the runners are within one hundred meters of it. The problem is that it goes from being a single large, stationary thing to being many small things that are flying quickly through the air. This transformation is accompanied by a *flash* and a *boom*, and suddenly the runners no longer have a boat. All they have is shrapnel, and it is flying in all directions, and one of these directions is toward them. They drop to the ground, assume defensive positions, and wait for the ringing in their ears that followed the *boom* to depart.

There were startled actions in the crowd around them when the engine made its dramatic transformation, but the frightful moment has passed and the good people of Lagos quickly return to their normal business—at least, that is what the ones that do not have a piece of outboard motor embedded somewhere in their body do. No one stops to ask the team of six people on the ground if they are all right, for they rightly assume that it is none of their concern. As it happens, all of them are okay, as if the hand of God tossed the engine pieces around in a way that avoided these six people. They stand up, brush the ever-present red dust off themselves, and take a moment to be pleased that they are alive and unhurt.

Then they all look at the smoking remains of their boat. A discussion is incipient, and it falls to Cayman to commence the proceedings.

"Shit," he says.

"Yes," Halim says, adding no further elucidation.

"We could just go through the city," X-Prime says. "Get a car or something, we all climb in, it wouldn't be that bad. Would it?"

The other five look at him as if to check to see if a piece of engine shrapnel did not end up lodged in the part of his brain responsible for logical thinking.

"We would make it," Halim says. "But it would take a long time."

"It's just getting more crowded," Groovetooth adds. "There's lots of people out there, most of them are mad, and the people they're mad at are right where we want to go. So they're jamming up the roads, and they're not being too good about letting anyone traveling south get through."

"Then it's the bridge," X-Prime says. "It doesn't look too crowded up here. We take the bridge."

Cayman looks at the other members of the group to see their reaction to this proposal, and they take it silently. Cayman has heard stories about this bridge, and he knows it is to be avoided if possible, but in the end it is nothing more than a long road, *abi*? And any road can be traveled.

"Maybe we could take Akuchi's bike, or find some other vehicle," X-Prime says. "Get us there a little faster."

Halim shakes his head. "No. You do not take vehicles on the bridge."

"Why not?"

No one chooses to relieve the *oyibos* of his ignorance at that moment. Instead, the four Lagosians who are in the group look at each other and nod.

"If the bridge is what we've got, then that's what we'll take," Akuchi says.

CHAPTER TWO

And now I must tell you something of the Third Mainland Bridge.

The bridge is a wonder and a marvel, mostly for all the wrong reasons. It is one of three bridges in Lagos that connects the heaven of Lagos Island to the hell of everything else, and it is the longest. Nearly twelve kilometers long, it is tons upon tons of concrete dropped into the water of Lagos Lagoon. It is an engineering marvel, in the past it has been the longest bridge in Africa, but it is my sad duty to tell you that it is quite ugly. There is no grace to it; it is a concrete road on concrete pillars and that is all it is. The designers lacked either the resources or the vision to make anything beautiful out of this project, and so they just built a road on the water. Nothing more, but, for much of its existence, nothing less.

Now, though, it is less. Much less. It will shock no one who knows anything about Lagos to learn that the bridge has been neglected for many years, and during that time of neglect parts of it have cracked and parts have crumbled and parts have gone down into the water. The people of my city, of course, are creative and entrepreneurial, and there are those who have found ways to make the holes in the bridge work for them, and thus it is still possible to traverse the entire length of the bridge, thanks to the efforts of those who would ferry you across the gaps. It is slower, it is more expensive, but in its backward, dilapidated way, it still functions. Much like everything else in the city.

This is the bridge Akuchi and Halim and Cayman and the rest are set to cross, and this is the journey they must make. Twelve kilometers south. Then their mission will end.

They are strong and healthy, these six. Traveling on foot, without obstacles or delays, they could travel twelve kilometers in short order—in, say, less than two hours. Given the various obstacles and delays of the bridge, Cayman believes they can make the trip in two and a half to three hours. The boat, of course, would have had them there in fifteen minutes or so, but the boat is gone and not to be dwelled on. Three hours is quick enough. If they get there in three hours, Cayman tells himself, everything will be fine.

So they walk, and they make progress, because the northern part of the bridge is in fine shape. The crowds are sparse, there are no people who wish to cause them trouble, and the travel is rapid. One kilometer, two kilometers are traveled, and less than fifteen minutes have passed. It is a wonderful pace they are keeping! It is good that they take this opportunity to make time, for eventually they will come to something that will slow them down, and then, just like that, "eventually" is now, and they see a gap in the bridge, one hundred meters long, and a line of people near the gap waiting for their turn on the ferry. The line moves down a rickety staircase to a platform, and the ferry is a line of boards spanning the distance between two pontoons. It has an iron hook at one end, and a rope runs through it and connects the raft to a cable that spans the entire hole in the bridge. Men stand at either end of the raft, grab the cable, and pull to propel the ferry back and forth, and the rope keeps the craft from drifting off course. When it is heavily loaded, the muscles of the men strain, and the ferry does not travel quickly. But it always moves.

There is a line, as I said before, but as Halim sees it, there are two lines. One line is for most people, and the other is for those who understand that they do not have to wait if they do not want to. That line is for him.

He walks past the occasionally resentful glares of the people waiting in line, with the other team members following him down the stairs. He does not care if they are angry with him, since he does not believe any of them will do anything about it. He also does not worry about how the ferry captains will react to his jumping to the front of the line, for they are capitalists. Any objection can be overcome with the right offer.

Unfortunately, Halim's timing is not good. He arrives at the lower platform just as the ferry reaches the other side and starts unloading one group of passengers and loading the next. It will take at least five minutes for the ferry to return. Not a large delay, it is true, but Halim has never enjoyed being still when he could be moving.

A glance at the black flag on the back of the ferry tells him that the Black Rogers are in control of this ferry, which is just fine with Halim. They are murderous scum, true, but they are murderous scum whom Halim understands. He can work with them, and that is all that matters.

The loading and unloading proceed at a reasonable clip. Halim looks at the water and finds it is almost pleasant to be here, as long as he does not think about the poisons that are in the water beneath him. The water is cooler than the air, so a breath of a gentle breeze occasionally stirs near his feet, and since the water tends to suck in the dust the air is somewhat clearer here. He does not like to wait, but it is not a terrible spot in which to be.

But then there is the puttering of a motor, and the spot becomes worse. It is a motorboat coming from the south, and the engine is struggling because it is overloaded. There is no flag flying from this boat, but as it approaches, the five people in it stand and, in unison, unsheathe curved, sparkling swords. That gesture is all Halim needs to see. These are members of the Razor Cutlasses, and they clearly have decided it is time for control of this ferry to belong to someone else.

Halim looks back to the two men pulling the raft across. They are straining, pulling hard, trying to get to the other side. There is panic in their eyes. Halim scans the area, looking for reinforcements. Surely the Black Rogers did not leave these two as the only guards on their ferry? But there is no sign of anyone else.

It must be the disease, Halim thinks. This strain of VITAS that has a good portion of the city dying while the rest roil about in perpetual near-riot. The Black Rogers are undermanned now, and the Razor Cutlasses are about to take advantage of the fact.

Halim reaches for his sword, but then thinks better and pulls out a carefully maintained Browning Ultra-Power. He prefers face-to-face combat, but any warrior must understand that there is a time to engage your enemies at a distance.

"What are you doing?" says a raspy voice, and it is Cayman. "Who are you planning to shoot?"

Halim waves his gun at the approaching motorboat. "Them," he says.

"Not our fight," Cayman says. "They're not coming to trash the ferry. They'll off the two guys on the boat, then they'll take over business. It'll only take a few minutes."

Halim raises his gun. "This is faster," he says. He fires, and one of the Razor Cutlasses drops into the water.

Cayman curses and drops to the wooden platform, which bobs lightly as he falls. Groovetooth and Agbele Oku move back, and Halim looks at the mage with scorn. Groovetooth he understands—this part of the fight is not her thing. But Agbele Oku could help if she wanted to. Instead, she is holding back, waiting. She will not be involved unless she feels it is necessary.

Cayman has a gun out that makes the pistols X-Prime and Akuchi are holding look like toys. Halim motions those last two back. They can be the second line of defense. If he and Cayman cannot handle this alone, then they do not deserve to travel any farther.

There is yelling on the ferry, and one of the Black Rogers has let go of the boat and dropped to one knee. He has retrieved an AK-97 from somewhere and is firing on the Cutlasses, but he is untrained, and the recoil from the rifle sends his arms skipping about, so his rounds hit mostly water. Then the Cutlasses, who have handguns as well as swords, make an accurate shot, and the Black Roger goes down.

Halim is squeezing off shots methodically. The Cutlasses had turned their boat after their first member fell, and they are running parallel to the broken end of the bridge, making them harder to hit. But the boat is not fast, and it does not take Halim long to adjust. He squints, aims carefully, and fires.

"Watch the—" Cayman says, but whatever it is he wants Halim to watch is lost in a peppering of gunfire. Shots from the Cutlasses dig into the wood beneath him, but Halim has made himself too small a target. They do not hit him.

Then Halim finds the range, and he manages to dispatch two of them with three shots, and Cayman kills one as well. There is one Cutlass left.

Now that Halim has found the range, it should be an easy shot. He is thrown off briefly as the Cutlass abruptly jerks to his right, his arm swinging out. Halim fires, and so does Cayman, and two splotches appear on the pirate. He falls into his boat.

"Dammit!" Cayman says as he jumps to his feet, and Halim wonders what he is upset about. The fight went quite cleanly, and Cayman cannot be upset about the death of the one Black Roger. They will get the ferry across just fine without that man's help.

Then a thin trail of smoke helps him see what had drawn Cayman's wrath. Just before he died, the last Cutlass took a final shot. Not at the Black Roger, not at Cayman, not at Halim, but at his own boat. He buried a bullet in the engine, and it did what it was supposed to. Fluid was leaking out. The engine was dying. It would have been a slow replacement for Akuchi's former boat, but it would have been better than walking. But now it was dead.

Halim returns his attention to his companions and finds that Cayman is glaring at him.

"What was that for?" Cayman says. "That wasn't our fight."

Halim jerks his head at the fallen pirate on the boat. "They were Razor Cutlasses," he says. His voice is so low that it sometimes hits a frequency that humans can feel, but not hear. "Yorubamen. They do not need to be taking this place."

Cayman rolls his eyes. "Can we stop with the tribal bullshit? At least for the rest of the day? I really don't care which group in your city doesn't like the other right now. Let's get the job done and save the other nonsense for another time. Preferably when I'm not in this city any more."

Halim makes sure he can talk calmly before he replies. "You only believe it is bullshit," he finally says, "because it is not *your* tribe."

Then, thankfully, the need for further conversation is ended. The ferry and the one surviving Black Roger have arrived, and the pirate will likely be more than willing to take Halim, Cayman, and the others on board, especially if they offer to help haul the ferry. They will be across in five minutes, and they will be moving. Halim wonders how Cayman can be dissatisfied with this result.

Meanwhile, at another point in the city, there is a person that I will call Sir for the moment because that is what everyone else calls him. You may wish me to call him by another name, his given name, but as long as I am telling the story you will have to content yourself with the way I am telling it.

Long ago, the people with money in Lagos discovered that there were two ways to escape the heat, the stench, the dust, and the other assorted miseries that pave the streets throughout most of the city. One way is to retreat to their enclaves on Lagos Island. Another is to build to the only parts of the city that remain untouched by the filth that is everywhere, and that part is the sky. The wealthiest and most powerful people combine the two, and live in high aeries above Lagos Island that allow them to pretend that the rest of the city does not exist.

Sir works in offices that are larger than the combined dwelling places of any six Lagosians, and he welcomes a stream of visitors who all have one thing in common—they all are desperately hoping to give Sir something that he wants, so that he might give them something in return.

This task is difficult for the current set of visitors, for their efforts to please Sir are both easy and hellishly difficult. It is easy because they have been tasked with reporting news to Sir about the conditions of Lagos, and thus all they have to do is deliver some sort of report, and they have fulfilled their duty. Sadly, though, most of the news they have come to report is very much not good. And so while they are diligently doing their job, they are forced to tell Sir very unpleasant things about his city, and they cannot be sure how he will react to this.

These messengers have tried to convince Sir that there are many convenient electronic ways to deliver the information he is looking for, but he brushes all their suggestions aside. He is not a technophobe, not by a long shot, but he believes news items should be delivered by people who know what they are talking about and who can answer any questions he might have. And so the largest news bureau in the city is not a professional organization, but is the force of hackers and reporters that roam the streets and the Matrix looking for news and reporting back to Sir. There is a steady stream of them, all day, moving from the subtle lighting and tan-and-brown carpet of the hallways to the blaze of sunlight streaming into the floor-to-ceiling windows of Sir's office. His windows face south, because everyone knows that the best views in Lagos are the ones that include as much of the ocean and as little of the city as possible.

Walking into the office can be nerve-wracking, because one never knows where Sir will be. He may be behind his desk, but more often he will be walking here, strolling there, or standing somewhere out of sight only to emerge silently and suddenly when a messenger enters, scaring the poor soul half to death by suddenly looming over them and snapping "Yes? Yes? What do you have to say?" Sir is a large man, and when he looms over you it is somewhat like an angry god looming over a sinful mortal.

He has been especially impatient with his messengers this morning, dismissing most of them before they finished their news. "Sir, reports say that residents of the mainland are demanding medications be released from corporate—"

"Sir, reports of Tamanous activity have surged, and many people believe they have harvested VITAS victims, which could of course lead to the spread—"

"Sir, traffic in the mainland is completely gridlocked. People will not leave—"

None of them finish, because none of them are saying what Sir wants to hear. Either with a wave of his hand, an angry shake of his head, or even just an icy stare, Sir silences the messengers and sends them away.

Then another messenger comes, an area boy with tight, ropy muscles and wide eyes that hunger in many different ways. He has been to Sir's office three times before, and each time he believed Sir was going to strike him before his message was complete. Even though the blow he has feared has not yet fallen, he steps into the room with worry and trepidation.

He walks ahead on the thick burgundy carpet and looks for Sir. There is no sign of him. He doesn't hear the sound of him pacing ahead, but then the carpet absorbs many noises. He can only see a corner of the large black desk, so he cannot know if Sir is behind it. He takes a few more steps, and then the desk chair comes into view. It is empty. The sunlight here is bright but not blinding, thanks to the polarized windows. He still cannot see Sir. He takes a few more steps, clears his throat and tries to say something, but a word will not form.

Then he hears a book—a *book*, of all things!—slam shut, and heavy footsteps coming toward him. Reflexes kick in, and the messenger jumps backward and almost runs away. But he holds his ground as Sir rounds the corner and towers above him. He doesn't say anything, and the messenger knows if he does not quickly say what he has to say, than things will not be well for him.

"Sir, I've been told, that is, I've been asked to say that the things—Sir, the packages—Sir, those three packages you've been concerned about? They are on the way. They have been retrieved, and they are on the way."

Then tension drains out of Sir. A day's, a week's, a month's worth of worries fade away, and Sir smiles, and the messenger is entirely unnerved.

"Wonderful," he says. "You have done well. What is your name?"

And for a few brief moments, the messenger cannot remember.

CHAPTER THREE

ONE HOUR BEFORE THE BRIDGE

Now, at this point, I must say that as I was describing how Halim and Cayman fought the Razor Cutlasses, I saw in my mind that I was not telling the whole story that needed to be told. The story showed how Halim is gifted with a gun, but that is not his native mode. To truly understand how Halim fights, you must see him in the way God intended him to be. You must see him hand-to-hand.

Fortunately for us, we do not have to go very far in order to see that. We only need to move slightly backward, two hours before the unfortunate Razor Cutlasses met their demise at the wrong end of Halim's gun, to see Halim in his true element.

Two hours before that encounter, one hour before he embarked on the Third Mainland Bridge, Halim was in the streets, alone, assured that Groovetooth was where she was supposed to be, and that he would soon meet her there. The streets were difficult to cross, as I have mentioned, and there was a certain amount of pushing and shoving involved in Halim getting to where he needed to go.

Halim is not holding a weapon. He is carrying many, yes, but none of them is in his hands. In his hands, he holds only a package. It is a box, not much larger than his palm, black, with some sort of fake leather exterior. It is oddly cool to the touch. It is sealed tight by mechanisms that Halim has not taken time to investigate and that he will not take time to investigate. For that is not his job. He is delivering the box to its intended destination, and that job does not involve knowing what the box holds.

Besides, for someone like Halim, the contents of the box are a simple mechanism, *abi*? A reason for him to travel from place to place, a reason for him to try to do something, and others to try to stop him. That is how he lives, that is where he is comfortable, walking forward against the current of people trying to stop him. The box he was carrying made it more likely for someone to want to stop him than if he was just walking alone, and he was just fine with that circumstance. He was tempted, occasionally, to lean into someone, to catch them extra hard with his shoulder and make them mad so that they would be goaded into fighting with him. But that would be a violation of his code of conduct. He can fight people, and he can even provoke fights with them, but he cannot provoke fights for a reason no better than the fact that he feels like fighting. If he did that, he would just be a street thug, and Halim is not a street thug.

He knows, though, that he does not need to pick a random fight with some anonymous passerby. There were people in the city who are quite willing to fight him, and they were looking for him, and there was a good chance that they were getting closer. There were some, four people, that he just dispatched, and it was not entirely unpleasant, but it was also not entirely fulfilling. So, he would be happy for another opportunity, and he had the feeling he would have one soon. Groovetooth had not told him anything about any other people out there, but Halim was beginning to believe that there was a selective nature to the hacker's knowledge, though how this selection occurred remained a mystery. Without Groovetooth's input, he was left to rely on his own instincts, which had been perfectly satisfactory for him a thousand times in the past.

And then some people moved one way and others moved another, and there was a group of five standing in front of him. One passerby looks at these five and points at them and yells, *"Anya onye ori!"* but Halim did not have the luxury of wondering what they were talking about. They had the rusted seams and inflamed scars of the hastily cybered, and two of them were either wealthy or connected enough to have guns. They were advancing, they were spreading out, and that meant it was time.

Then there was no noise beyond this circle of six people, Halim and his five seeming assailants. The city sounds, the whining engines, the yelling voices, all of it disappeared. Instead it was just his feet scraping over the dust, the cotton of his robe rustling as his hand reached underneath it, the sound of metal rubbing leather as his gun came out of his holster. There were *pop-pops* of

guns from the men down the street from him, and bullets sliced
the air near his head and one hit his chest. It thudded harmlessly
into body armor—it would leave a bruise and a hole in his robe,
which was irritating, but it would not slow him down.

The scraping was loud because Halim was close to the
ground; he was moving fast but felt slow because he could
carefully consider each move. He moved his arm and saw a red
crosshair flying past him through the air, and then it turned yellow and Halim fired. He rolled, he kept moving, and when he
was on his feet his sword was in one hand and gun in the other,
and the heavy breathing of the four goons around him was like
music. His vision narrowed, with the four men in sharp focus and
everything else a dark blur. He felt his robe brushing against his
legs, he saw motion, he reacted. His sword blurred, his gun fired,
he heard grunts. The quieter the grunt, the better, he had always
felt. If they grunt loud, then he had left them with too much energy and life. When they grunt quietly, he has hit so hard and
fast that their body cannot muster any significant sort of reaction
besides falling to the ground.

He was moving quickly, sweat was running down his forehead, but he felt as if his heart rate had slowed. His breathing
was even.

Movement was rapid and fluid. Forward left, swoop down,
lunge, cut, step ahead, skitter right, flow back. Never slow down,
never give them a clean look. He did not look at any of their faces,
he could not describe any of their faces if asked, but he knew their
fighting styles. Two of them are down, three are left, and they
are a brawler, a dodger, and a counter-puncher. As he moved, as
he whirled, Halim could see how they would work together, and
knew he would not let that happen. He had identified their styles,
but they did not yet know what his was, or indeed what *he* was.

They moved, cautiously, staying together, waving a board
with nails through it, a chain, and an iron bar. Halim had a gun. He
could shoot them and be done. But Halim had never been one to
prematurely end a fight.

He moved the sword from hand to hand, spinning it, and
it was all rather unnecessary but quite pretty. His sandaled feet
brushed across the street like dust in the wind, stepping light,
keeping his assailants from landing blows, from knowing what
he would do next. He enjoyed watching them feint, he enjoyed
watching them lunge, and he played with them like they were yo-

yos, moving them toward him, then pushing them away. Then he tired of the game, and his sword blade moved with purpose, and blood made the dust even redder. Halim felt the impact of each blow in his arms, the slowing when the blade hit flesh, the complete stop when he dug into bone, the rough, rumbling pull when he brought his hands toward his stomach and removed the blade from a victim.

There was still more red, red filled his vision, he stepped through red and into red and made more red with every move. Every motion he made flowed into another motion, every move gave power and speed to the next one, like a creek flowing into a stream flowing into a river. Then there was the moment, the single moment everything had been building toward, when it was silent around him, no noise, no scraping of feet or panting of breath, and everything was still. He did not have to move anymore. Every muscle in his body was awake and loose and poised, his brain was alive and sharp, and he was standing tall above the five forms lying on the ground near him. He breathed the moment in deep, his tusks brushed his upper lip, then he exhaled, then it was gone.

The noise of the city around him returned, flooding into his ears. People were shying away from him, especially from the dead people at his feet, but at the moment no one was doing anything about it. No one was calling the authorities about the situation because, as far as they were concerned, Halim *was* the authority, the only one that mattered.

He could see everything again, the buildings, the people, and the blue of the sky peeking through the red dust in the air. He cleaned and sheathed his sword. It was over. This moment was gone. He moved forward so that he might find the next one.

CHAPTER FOUR

The moment Halim had with the Razor Cutlasses, that was not a moment. That was a gunfight, and it is not the same. He had not even had to move that much during the course of that fight. He just dropped to the ground and fired. It had no poetry to it; it was just a simple transaction in which living people were traded for dead ones. He will have to wait a bit more for his next moment, but he would be happy to know that it is not far off. But he did not know, and I am powerless to go back and inform him.

At the ferry, the six runners are, of course, the first people on the raft, and after that there is a pause, as few people are anxious to be the first going onto the raft with them. They look at each other and shuffle, hoping that as they lean toward the ferry that will make another one take a full step, and then they will know it is okay to board, and they will move on. And it happens—one steps forward and many others come in a surge, a push so rapid that the raft heaves under their feet. The surviving Black Roger collects the toll from all passengers, then mans his position by the cable. Cayman is at the same position on the other end of the raft and he starts pulling and the raft moves across the water. The people on the raft, they are very still and quiet. They wait to get to the other side, then they hurry hurry off.

Now comes one of the great secrets of the Third Mainland Bridge. Back in the old time, when the bridge was mostly for cars, you only got on or off at the ends. So a place like this, one of the isolated pieces of the bridge that has collapsed sections on either end, you would expect to be less crowded than the ends. Because people here just passing through, *abi*? No new traffic?

But this is the Third Mainland Bridge of today, not of some other day. There are jutting peninsulas of land that let you walk to it, and boats that let you row to it. And why would people come to it? Because there are pirates, and the pirates have money, and there are flat surfaces away from much of the dirt and chaos of the city itself. Parts of the bridge, they have become their own villages, with merchant booths and shanties and even huts. They are built poorly, held together with wattle or with gravity and a fond wish, but they are there, plywood boards leaning against each other or corrugated metal sheets forming huts that hold incredible heat, and all other manner of improvised, poorly made structures.

And so the walking has become more difficult. The pathway is narrower, the people are more numerous, and they are not still. They are running and biking back and forth, they are haggling and trading, they are fighting and occasionally dying, because there is money coming in here from either end, there are pirates collecting tolls at each gap in the bridge, and where there is money, there are people who want it.

Cayman tries to push his group to the same pace they had made on the north end of the bridge, but it is impossible, so he must go slower. He can see the skyline of Lagos Island ahead of him, maybe eight kilometers away, not so very far, really, but at the same time impossibly distant. He is angry that it is so far away, and his anger is going to be taken out on someone.

Halim is nearby.

"That wasn't our fight," Cayman says.

"You said that already," Halim replies.

"I know. But I'm not sure it sunk in yet. I didn't think I needed to tell you that there's some fights we don't need to get into, but I guess I do."

"It got us through faster. We would have had to wait for the fight to play itself out, and then for the Cutlasses to figure out what they were doing with the boat. I didn't want to wait."

"Yeah, yeah, but it was just...it's..."

"Do you still need me for the remainder of this conversation, or could you just yell to yourself?"

Cayman gives him a glare that he knows will have no effect, and then mumbles to himself for a time as they walk on through the thickening crowd.

The most noticeable thing in a random setting is something that is not random. Cayman has been traveling this way and that to push his way through a particularly crowded section of the bridge village, and he is tall enough to notice that he keeps seeing the same head-tops ahead of him, bobbing when he bobs, weaving when he weaves, and coming closer and closer. It is possibly a coincidence, but very probably not.

"Now this one," Cayman says, "this one is our fight."

Cayman turns to look down at Groovetooth. He raises an eyebrow, but she only shrugs back. There are a few PANs here and there, but no grid. No access to the larger Matrix. No AR overlay. The bridge is bustling, but to her it is eerily empty. I can tell you that she has not been at all comfortable since they set foot on the bridge, and she has nothing useful to tell Cayman about what may be happening.

Cayman looks forward again. He does not even bother asking Agbele Oku if she is going to help, because he has already learned that Agbele Oku only helps when and if she cares to. He believes that she will intervene when necessary to save the lives of anyone in the group—at least, he sincerely hopes that is the case.

Guns are of limited use in such close quarters, unless you are eager for the type of accidental shootings that tend to make fights bigger, bloodier, and more noticeable than they need to be. It is so crowded on the bridge that long blades like Halim's sword will also not be very useful, for there will not be enough room to swing it without hitting either a building, which could collapse it, or an innocent person, which would make the fight overly complicated. And so Cayman opts for a dagger, and Halim flexes his forearm so a blade snaps out of it and locks into place.

Cayman keeps his dagger low, thinking that perhaps the people coming toward him will be willing to talk before any combat ensues, but he is honest enough with himself to admit this will probably not happen.

Then there is enough space and the crowd parts, and Cayman can see more than the tops of the heads of the people coming toward him. They are two humans, a dwarf, and an ork, and there is enough ink in the tattoos on their bodies for me to write out this entire story in longhand. The ork has a brand on his cheeks, the letters "A" and "E," but the rest of his skin is so scarred and uneven that the brand gets lost in the landscape of his face.

They move with the grim determination of people who have done this kind of job before, and know how to accomplish it even if they do not enjoy it. Perhaps they would spread out as they approached the runners if they could, but there is not enough space, so they move ahead in a tight square. They, too, have weapons out, and Cayman looks at them and sees he is in for a good, old-fashioned knife fight.

Cayman believes you cannot overestimate the importance of landing the first blow in a knife fight. He firmly believes that the first person to bleed in such a fight almost always loses.

So when the four come forward with their weapons ready, Cayman advances quickly and aims a blow at the heart of the target closest to him, one of the humans of the group. The target is ready for this, of course, and moves quickly to block the blow, but the direction of the blow has already changed. Cayman has anticipated, is pulling his arm back and away, slashing across the target, and the blade drags across the man's arm, cutting through skin and into muscle and tendon.

To his credit, the attacker doesn't drop his weapon, a metal rod with an unfortunately jagged end. But he hesitates, and that means Cayman can control the fight.

If he wanted, Cayman could play with the target like he was a marionette, pushing here, pulling there, and watching the man react to every move he made. But there was no reason to mess around.

And so Cayman proceeded with various stabs and slices that I do not have the heart to describe in detail, because there is something about knives that puts a cold knot in my stomach. Please be assured, though, that Cayman does some things that are very bad to his target, things that involve hard slashes and multiple kinds of bodily fluids and grunts of surprise and pain, while next to him Halim is doing things that are worse. And the whole time Cayman is waiting for one of the other members of the group to move on him, because this is not a trideo where the combatants attack one by one, politely waiting their turn instead of ganging up on the hero. So he expects to be hit from another direction at any moment, and it is because of this awareness that he sees the ork moving around him and heading toward the people in back of him. Heading toward X-Prime.

Cayman runs. *That boy, that X-Prime,* Cayman thinks, *cannot defend himself against a fly, let alone a charging ork.* And the boy (who is actually more than thirty years old, but will forever be a boy in Cayman's eyes) seems to know it too, as there is panic in his eyes. Both of his arms are wrapped around a package, the package they had retrieved just over an hour ago in an extremely annoying fashion, he is clutching it to his chest and leaning backward. Like a stupid boy, a boy who does not know how important it is to keep his balance. He will have few options against the ork now, he will be pushed around and pummeled at will unless Cayman helps, and the ork knows it, he is closing fast, Cayman can hear a guttural growl in the ork's throat, his blade is ready to slash X-Prime as soon as he is in range, and he is quite unprepared when abruptly one of X-Prime's arms unfolds, and there is a holdout pistol in his hand and he fires it at the ork's head.

A holdout pistol is usually not enough to stop a charging ork, particularly the little lemon-squeezer design X-Prime is holding, but it is enough to startle him. The ork's growl becomes a roar, his head leans back, and Cayman gets a clear view of the flechette sticking out of it, but the ork is still moving forward, and now he very much wants to rip X-Prime into many small pieces.

X-Prime, though, did not just sit there and wait after he fired his gun. He was already moving when the round fired, sliding to his left, and the ork had to adjust, turning and moving and waiting to slash into the short, annoying man, but the delay and the move to his right have cost the ork, because Cayman is there now and his knife, which was already red, is prepared to do more work. Cayman slashes up and pulls his arm to him, cutting the ork under his arm. It's a hard cut to make, there is armor and tough ork skin to get through, but Cayman is slashing hard, and he found a way through the defenses. The cut is not deep, but it assuredly hurts.

The ork howls, starts to turn, but then there is a second flechette sticking out of his eye now, and that will have an impact. Ruining a creature's eye, Cayman knows, is not always fatal, but it is most certainly always critically demoralizing. People do not just jump up to fight more when their eye has been ruined.

The ork goes down. Cayman sees that X-Prime is now standing with exemplary balance and poise, and for perhaps the hundredth time he wonders how long it would be before he stopped underestimating this boy that he had been forced to mold into a runner a number of years back.

He shakes his head and starts to speak but the ork takes the opportunity to remind him that two flechettes are not normally enough to finish an ork. He is on the ground and his right foot flies up, an awkward but swift kick aimed at X-Prime's gut. X-Prime is balanced, but he is not ready for the speed of the blow, while he moves back the foot catches his arms and the ork's toes hit the box he was carrying and send it flying.

Now, it may be that you have not fought in a crowded place very often, so it is my duty to inform you that shooting a bullet horizontally into a crowd presents problems, while firing a bullet downward is a simpler, less perilous affair. Cayman has his hand-gun out, a weapon with much more punch than X-Prime's little holdout, and he fires it so that the bullet makes a path into the concrete of the bridge by way of the ork's skull.

X-Prime is already retrieving the package that had been kicked out of his hands. It had hit the ground near Cayman and broken open, and X-Prime is furtively stuffing the contents back inside and closing the box. He is fast and smooth, but Cayman gets, for the first time, a look at what it is that they are carrying. The first thing he sees is the hair, black and wiry and curled, and then he sees the odd, leathery fabric that is holding the hair, and when X-Prime scoops up the object he sees the brown and crimson underside of it with all its ragged edges, and then he recognizes it for what it is.

They had been tasked with carrying three packages to Lagos Island, and Cayman now knows that one of those packages held, until very recently, a human scalp.

CHAPTER FIVE

FOUR HOURS BEFORE THE BRIDGE

Everyone knows that a professional runner only knows what they are supposed to know and then does not worry about other things. When you are at an oasis, you do not concern yourself with how much desert is around you, and when you are in the desert you do not waste time thinking about oases. You worry about what you have to do, and that is all.

But a runner may be good and professional, but a runner is still a metahuman, and a metahuman is generally curious, which must be the way, or all our collective species would not have survived as long as they have.

We should take a moment and look into the minds of Cayman and X-Prime when the box opened, and what we will see is something we will not understand until we first look at them when they found the package, four hours before X-Prime dropped the package on the bridge.

They were in a dumpster. Or, to speak correctly, they were next to a dumpster, having a discussion about going in it.

"Get the hell in the dumpster," Cayman said.

X-Prime looked at the dumpster, which once was white, but now was mottled with many colors, most of which were unspeakable. "Mmmm, no."

"I wasn't asking."

"I'll just look in it and see if I see a package." X-Prime stood on his toes and scanned the inside of the dumpster. "Nope, don't see anything that looks like a package."

"Who says it would be on the top?"

"Who says it wouldn't? Why would someone bury it in the dumpster?"

"Maybe they didn't bury it," Cayman countered. "Maybe it's just been there a while and now it's covered."

"You know what they're paying us for this job, and you think that whatever it is we're picking up, the thing that is worth so much to them, might have been left sitting in a dumpster for a few days?"

Cayman looked around. Other than flies, X-Prime was the only form of life he saw. There were empty tan buildings, most with at least one portion of collapsed roof, and there were empty lots filled with the type of rubble that is left once the scroungers of the sprawl have given everything careful repeated goings-over. "I think it might be kind of safe here if they did. Anyway, the point is we're supposed to be good at what we do, and being good means being thorough, and you weren't thorough when you looked in the thing just then. So get in there."

X-Prime did not say anything for a time. He opened his eyes a little wider, which made him look even younger and more inno-cent than was his custom. He remained silent.

"What?" Cayman finally said.

"Where's the threat?" X-Prime said.

"What threat?"

"The threat of whatever it is that you're going to do to me if I don't do what you say? Come on, there's plenty of stuff here you can use. Maybe you'll break my back over the edge of the dumpster. Or maybe you'll go to the other side of this wall—" At that moment X-Prime pushed a corrugated metal wall near the dumpster that wobbled with ominous creaks and moans "—and push it over on me. Get creative! Make me scared! It's, you know, your thing!"

Cayman's eyes narrowed and he struggled for control, so that his voice would be even when he spoke. "I'm not going to threat-en you. I don't need to force you to do your job. You're a shad-owrunner. A professional. You know what it takes to do things right—at least, that's what I'm counting on."

X-Prime, he returned his eyes to their normal width, and he made sure he waited for a few seconds before moving, but then he turned and scrambled into the dumpster. He pulled himself up to sit on the edge, swung his legs around, then pushed off so that he landed feet first on the garbage inside. It made a soft, squishy noise. Odors of rot were freed by the impact of his feet.

"That thing you did just now," X-Prime said. "That professional thing. That was a low blow."

Cayman smirked and waited for X-Prime to complete his search.

This took a few minutes, and X-Prime uncovered a wide variety of smells that helped him expand his definition of the word "repugnant." He found many things that were revolting, nothing that had any intrinsic value, and no package like the one he was looking for.

"It's not here," he said, climbing out of the dumpster and wiping the larger pieces of dirt and muck off him. Cayman thought about asking him to check again, but then decided they could move on.

Their instructions were not very specific. They were told to find the item they were looking for in a dumpster near the Esogbue Iron Works in Ikeja. Groovetooth told them what she could about the factory, but the factory had changed names many times and had opened and closed and re-opened many times, and in the end all Groovetooth could do was suggest an approximate location, and say that Cayman and X-Prime should just search through every dumpster in the area, which is always an easier suggestion to make when you are not the one who has to carry it out.

There are a fair number of dumpsters in the area, because industry always produces things it does not need; in fact, the two men have seen more dumpsters than people since they have been in the area, since most of the industries in this area are no longer functional, but the dumpsters were left behind, because who wants to claim a dumpster, especially since when it is quite possibly full of toxic materials? The few people seen in this area were squatters, who do not move around much, and the people who work here, who were not permitted to walk around when they should be at their stations doing their work. And so the streets were as empty as the dumpsters were full.

Cayman and X-Prime walked behind a speckled brick building, walking through an alley with potholes so deep they might well be concealing alligators. They walked by one dumpster that was so eaten by rust that it was a piece of red-brown Swiss cheese on wheels, and if you have never seen a piece of red-brown Swiss cheese, than you have never shopped in a Lagos open-air market. They walked by this dumpster and they looked in it and that was all it took to tell them that there was nothing in there to interest them. Because metal pockmarked with rust was not what they were looking for.

"So all the scheming, all the planning, all the manipulating that have made this run what it is has left us here," X-Prime said, continuing a conversation from a bit earlier as if it had not been interrupted. "Is that fate? Is that destiny? Clearly someone wanted us to be here, and it's someone more powerful than us, because if they weren't more powerful than us, they would not have been able to get us to go someplace where we'd obviously rather not be. But they might not have even thought about us, the two of us, as people, when they came up with this part of the mission. They put the package here for whatever reason they had, and we're here more as an accident, as a side effect. Nothing more."

"Is this going anywhere?" Cayman asked.

"Just thinking out loud. See, the thing is, we're just a sideshow in this plan. It's about something bigger than us. We are, at best, tangentially related to the plan, which means it doesn't matter what the plan is. It's moving on its own course, and we're briefly caught up in the gravity of its passing, but soon it'll move by us and leave us alone again. So the size of it, the shape of it, doesn't matter much to us. We don't matter much to it, so I can't see why it, whatever it is, should matter to us."

"Because things matter," Cayman said stubbornly, but if you pressed him he probably would not have been able to say just what he meant by that.

Then there was another dumpster in front of them, much like the one that X-Prime searched before. White was its base color, but red dust and rainwater and mold and the foul substances that can often be found in cities with substandard plumbing and significant homelessness can add a great mottled variety to the metal. Both men walked up to the dumpster, and both stopped at its edge.

"Your turn," X-Prime said.

"Who says we're taking turns?"

"It's only fair."

"Who said I'm interested in being fair?" Cayman said.

"You do. You're the one usually talking about how fair you are, except for when you're trying to take advantage of me, which happens a lot."

"And is happening now. Get in there."

"No. I did the last one."

Cayman thought about puffing out his chest and preparing a significant amount of bluster to throw in X-Prime's direction, but then he thought that perhaps he had used that particular tool too often and if he kept using it, it would become dull and ineffective. But a good boss always has more than one management tool at his disposal, so Cayman chose a different strategy.

"This is ridiculous," he said, "standing here arguing about this. I'll search the damned thing, and I'll show you how easy it is."

With a single smooth motion, Cayman jumped forward, grabbed the edge of the dumpster, pulled himself up hard, tucked his legs in front of his chest, and vaulted over the edge. He landed in the assorted refuse with a sound that was first a rustle, then a squish, then a *snap*, then a *squeak*.

The dumpster came alive. The boxes and papers and empty bags on top started bobbing up and down as if they had suddenly been swept into an angry sea, and Cayman's eyes bulged. He yelped, then jumped backward, quickly sitting on the edge of the dumpster, his feet just above the garbage in the bottom half.

It was still alive in there, roiling and swarming, and the source of the movement started to become more clear. Pink flesh, wrinkled and mottled, showed beneath the garbage, with darker pink tails and furiously twitching ears. Then one of them jumped up on its hind legs to show its uneven, sharp teeth and its angry eyes.

For its trouble, that devil rat was shot by Cayman. He thought about spraying bullets into the dumpster until they were all dead, every last clammy, evil-eyed one of them, but a missed shot hitting angled metal could have effects that Cayman would quickly regret.

"Get off!" X-Prime shouted, and Cayman did not bother to yell at the boy for saying the obvious. He wished he could just drop a grenade into the dumpster and take care of the creatures then and there, but if the package they were supposed to pick up was in there, that would be very bad for them. So the devil rats must be eliminated through more conventional means.

Both fortunately and unfortunately, the devil rats had a way out of the dumpster—fortunate in that it got them out of the place that Cayman and X-Prime did not want them to be, unfortunate in that it meant they had to deal with the creatures being all around them. The rats squirmed through a hole in the base of the dumpster, squirting out one by one, and some of them disappeared into dark shadows, but not all of them. There was enough red dust in the air to filter the sun, and devil rats were not prone to backing down from a fight. They were quick, nimble, scurrying over the broken asphalt on twitching legs, and they were large, their size and hairlessness making them sometimes look like horrible crawling mutant babies.

X-Prime had his little lemon squeezer out, and what he lost in stopping power he made up for in accuracy, as most of the flechettes found their way into a devil rat's skin. The rats were moving so quickly that the target on Cayman's heads-up display was making him dizzy, bobbing here and there, changing from red to yellow to red, but Cayman had dealt with moving targets before and he knew how to react almost before his target actually moved, and he fired rounds into scuttling rats that stopped them in their tracks. But the other rats, they were coming, the dead bodies in front of them did not disturb them or slow them, they scurried over the bodies and bared their teeth and hoped to get a taste of human flesh before they were killed.

X-Prime was slowly moving backward, giving space to Cayman, so Cayman pulled out his sawed-off shotgun and sent out blasts that did not need to be targeted because they were brief hailstorms of lead that pulped anything in their range. The shotgun was in his left hand, the handgun in his right, he grabbed shells and reloaded when he needed to while trying to keep firing the whole time because he had been on the streets of the city, and he had seen the plague that was killing people here and there and everywhere, and he knew what could happen if the rats got a bite of him. A few had already tried when he was in the dumpster, but they received nothing more than a mouthful of boot leather for their efforts, because no matter the climate, no matter the environment, Cayman always had heavy boots on, and this day only firmed up his resolve to keep it that way.

The rats were dying steadily, yet somehow coming closer, because you can always gain ground when you have no care for your own life, and they were getting perilously close to X-Prime, whose legs were not protected by anything more than canvas pants. X-Prime was moving too much, dodging back and forth, for Cayman to be able to shoot to help him, but if Cayman could clear enough rats near him he could move in and help with a blade, so he shot and shot and hoped he could kill the ones in front of him fast enough, and he looked at X-Prime and saw one particularly large rat coming closer, it was only a meter away from the boy and closing fast, and X-Prime hit it with a flechette but it did not seem to care, it leaped forward, mouth opened, aiming at X-Prime's vulnerable shin, and X-Prime could not stop this beast with his gun because it was coming too fast, and Cayman tried to run and get a shot off but he was not sure he could find the angle, and the boy's foot moved forward with a kick, which was not a bad idea but it would not be enough, because the rat would just react by grabbing the boy's leg, wrapping around it and biting, but Cayman saw a glint of metal as the foot moved forward, and the boy's toe caught the rat right in the belly, and Cayman swore he could see the rat's eyes widen even though he was behind the creature, and the rat suddenly stiffened and then went limp and then fell to the ground, bleeding through a wound in its gut, and Cayman reminded himself that he should not forget that the boy is full of surprises.

It was as if that single kick took the steam out of the rats, and the tide of them slacked off. There were a few more to kick and shoot here and there, but they became less of a threat until they disappeared altogether, either dead or searching for less well-armed prey.

Cayman walked over to the dumpster, looked cautiously inside, then sat on the edge and poked around with the barrel of his shotgun. There was no movement inside, which was a significant relief to Cayman. Not only that, but as his shotgun moved around the rubbish shifted and all of the sudden there was a package, a simple black package, sitting uncovered and waiting for them. There was a bit of rat leavings on the box, but other than that it seemed in fine condition.

"Ah-ha!" Cayman said, and X-Prime walked over and looked in and saw what he saw.

"See, that's what they should have told us in the first place," he said. "That the package was in the one with the devil rats."

CHAPTER SIX

There are times when a group must stop for a moment to take stock of where they are and what they are doing, and if you happen to be in a moment where you find that, without having any knowledge of it, you are carrying a human scalp, that is one of those times.

This is not to say that the group stops moving. Cayman is already impatient enough to get to Lagos Island that he is not going to stop just because they need to talk. Walking and talking is fine with him, so long as there is no one trying to attack him.

"Why is someone sending around a human scalp?" Agbele Oku asks, a note of anger in her voice.

"Why do we care?" X-Prime says. "If we had done all this right, we wouldn't even know what's in the box. That means we can do our job without worrying about it. So let's keep the box closed and forget about it."

Agbele Oku's eyes narrow. "Have you trafficked in human body parts before?"

"Not that I know of," X-Prime says, "though we did cut off this one guy's cyberarm once."

"Then maybe this is easy for you," Agbele Oku says. "For me, I am not making the adjustment so easy. We have a body part, and I want to know why we're carrying it."

Halim is walking and looking straight ahead. "There's no one here who could tell you anything about it. I wouldn't worry about it."

"There are ways we can find things out," Agbele Oku says. "Maybe Groovetooth can do some quick research. Do you have access here?"

Groovetooth lets out a short bark that they all take to mean "no."

"I don't like this," Agbele Oku says. "And I do not think I will like dropping this off to a person who would want such a thing."

"I think you'll like it once you get your cred," X-Prime says.

Speaking at almost the same time, Akuchi says, "You don't have to like it. I'm not sure I like it, but that doesn't change much. We have the package, we are paid to deliver it, we need to deliver it. We can worry about the whys of what we're doing later."

"When you try to worry about it later, you generally worry about it too late," Agbele Oku says, though her tone is resigned now.

The crowds have thinned somewhat at this part in the bridge because they are farther away from land, and it is more difficult for people to come and go here. Cayman finds the sparser crowd appealing, as he can walk faster and try not to get involved in the conversation behind him. The wind is at his back, pushing him toward the island, and it doesn't seem all that far off anymore, maybe only eight kilometers, maybe less. They will make it, the scalp and whatever is in the other two boxes will be dropped off, and it will be over. And they will not even have to bother knowing anything about what the other boxes hold.

"What do you suppose is in the other boxes?" X-Prime says.

Cayman stops and whirls on him. "Why do you care?"

X-Prime shrugs. "I don't, really. Just seems like it might be interesting. I mean, that one box is kind of neat, if gross. So the other two—"

"Are none of our business!" Cayman thunders.

Agbele Oku has stopped. In her green-and-black gown with her long neck and sharp features, she looks like some kind of queen. "Maybe we should open them. That might help us learn more about what we are doing."

"We're not opening *anything*!" Cayman says with as much command as he can put into his voice.

"We learn what is inside, we get more information," Agbele Oku says. "Groovetooth, the more information you have, the better, right?"

"Don't drag me into this," Groovetooth says, looking skittish and nervous. She keeps looking around, looking back over her shoulder, and Cayman figures the lack of AR and Matrix access has her unnerved.

Agbele Oku pulls herself to her full height and the breeze

makes her robe billow out in front of her. "We have a duty—" she begins, but Cayman cuts her off quickly.

"To do our job!" he says, and he continues south on the bridge.

The wind feels good against the sweat on the back of his neck, and Cayman considers walking backward for a time to let the breeze blow on his face, but that would mean he would be facing the rest of the group, and possibly make them think he is inviting conversation, which he most certainly is not.

It is because he remained facing forward that he sees the line of women standing in front of him on the bridge. They have picked a spot where some of the bridge had crumbled and it had narrowed to half its width. That meant that a group of eight women could form a line across the entire bridge, which they did. Cayman notices that they are well-groomed group of women, all in clean robes and all with alert eyes. They look watchful but not hostile, standing casually, some with their arms folded, others with their arms at their side or a hand on their hips. They do not look threatening, but they also do not look like they are about to move.

Cayman waves an arm toward Halim without turning to him. "Don't get any weapons out. Please. Let's not kill them if we don't have to."

Halim says nothing, and Cayman takes a deep breath and then lets it out.

He keeps harboring a distant hope that they will approach this group of woman, walk through them and past them, and move on without anything happening. There are many, many people in this city, and many, many people on this bridge, and it is possible that these women are looking for someone else on this bridge, and not this group. *Why should everyone be looking for us?* is what Cayman thinks. *People in this city, they have other business to do.*

But Cayman's hopes are soon dashed when he comes within twenty meters of the women and one of them steps forward, a short woman whose feet are apart so she looks firmly anchored to her spot, and the wind barely seems to be touching her, her robe and her long braids are not even moving, and her face his round and calm.

"You are the people with the packages," the woman says, and it is not a question.

"There's lots of people with packages," Cayman says, not because he is the leader or the spokesman, but because he figures if he speaks first he can prevent some of the others from saying things that might be more inflammatory than the nondescript words he offers.

"Yes," the woman says, "but you are the people with the packages we are interested in."

"These packages are going south," Cayman said, "whether you're interested in them or not. Sorry."

"Do you know what is in the packages?" the woman asks.

Cayman hears Agbele Oku draw in breath behind him, so he speaks extra quickly. "No," he says. "That's not our job."

"We have reason to believe the objects you are carrying concern us," the woman says.

"Okay," Cayman says. "And who are you?"

"We are some of the many Daughters of Yemaja," the woman says.

"Oh, good," Cayman says. He has not been in Lagos long, but he has already heard at least five stories about the Daughters, Awakened women who dedicate their lives to seeking justice for women, which, given the way Lagos tends to treat its women, is a very demanding job indeed, and he braces himself for a lecture and hopefully nothing more.

"We have reasons to believe that you are involved in business that concerns us," the woman says.

"What?" Cayman says.

"We have reasons to believe that your are involved in business that concerns us," the woman repeats.

"Okay, just checking to see if you were actually going to say it the same way twice. What do you want from us?"

Then there is a pause, and Cayman looks, and he thinks he can see hesitation in the woman's face, but when she talks she retains her confidence and authority, so he wonders if he imagined it.

"We want to discuss what you are doing and where you are going."

"Oh," Cayman says, then he shrugs and walks forward.

"I think we should talk to them!" Agbele Oku says behind him, and Cayman rolls his eyes and thinks of *course* Agbele Oku has sympathies with these people, but it does not matter much to him, and he continues walking.

"You think we can just be ignored?" the woman says as he draws near.

"Yes," Cayman says.

"Do you know who we are?" the woman says as Cayman passes her.

"Vaguely," he says, and then, against his better judgment, he pauses, though he does not turn around. "Look, I'm sure what you're doing is important and all, and God knows the women around here need someone to stick up for them, but if you want to make a play, you better make it, because you're not going to intimidate us into doing anything."

He can feel the force of Agbele Oku's glare on his neck, but it does not concern him much. There are always times during a job when someone on the team is mad at someone else, but Cayman knows of one sure way to make everything okay—finish the job with everyone alive and everyone paid. If he worries about those two things, the rest of life tends to take care of itself.

"We are not here to force you to do anything," the woman says. "We had hoped you would be reasonable, and would help us interpret some troubling information we have heard. We keep hearing about things that are happening across the city, and many of these things keep coming back to you and your team."

"Sorry, this isn't how the business works," Cayman says. "You don't get to learn our secrets just because you're curious. We've got allegiances to worry about, and none of them are to you."

"What about to justice? Are any of you allied to that?"

Cayman finally turns and sees the furrowed brow and taut neck muscles of the woman. Behind her, Agbele Oku is opening her mouth to speak, so Cayman speaks faster.

"We're always happy to be allied to justice whenever justice comes up with a good cash offer," he says.

But that does not keep Agbele Oku from talking. "You don't speak for all of us!" There is a tension, a strain in her features that Cayman does not understand, but he is not about to ask her about it.

"Right now, I do," Cayman says. "We don't have time to waste. Let's go."

The woman has her hands on her hips, balled into fists. "We do not use violence easily, but we will use it. You're not going to get by us with a more satisfactory answer than that."

Halim has his arms folded, and if the Daughters know anything about him, they will know that from that position there are at least three weapons he can draw within 1.2 seconds. He does not speak, but his eyes and his posture say everything that he needs to say, and what it says is that unlike them, he *does* use violence easily, and his patience has been frayed to the point of being on the edge of using it.

Then, suddenly, the mouse is at Cayman's side. He never sees her coming, he blames her size, but there she is, and her nose is even twitching.

"Maybe we all want the same thing," Groovetooth says. "Maybe we all want to know more about what's going on. Maybe we could find out together, open the boxes or something."

"There's another person you don't speak for," Agbele Oku says, and Cayman finds the smugness in her voice very irritating.

"We're not opening any boxes!" Cayman says, and he keeps waiting to hear the sound of an unsheathing sword that means Halim's patience has run out. "We are moving on, and I think the Daughters are too smart to cause a problem about it."

"I wouldn't count on that," Halim says.

There are many frantic looks going this way and that, both groups are intermingled, their battle lines are not clearly drawn, so each person has to look quickly back and forth to see what the others are doing, and to make sure the seemingly inevitable fight has not started yet.

"Let me talk to them alone," Agbele Oku says abruptly.

Cayman rolls his eyes. "You? You talk to them, you'll be on their side in five minutes."

"I'm a professional," Agbele Oku says. "Let me talk to them."

Cayman does not really want to do that, but he also does not want to get into another fight. It's already been a long day. He waves his hand and hopes she can take care of things quickly.

CHAPTER SEVEN

THREE AND THREE-QUARTERS HOURS BEFORE THE BRIDGE

Did I mention that the whole team has had a long day? They did not just wake up after a full night's sleep and decide to go walk the bridge. No, by the time they arrived at the bridge they had covered much of the city, running here and there, in three separate directions at least, so that their walk on the bridge is not done with the fresh steps of energy, but with the heavy paces of people who are strong and fit, but still need to rest on occasion after all they have been through.

Let us see what Akuchi and Agbele Oku were doing earlier in the day. You remember how Akuchi rode his cycle, *abi*? You remember how he can navigate through the streets? He had Agbele Oku with him most of the day, and she kept her face impassive as he drove, because when you are a shadowrunner, you learn very early on that if you look impressed at something that means you likely have not ever seen such a thing before, and to admit that kind of inexperience is to give an advantage to those around you. So you keep your face blank and bland, and if you see someone drive a cycle through an alley barely a meter and a half wide and then put that cycle into a wheelie and then hop over perilously deep holes in the road and then bring the front wheel down at just the right time to squish a large devil rat that seemed determined to get in the way, you just nod and say "Not bad" in a tone so quiet that you are not sure if the driver ahead of you heard it.

There was a point in the day where Akuchi and Agbele Oku came out of an alley into a dusty street and kicked up a cloud behind them. They were lucky to find a street there, but ahead of them their luck ran out. A thick vine, thicker in parts than Akuchi and Agbele Oku and the cycle put together, had gone and taken the street away from metahumanity and reclaimed it for nature, or at least for itself, for it is very possible that of the things the vine represented, "nature," in its purest sense, is not one of them. It had spread many tendrils here and there, it had gone up and down through the asphalt and concrete, it had shattered the road and made it rubble. The buildings on either side of the road were mostly gone, they were ivy-covered, they had tree limbs poking through them here and there. Agbele Oku swore she could see the plants growing before her eyes, reaching out and expanding, but of course she could not, for they grow fast but they do not grow *that* fast. But no matter how fast or slow they were, they had blocked the road, and Akuchi had to find another way to go.

And so they go through another alley, this one wider than the first, and made even wider by the fact that the buildings that used to shape it have mostly gone away. The alley seemed harmless, there were no creatures in sight, but this was Alimosho, and if you are in Alimosho and you do not see creatures there, it is because they are just out of your sight doing something horrible, so you should not feel the least amount of comfort.

The breeze switched and blew from the road ahead of them, and Agbele Oku got a hint of what that nearby horrible thing was. It was a thick odor, it had its own substance, it was a mist that pushed into her head and made everything in her clench. It was cloying, rotten, and dead.

If it was not for the noise of the cycle, she would have heard the noises ahead of her before she saw what made them, but as it was she had to wait until the motorcycle emerged from the alley to see the large, shiny, black bugs swarming on top of a pulpy, red-and-brown mound, and maybe she could not hear them over the noise of the cycle but she at least imagined she heard them, the clacking of their legs on the ground, of their shells against each other, as they squirmed and pushed and maneuvered to find the tastiest spot on whatever dead thing was beneath them.

Agbele Oku's first instinct would be to run, run in the opposite direction, but Akuchi knew the roaches had what they wanted, and so were not likely to be distracted by anything else. He gave them a wide berth, of course, so they did not think he was threatening their food, but he drove by them and the bugs seemed not to notice, and Agbele Oku made a point to look away from them because she did not want a detailed image of them and their meal burned into her skull.

She wanted to be out of here. She tried to imagine leaving Alimosho, but she could not picture it, because she could not quite imagine how she was going to conclude her business here. She had not had nearly long enough to think about it, and she certainly had not had enough time to keep from feeling like what she was going to do was a betrayal.

There were plants all over, the air here was moister than the rest of the city, a little cleaner thanks to the plants scouring it, and normally Agbele Oku would find this refreshing, except she could almost hear the sound of the plants breathing, as if their thick stems and rough husks hid moving lungs and beating hearts. She wished she did not have to deal with the sort of people who test others by asking them to come to places like Alimosho, but this was her lot in life. She held tight to Akuchi, and hoped they would find their target soon.

No sooner did she think this than the cycle turned a corner and there were a group of people in the street. They were walking to one side, moving slowly, and Agbele Oku saw the shamble of shedim in their walk, but then the cycle came closer and she saw she was mistaken. It was a group of women, all in brown and black bodysuits, each one wearing a different shade that matched their skin. Their uniforms, for that was what they appear to be, bore no markings. The slow movements of the group resolved themselves into a formation, and they stood behind one of their number, a woman whose skin and clothing were the color of the inside of the mouth of a desert cave at sunset.

Akuchi stopped the cycle a respectful distance from the women and climbed off slow enough to ensure that Agbele Oku was off first. This had all been discussed, this was her job to do, and he was not going to get in the way of her doing it.

She moved smoothly, unhurried, confidently. She had done this before, she told herself. They would not show her anything new, they would not tell her anything she was not ready to hear. She was tempted to make some remark about the surroundings, about their reasons for meeting in this piece of hell, but she didn't. She acted like she did business in Alimosho all the time.

"I have something for you," she said as she walked up, almost swaggering. "Something you'll be interested in."

"That is what we hear," said the woman in front. Her cheek-bones could be used to polish diamonds.

Agbele Oku reached into a pocket and pulled it out, spreading it with both hands. It was a beaded leather hair string—pretty, but not especially fancy. "I don't have to tell you what this is," she says, "assuming any of you are good enough to use it."

She gave the women a minute to look at the string. "You see it," Agbele Oku told them. "You see how much juju is in here. Whatever is in that box you have, surely it is not worth as much as this."

Some of the women are nodding, and Agbele Oku saw the looks they were giving to each other. She had them. She began to think, as any trader would, that perhaps she should have asked for more.

But there was a woman in the back, a woman whose black hair had thinned to sparse wires, whose eyes widened and nostrils flared. She said a word.

"Atinuke!" she said. "Atinuke!"

The other women turned to her. The woman with thin hair pointed to the hair string and said it again. "Atinuke! That is Atinuke's!"

The lead woman turned her back entirely on Agbele Oku, and of course Agbele Oku was dismayed to find out that she obviously was not considered to be much of a threat.

"Are you sure?" the lead woman said.

"Can't you see? Her aura is still on it! It was created by her hand! That is Atinuke's hair string!"

Some of the other women murmured in agreement, and despite her best efforts, Agbele Oku felt the confident set of her jaw stiffening and becoming artificial.

The lead woman turned back to Agbele Oku. When she spoke, her voice was low, almost a monotone.

"After the SURGE, when parts of the city were burning and metahuman females were attacked on sight, Atinuke saved fourteen women in three days, helping them get to safety. She has brought women out of brothels, out of piracy, out of conditions that would make a young girl like you want to slit her throat rather than live one moment more. Atinuke was a true Daughter of Yemaja, and that is her hair string. How did you get it?"

And Agbele Oku was ready. There was still a knot in her stomach, a knot that had been tied there the moment she understood where this string had come from, but she at least had not been surprised.

"Yes," she said, "it is Atinuke's. I bring it to you with great sorrow, but I am also honored to return it to you, Atinuke's sisters, who meant so much to her."

The lead woman was not swayed from her purpose. "How did you get it?"

"It was given to me by an associate. He got it from some area boys. That is all I know."

"Street thugs did not just happen upon Atinuke's fetish! Your associate did not come across it by accident! How did Atinuke lose it, and why do you now have it?"

"I have it because I wanted to get it back to you," Agbele Oku said. "I don't know what happened to Atinuke. I wish I did. Atinuke was good to me, once. I can't say I really knew her, but she helped me, like she helped so many others." Agbele Oku heard the sentimentality in her voice and did not like it, but she also knew that it was what the Daughters were ready to hear. "Once I discovered that I might be able to recover it for you, I knew I had to do it. My associate was able to make a trade for it, and I was able to bring it back to you."

"So you can make your own trade!" said the older woman with the wiry hair.

"No," Agbele Oku said, even though she had been trying to do just that a moment before. "All I want to do is return it to you. It belonged to a Daughter, so it should be returned to you." She stretched out her arms. "Here. Please."

The lead woman quickly grabbed it. "You want a reward," she said. "I can see it."

"I want nothing other than to help the Daughters."

The lead woman started to sneer, but others behind her had softer faces, and they were talking quietly, and one of them tapped the lead woman on the shoulder and whispered something in her ear. The lead woman nodded, then spoke.

"We do not know what is in the package you want," she said. "We have been asked, by people we respect, not to open it. We have also been told to give it to someone who does not seem to want it."

Agbele Oku tried not to let excitement drift into her face as the lead woman continued speaking. "You may not be the person who is supposed to receive it, as you clearly want it. But you are willing to act like you don't want it, and perhaps to walk away without it. That may be enough."

She quickly jerked her head, and one of the women behind her made a box materialize seemingly from nowhere. It was a black box, sealed in some way Agbele Oku could not see, about the size of a devil rat's head. She handed it to Agbele Oku, and Agbele Oku wasted no time in grabbing it, perhaps grabbing it too quickly. But it did not matter. They did not move to take it back while she profusely thanked all of them while backing away, moving toward the cycle so she could leave and take this box to where it belonged and be done with it.

She got on the cycle and then turned to wave to the Daughters behind her, but they were gone.

It was not much later than this when a woman with a long, flowing robe and a headdress with a horizontal piece of carved wood almost as broad as her shoulders was admitted to the office of Sir. There were goose bumps on her skin, and she did not appear at all accustomed to being in air conditioning. She had a mild face that made people who did not know her ask her for advice. Sir, though, was immune to that effect.

The woman, whose name was Baindu, spoke without being asked to, which was unusual in Sir's experience.

"The package has been handed off as requested," she said. "The woman who received it was even led to believe that she was supposed to receive it, or some such nonsense."

Sir rolled his eyes. "That was unnecessary. Why do people always have to come up with a story? Why not just say thanks for the string, here's the box, have a nice day?"

"We do not share all information about our workings with everyone," Baindu said. "Not all of our group who was there was working from the same script. The story was as much for them as it was for your operative."

"Fine, as long as it's where it's supposed to be." Sir returned to the pacing he was doing before Baindu arrived. He walked across the office, turned, and was surprised to see that Baindu was still there.

"I appreciate the fact that your people handed off the item.

The payment has already been arranged and will be made. Good day."

Baindu, however, did not move. "You are using us," she said. "Most days you have no use for us, but when it suits you, you decide to make us your couriers. It seems—less than respectful."

There was much truth to this, but Sir of course knew it would do him no good to acknowledge it.

"This is not a matter of respect," Sir said. "I have a job with many facets to it, and one of them is keeping the peace in the city."

Baindu snorted.

Sir smiled. "Yes, it's a relative term. Sometimes all I can do is avoid actions that I know will directly lead to violence."

"And you believe this is one of those times."

Sir turned and looked out his window, and the ocean glittered while he quietly counted to ten. Then he turned back around.

"Since you know my position, you'll understand that if I tell you what you want to know, you'll have to promise that the Daughters will not engage in any reprisals."

Baindu pulled herself somewhat taller. "I will make no such promise. We have our mission, and we cannot decide to ignore it simply because it is inconvenient to you. You say you want to keep the peace—if you are letting the guilty walk the streets un-punished, that is not a peace worth preserving."

The next part was difficult for Sir, but since all politics involve a degree of performance, he had some experience that he could call on. He could not turn to the window, because he had already used that particular move, so he returned to his pacing, a few strides towards the bookcases, a pause, a turn back to Baindu. A few steps toward her after a short pause.

"My mission," he said, "is keeping the peace as much as possible. That includes punishing wrongdoers when I can." He managed to look completely serious when he said this. "These packages that are coming to me, including the one your people acquired and passed along, are evidence. Evidence of a crime against a very prominent woman."

"Who?"

Sir gave her the name, and that was the end of their conver-sation. Baindu's eyes flashed, and she was gone. Sir watched her leave, and hoped, for their sake, that the runners would have the packages in his hands soon. Since now there was yet another group who wanted them.

CHAPTER EIGHT

So, the Daughters were in one part of the city and some of them, later, are in another, and they are repeatedly engaged in conversations that are not particularly helpful to the blood pressure of anyone involved.

Cayman taps his toe on the ground in impatience—he really does this, which X-Prime always finds funny, because it makes him look like some old lady from a twentieth century 2D movie. Agbele Oku is not paying attention to these men, for she is engrossed by the conversation she is having with the Daughters of Yemaja, finding for the second time today that she is in the unfortunate position of trying to convince some Daughters that she is in fact a person of good intentions. Cayman wishes he could hear what she is saying to them, but she has been careful to keep her distance and her voice low, so he must wait and hope she is being useful.

You are fortunate to have me with you, then, because I am not burdened by the same restrictions as Cayman. I know the words that were said, and so you do not have to strain to hear them or act in ignorance. You only have to listen to me.

"You don't need to worry about us," Agbele Oku tells them. "We are on your side."

"Really," says the leader of the group, who introduced herself to Agbele Oku as Mariam.

"Yes. In fact, some of your people gave one of these boxes to us just a few hours ago. If you wanted to have it, your people should have kept it. But they gave it to us."

"Yes. That was a mistake."

"Then why did they do it?"

Mariam chose her words carefully, speaking slowly and evenly. "We have spent much of the day learning things we did not know. We are very careful about who we trust, but it seems we have not been careful enough."

"That doesn't really tell me anything," Agbele Oku says.

Mariam's expression does not flicker, and clearly Agbele Oku's lack of understanding is not causing the Daughter any great pangs of guilt. Agbele Oku would love to use a spell, something that could help her get a better read on Mariam, but she does not doubt that each and every Daughter around her on the bridge is Awakened, and that anything she did would be noticed. That would not, of course, do much to help convince the Daughters that she is someone that can be trusted. She has kept a careful eye on Mariam's aura, but all its blue-purple colors are telling her are that Mariam is Awakened and that she is calm. There was a brief flash of red before Mariam began talking vaguely about the things she had learned as the day had passed, but Agbele Oku would have been able to perceive the anger behind her level tones even if she had been blind, both astrally and physically.

"If it were up to me," Agbele Oku says, "we would give you the box. But it's not. There's five other people, and they have a job to do, which is important to them, so they are not going to give up the box easily. We could fight over it, but why not look for some other way to help us both get what we want?"

"How will we do that, when what we want is the box?" Mariam quite reasonably asks, but there is a yellow tinge now to her aura, and Agbele Oku hopes that represents openness to discussion.

"Why do you want the box?" Agbele Oku asks.

"Because it contains something important to us."

"Do you know what is in the box?"

Mariam pauses only slightly before answering. "No. Do you?"

"No," Agbele Oku says—thankfully, the box the Daughters want is not the one that had already broken open, so her answer is the truth. "How do you know it is important?'

Again, the very careful tone appears. "We know someone who knows what is in the box, and that is what he told us."

"Is this someone you can trust?"

There is another red flash, so brief that Agbele Oku must wonder if she actually saw it or if was just afterglow from the blink of her eyes. "No," Mariam says. "In many respects, it is not. But in this respect, we think he is telling us the truth."

"Can you tell me who this person is?"

"Absolutely not," Mariam says, with no hesitation.

Agbele Oku feels the impatience of the other runners, and she worries that Halim might be preparing to attack at any moment, to use the virtue of surprise to offset the Daughters' magical advantage. Both his face and his aura are calm, but she has looked at him when he is fighting and there is almost no change in the color of his aura—in fact, there are parts of it that become a richer, cleaner blue and green when he is fighting, showing that he is more at peace than he is at other times. So she cannot guess what he might be about to do.

She tries a new tack. "You don't know what's in the box, but you think it's important. What's important about it?"

"It is evidence of a wrong."

"A wrong you want to correct," Agbele Oku says, which is not that difficult of a guess because righting wrongs is a major preoccupation of the Daughters.

"A wrong we *will* correct," Mariam says.

"And if we deliver the boxes to our employer as intended, you're worried you'll never know what this evidence was."

Mariam nods.

"How soon do you need to know what is in the box? I know it is important to you, but can you wait to find out?"

Red and orange blaze quickly but brightly. "Justice should never have to wait."

"Of course. But neither should payday. We're delivering this package as soon as we can, and after that we're done with it, and you can do whatever you want with it."

"Who are you delivering it to?"

Mariam says that last line with a rapid nonchalance, but it does not fool Agbele Oku.

"You don't want to reveal your contact, I don't want to reveal my employer. Assuming I knew who it was, ultimately, which I don't."

"Then how do you know we will be able to do anything with the package once it is delivered? Maybe it will just disappear, and no one will ever see it again."

"Then we'll find out what's in it for you, before we give it away."

And that, sadly, after all the other lines, after all the things that are said that he does not hear, that is something that Cayman in fact hears, and he does not like it one bit.

"No!" he says, storming over, surrounded by dark, angry red. "We are doing this job *right*! No changes! No screw-ups! We're not opening anything more!"

"Okay," Agbele Oku says mildly. "Then we'll sit here and negotiate for a while longer, maybe fifteen minutes or half an hour, and then maybe we won't come to an agreement, and the Daughters will try to take the box by force, and we will have to kill them, and we'll do our best not to die while we're doing this. But that won't change the mission, will it?"

She has not known Cayman long, only for this mission, but she has seen enough to know that he is pragmatic beyond any other impulse. She knows how he will respond, and she knows he will scowl when he does it.

And so he does. "Fine," he says. "When we get to the Island, when we're near the delivery point, if everything's okay, we'll take a peek. You can assense it, cast a spell on it, whatever. All right?"

"I think so," Agbele Oku, and she turns to Mariam. "You won't have to wait long, and you'll find out what is in the box."

"We'd learn more about it if we actually had it," Mariam says, but aura or no aura, Agbele Oku knows how she is leaning.

"None of us gets just what we want," Agbele Oku says, looking at Cayman and then Mariam. "But we all get something. What more could we ask for?"

Mariam looks Agbele Oku up and down, and she can feel the force of the other woman's gaze, and she knows this is how a book feels when it is in the hands of an expert scholar. Then Mariam looks her in the eyes.

"We will find you soon," she says. "And then you will tell us what you know."

And then the deadlock is broken, and the Daughters walk one way, Agbele Oku and the others another way. No one has had to die, and Agbele Oku hopes there is some force in the universe, somewhere, that acknowledges that fact and credits her for it.

CHAPTER NINE

THREE AND A HALF HOURS BEFORE THE BRIDGE

And as I think about Agbele Oku walking away from the Daughters and feeling calm, I cannot help but feel that there is another conversation I should have related, that perhaps when I was telling the story of Akuchi and Agbele Oku in Alimosho, I should have continued it and told the story of Akuchi and Agbele Oku leaving Alimosho. They were eager to leave, because who would stay in Alimosho except the desperate, the insane, and the people who dearly love hideous bugs and the undead?

Akuchi wanted to take the same way out that he took in, but Alimosho has a way of changing underneath your feet—plants grow where they weren't before, creatures crawl in new areas, and the movement of the sun across the sky casts light into new places and reveals dangers that you had overlooked before when you had passed by blithely without knowing how close you were to someone who would craved the taste of your flesh and was a half meter or less from being ready to claim you for their own. Not for any personal reason, of course, but for a deep and abiding hunger that comes when you crave something fresh in a district where everything is rotten.

He turned down the alley he thought had brought them there, then he had emerged onto one of the streets choked with vines and broken pavement, and he knew he was generally traveling in the right direction, but he cannot be sure how long it will take for him to get out or if he will run into dead ends, which is an unfamiliar feeling for someone who cannot see any image of intersecting lines without knowing which intersection in Lagos those lines resemble. But there were times, years ago, when most of what he did was improvisation, and those skills have not gone away, and he is not entirely displeased to have the chance to use them again.

There was a street that looked promising, broad and reasonably intact and heading east. But perhaps it was too promising, too broad, because if a street was taken too often, then there would be things attracted to it that wanted to encounter the things that used that road. So ahead of him, Akuchi saw a group of people-looking things, and they were moving slowly with their arms extended, and he knew they were shedim.

He had encountered shedim before, and he knew some of them find it strangely amusing to imitate zombies from trideos. And sometimes it was not just done for laughs—there are people who find the shedim morbidly fascinating, especially the shedim of Lagos, who have access to a full range of bodies, including those that have died violently or decomposed somewhat, and people approach them as hideous displays of anatomy in motion, where they can see muscles flexing as the shedim walk, and they come a little closer because they know that if anything bad happens, they can just run off, dash away from those slow trideo zombies, and then they get close enough and the shedim move at their normal speed, and there is no lurch or shamble to them, only hunger, and hunger helps make them faster.

So Akuchi was not fooled. He saw the shedim grouped to one side of the road, shuffling slowly ahead, making it look for all the world like he could just move to the road across from them and pass safely, and he knew that was the last thing he should do. He quickly turned the cycle so he could go back from where he came, and that was when the second group of shedim came out of a building behind him, and these ones were not putting on any act, they were running, ready to throw themselves in front of the bike, to do whatever it took to stop the cycle and get the fresh meat that was on top of it to hit the road so they could taste it.

Then there was a wall, coloring the air purple ahead of him, and it was right in front of the shedim, slowing them down. It was not there for long, they pounded it, and it was gone almost as quickly as it appeared, and the shedim were moving ahead, but there was a gap and Akuchi took it. He wasn't going to admit he needed help, but at that moment he was grateful to have Agbele Oku on the cycle with him.

He could feel the road. The dark asphalt was warmer than the green leaves, and the leaves were smoother. He could feel rocks, he could feel rusted metal, he could even feel the odd squish of unidentifiable, rotten matter. None of it hurt, because he was feeling it with reinforced polyurethane, and blows that would hurt his other skin didn't do anything to that. The tires gave him a rolling grab on the road, almost as if he was continually seizing the pavement and heaving the cycle forward on top of it, pushing left, edging right when he needed to. He had sensors giving him all sorts of information about his surroundings, but he didn't bother to translate that information into some tacky visual interface. The data went right into his head so there were just things he knew, where to go, where to not go, things he knew even if he did not always exactly understand *why* he knew them.

He felt the shedim as he passed them, felt both pulled toward them and repelled away from them, but the inputs from his cycle were far more powerful than the juju the shedim tried to implant into his brain. They reached out as he wheeled by, he leaned, he felt Agbele Oku lean with him, and they were past.

He saw an alley, he turned into it, and there were bugs in the alley. Large ones, with smooth, hard brown backs and quivering antenna moving every direction at once. Maybe he could drive over them, maybe he couldn't, but he did not need to worry about it because Agbele Oku had apparently decided she had enough. He felt a pulse of heat pass over his right shoulder, and when he drove over the bugs, crunching and squishing, they were on their backs with their legs twitching.

He came out of the alley and saw a street with an uncertain passage through twisted metal and spined plants, but even though it was not certain if the passage was in fact there, it was enough for Akuchi; he cut through the path and did not know everything he was avoiding but avoided it anyway. And soon the plants began to recede and the road began to clear and it was safe to talk. He made himself heard over the noise of the cycle's engine.

"Have you ever had a whole group of people pissed at you before?"

"What?"

"The Daughters. They seemed like they might not be happy with you, and you didn't seem to like that. Have you ever had a group like that pissed with you?"

"I am an Awakened woman in Lagos," she said. "Many groups hated me as soon as I was born."

"Yeah, but that's hating you as a concept. What about hating you specifically? Personally?"

"Not that I'm aware of."

Akuchi nodded. "It's a first-time thing, then. Anytime you do something for the first time, you feel a little nervous. More than a little, if it's a big thing. But then you survive, and when it happens again, you go in knowing that it's a thing you can get through. That's what will happen. The Daughters might be a little mad at you, but you'll survive. The next time you have to cross a group, it won't bug you as much."

"Who says this is bugging me?"

"Your face. Your words. You were practically begging them to like you."

"I did no such thing!"

"Look, let me tell you a story. I got my start with the area boys, like a lot of Igbo. First thing you learn when you're an area boy is who you can mess with and who you can't. Second thing you learn is if you don't keep increasing the total number of people who you can mess with, you'll just be a lousy street thug your whole life. So you work to get better and better, catch bigger fish.

"I was driving back then, too, and driving's a good way to start. Usually you're part of someone else's plan, and usually no one sees anything of you besides a windshield or a helmet. I was involved in plenty of jobs that might have been over my head, but all I was doing was driving getaway or playing courier. Doing jobs that no one really cared about.

"But then I got the chance to do something else. Some Yoruba merchants had managed to secure some sapphires for themselves, and they were coming down from Kaduna in an armored van. The planners had thought it over and decided the best way to get our hands on those sapphires was to take them from the van, so they'd need some transportation. I was going to be it. It was your basic van robbery—stop them, blow the doors, shoot whoever is in the way, grab the stuff, and get out. We met the rig when it was coming in the city, and everything went just like it should—except one thing. I had tinted windows, I was nice and covered up, but when I skidded in to pick up the gems, I was turned a little sideways. And I never stopped to think that there was a camera inside the truck. So I was leaning over with the car doors open when the guys with the gems jumped in, and I looked at it. I looked right at it, saw the camera in the other van, and I knew that no matter what we had done to that damn van, that camera was still working.

"They had my picture. I knew there weren't any police that would do anything about it, and I didn't think it was big enough for the Yorubas to bother to track us down. But they knew who I was, and that shook me.

"I didn't sleep for days. I didn't go out much, and when I did I flinched whenever I saw anything that looked the least bit Yoruba. They were looking for me, I thought. They were coming for me.

"But none of them were. The first ones I saw, I crossed the street to avoid. Then others, when I saw them, I looked away, or flinched a little. But none of them did anything, or even paid attention to me. My life after the heist was pretty much like it was before the heist. Except I had a little more money.

"So the next time I did something that was going to hurt the Yorubas, I didn't worry too much. I was still cautious, of course. Still careful on the job. But after it, I didn't flinch each time some Yoruba came in sight.

"I've crossed paths with plenty of Yorubas since then. The Seven Kings War presented plenty of chances, and I took a lot of them. And I'm still doing my same basic thing. Maybe the Yorubas can afford to ignore me, since they won the thing. But whatever the reason, I'm safe for now. They might come after me some day, and I'll be ready if they do. But I'm also ready to just keep living my life."

He did not say anything for a while, and neither did Agbele Oku. The cycle kept up a steady whine, and they started to occasionally pass people in the streets. They were definitely out of Alimosho.

"It's easy enough," Agbele Oku said. "I just should not flinch."

"Right," Akuchi said. "It's the only way to live."

He took a right, and all of a sudden there were many more people. The streets were crowded, people were surging, and they did not look happy, which was not unusual for Lagos, but it put Akuchi on edge—his senses told him what to avoid, and they were telling him to avoid the whole thing.

"We'll try to skirt north of this," he said, "but if we can't get around everyone, we'll have to go through some of them."

"Okay," she said.

Akuchi turned north. It was good, he knew, to take the most direct route to where you were going, but it was better to make sure you survive long enough to get there. The path of less resistance was always better than the path that left you dead.

He would make his way through the city, they would get through the crowd, and soon they would be at the boat. *And everything from there,* Akuchi thought, *would be clear.*

CHAPTER TEN

It only took a few hours and an exploded boat, but at the moment it seems Akuchi's prediction of everything being clear has finally been realized. The Daughters of Yemaja are behind them. The bodies of whomever it was that assaulted them are behind them. The clash between the Black Rogers and the Razor Cutlasses is behind them. They have only six kilometers or so to go, they have made it to the halfway point, and in perhaps an hour they will be where they want to be.

Cayman walks with his eyes fixed on the Lagos Island skyline. When he was a young man, a boy young enough to worry about frivolous concerns rather than focusing intently on matters of survival and related topics, Cayman had engaged in a fierce debate with a friend of his about running style (and let me say at this juncture that you can be assured that this story is a true account of Cayman's past, but even if it was not, it would be a completely accurate representation of how Cayman thinks, and so it fulfills any definition of "truth" that matters). Both boys liked to run, partly because it was a pastime that required little in the way of equipment and socializing. Cayman had seen his friend running, and his form was terrible. His head was bowed, he stared at his shoes the entire time he ran; he looked as though he was running to try to get in front of a heavy sorrow but was not succeeding.

Cayman pulled his friend aside and informed him that his running style was not correct.

"It's always better to look at your goal," Cayman said. "Keep your eyes on where you are going and you'll get there faster."

The boy, who had glasses that always slipped down his nose, pushed them back to their proper position. "I don't like to do that," he said. "It just reminds me how much farther I have to go, and sometimes it seems like it's not getting any closer."

"That's why you look at it!" Cayman said. "So that if you're not getting there fast enough, you can run faster!"

"That doesn't help. I like to look down for a while. Then, when I look up, I'm surprised at how far I've come. Or sometimes I look from side to side, and I see something interesting, and that makes me forget for a little to think about running. It's a nice distraction."

"Distraction?" young Cayman said, outraged in the disproportionate style of fourteen-year-old boys. "Running is what you're *doing*! You shouldn't be distracted from it!"

But the other boy only shrugged, looked down at his shoes, and said "Sometimes I like to look down."

Thirty years, give or take some, had passed since that time, and Cayman still did not understand his friend. There will always be time to look down or from side to side when you are done with what you are doing. He would not be distracted—he would keep looking at the Lagos Island skyline until he was directly under it.

They are making wonderful time now, they are almost jogging, and Cayman is remembering the one-two-three-four-*in,* one-two-three-four-*out* breathing rhythm from his running days, and he knows he could keep up this pace forever if he needed to.

The huts, the booths, and the crowds are gone. They must be far away from any entry points to the bridge. Traffic is scarce—in fact, Cayman thinks it has been a few minutes since they have seen a single person coming from the south. That is, of course, fine with him. The less distractions, the better.

Then a possible cause of the lack of northbound traffic makes itself known. Ahead, Cayman can see one of the bridge's many broken spots. It does not look to be large, Cayman can see the clean shear at the other edge of the break. The gap is perhaps twenty meters long, making it much like the other gap, but there are no people at this one. No line on either side waiting to get across, no stairs down, no platform, no boat crews in the water. This does not please Cayman, as it makes it more likely that he will have to get into the water of the lagoon, and he does not believe there are enough vaccinations in the world to protect him from everything that is swimming in that fetid mess.

He could perhaps ask Agbele Oku to build a horizontal barrier that would serve as a bridge for them, but that would be asking for a lot of effort from her to provide what he knows is a luxury. There will, of course, be the small matter of ascending back up onto the bridge once they are on the other side, but it is situations like this that justify Cayman's belief that, no matter how technology advances, a rope and a grappling hook will always remain one of the most useful items in the world (he is, however, grateful for the technology that combined those two things into a wonderful, single gun). In fact, he could shoot the hook across the entire gap, and most of the team could go hand-over-hand to the other side. Only the last person would have to jump down in the water so he could bring the gun along with him.

As they walk closer to the gap, Cayman realizes it will be even easier than he thought. The far side of the bridge crumbled, but the north side, it stayed attached, so the bridge swung down and now forms a ramp that leads down into the lagoon. It is a very steep ramp, and a misstep on it will result in a very unpleasant roll into the water, but the bottom of this ramp is only five meters or so from the other side of the bridge. He can picture it already— shoot the hook into the top of the bridge, get the winch moving, jump in the air, pull your legs up, and swing forward while the winch takes up the slack. His legs might get a bit damp, but that's it. Then he will simply toss the gun back to the next team member, and they will all ascend, and they will be on their way.

His plan changes, however, when he takes a closer look at the water.

It is darker at the base of the ramp. None of the water in Lagos Lagoon is a natural color—it is dark blue, dark green, oily, and bubbles in unpleasant and inappropriate places. But here, in this spot, it is even darker, and some of the bubbles are red. And there are things floating in the water, things Cayman cannot and does not want to identify, but he is pretty sure those things used to be a part of something living not long ago. He does not believe that they just drifted there.

He stops at the top of the ad hoc ramp. "I'm pretty sure we don't want to go down there," he says, and just as he does the water roils and a flash of scaly leg and tail appear at the water's surface. Then another tail.

Halim is standing next to him. "Ammits," he says. He watches the water for a moment. "Plenty of them."

"What are they doing here?"

Halim points to the ramp. "Food is sliding right down to them. It's like a vending machine."

"The ammit Stuffer Shack," Groovetooth says.

"It's not a problem," Cayman says. "We can go hand over hand." Then he turns to X-Prime.

X-Prime has been with Cayman too long, knows too well how he thinks. "Oh no," X-Prime says. "If you're making the plan, you get the hard part."

Cayman scowls. "I wasn't going to ask you anyway," he says, and it is true. He is often hard on the boy, yes, but the number of unpleasant things he considers doing to him are far greater than what he actually does. And he has always been reluctant to come up with a plan where the truly difficult part is assigned to someone else. "I'll fire the grappling gun across the way, then tie it off on this end. You all can go across, and when you're done, I'll follow."

No one asks Cayman how he'll get there, and he finds that very disappointing. It was a good little plan, and it would be nice if the other runners would recognize that. But they just assume that he will take care of himself, and he cannot say that he blames them for that assumption.

The grappling hook does not take hold on the first shot, pulling out amid a shower of concrete. Chunks splash into the murky water, and immediately the water froths around the ripples, and Cayman counts and he sees at least five massive bodies churning through the water, looking for something to eat. He looks at the steep ramp leading down to the water and is grateful that the giant crocodile-like creatures below are terrible climbers.

On the second shot the grappling hook finds an anchor. Both Cayman and Halim pull and pull on the rope and it does not come loose. There is no guarantee that it will stay that way, but it must do. Cayman ties the rope around part of the railing at the other end, and he leaves the gun barrel dangling helplessly off the side of the bridge. He yanks the rope a few more times to make sure it is secure, then there is nothing more he can do.

Groovetooth walks to the edge of the ramp without anyone telling her to. This is not the first time she has been the smallest member of a group, and she knows what she is expected to do. She gets to test the grappling hook's hold on the bridge.

In combat, in driving, in almost any situation, the other runners have made sure to put Groovetooth in the back, and so she is going to take advantage of this chance to be in front and she is not going to be timid about it. She takes firm strides to the edge of the bridge, she bends her knees when she approaches the edge, and she jumps, almost dives off the end.

Perhaps it is not as dangerous as it looks, because there is the ramp beneath her that would catch her if she fell, but it is steep and she may not be able to get a hold anywhere, and so there is a good chance that she would slide all the way to the bottom and find her way into the mouths of the ammits waiting patiently below. But the thought of failing, the thought of missing the rope, it does not cross her mind, and she grabs it and pulls so her legs swing beneath her, giving her some forward momentum that she uses to carry herself a meter or two. Then she slows, and she is dangling over the ramp and the ammits, and she has to move at a slow, unspectacular pace. But that first jump, she thinks, was fun.

She makes her way across, and the hook seems completely sturdy in its place. She takes up a position near the embedded hook so that she can keep an eye on it in case it is considering wiggling loose, and then Halim is on his way, which Groovetooth resents a small bit because it is as if they feel she is helpless on her own and she needs the big man and his sword to keep her safe. She resents the decision to send Halim even more when she feels a small breath of relief that he is on his way.

Halim makes it across smoothly, taking swings along the rope that are as long as his walking strides. He is then with Groovetooth, and Akuchi, Agbele Oku, and X-Prime take their turns. Then Cayman is the only one left on the north side.

He has studied the ramp while the others have been making their way, and he has concluded there is no way he can just leap from the top, swing down, then have the gun's winch pull him up. The slope of the ramp will not allow it—if he jumped, his ass would scrape on concrete before the winch could take up enough slack. This means he will have to move to the bottom of the ramp and go from there.

He pulls out his rifle and sprays the water at the bottom of the ramp with bullets. He cannot afford to be as thorough as he may like, as ammunition is limited, and the supply he is carrying on him must last him all day, but Halim adds some fire of his own from above, and in a few spots the water darkens to a red-violet color. He hopes these wounds are enough to slow the ammits, or even scare them off. He thinks this because he has not been in Lagos long, and his understanding of ammits is very limited.

Cayman cannot walk straight down the ramp, as it is far too steep. He is left to serpentine, crossing the ramp slowly one way, then the other, gradually making his way down. He keeps an eye on the water at the bottom of the ramp, looking for any sign of ammit activity, but it stays calm, so they have either left or they are being quite crafty.

Then the bridge bucks beneath him. It is as if he is no longer standing on concrete, but rather on a gigantic slab of grey jelly, and it shakes in every direction and resists any effort he puts forth to keep his feet safely in a single place. Both of his knees are moving in different directions, and his ankles, too, have become very independent minded in their movements, and his arm shoots out because he is going down.

It is regrettable that the arm he uses to try to catch himself is the one that holds the rifle, which means that the weapon is no longer pointed at the base of the ramp. Shaken by whatever it was that heaved the earth underneath Cayman's feet, the ammits have re-emerged, nervous and unhappy, and like so many other creatures on this earth when they are unhappy and nervous, ammits have a great propensity toward eating. Their great mouths open, their sharp teeth are studded with flesh from their last meal, but they are hungry nonetheless, ready for the next piece of food to slide into the red darkness lurking behind the teeth.

Cayman is falling now, a kind of rolling tumble, and he knows he has nothing to lose, so he activates the grapple gun's winch and it starts its slow wind. It is not totally taut, of course, but it gains a little tension, it is a pivot point around which Cayman can rotate his body and attempt to get straight. He rolls, moves onto his back, he is just sliding now, not rolling, he feels small rocks under his back that help lubricate his movement downward. He hears a few *pop-pops* and knows that Halim is trying to harm or at least scare the ammits before Cayman reaches them. He appreciates the effort, but he knows it will not be enough.

He is getting more in control now, he has his rifle pointed in the general direction of the water and he fires, and some light water spray hits his face a few moments later. He sees the horrible bloody murk coming closer, he smells it, and it smells of mold and iron and dead plants, and he dearly wishes he did not have to come into contact with it, but that now seems quite inevitable.

Cayman pulls his legs up as the water comes closer, and then his feet break the surface, and he kicks, kicks hard, not at anything in particular, just a hard kick forward. And he makes contact. Contact so hard it feels like he might have just shattered his shins. Then there is movement under his feet, a rough surface bumping under his boots, and he knows it is the skin of the ammit that he just kicked. He hopes he has not just made the creature angrier, but then he knows of no creature in the entire world that does not become angrier when you kick it.

He is now mostly underwater, so he swings his legs back, beneath and behind him, reaching for the submerged portion of the ramp. His legs bend as they find the concrete, then they spring forward, catapulting him toward the other side of the gap. The water he cuts through froths purple and yellow, and around him it churns. He pivots the rifle he holds in his right hand and swings it wildly, butt out. It hits nothing. Then something bumps his left ankle, and Cayman knows he doesn't have much time to react, so he kicks his left leg forward, his right leg back, and there is a light tug on the back of his left foot, and for a moment he fears it is caught, but then the leg pulls free. He then thrashes his legs, kicking wildly, occasionally making contact with things, once so hard that he wonders if he broke a toe, and he thinks that perhaps he is kicking submerged pieces of concrete instead of ammits.

Then he feels a tug on his left arm and it is the greatest feeling he has ever felt. He bends that arm, pulling his entire body behind him, and he rises out of the water. The winch has finally taken up the slack, he is directly below the other side of the gap, and he is moving up. The ammits know they are very close to losing fresh meat, and they thrash after him, but most of them succeed only in getting in each other's way. There is one, though, whose large scaled back breaks the water, who looks like it is perhaps the same size as the exploded boat back at the north end of the bridge, that has found a clear path toward Cayman. Even with his arm bent and his legs tucked under him, Cayman has no more than a meter's clearance of the water as he slowly moves upward. He very desperately wishes he could fire his rifle, but he can't be assured the barrel is clean and having the thing misfire and break on him now would be bad in case he needs to use it later. So he watches the ammit approach as he slowly rises into the air, and the ammit makes its lunge, breaking the surface of the water, but ammits are built for lunges, not leaps, so it does not get very high. Still, its teeth are many and sharp, and it has the crocodile grin of confidence on its face as its mouth opens. But Cayman wheels a leg around and crashes his heel on the ammit's snout, shutting it quickly. His other foot is near the ammit's neck, so he steps on the ammit and then pushes off, like he is running. Then he *is* running, dashing along the ammit's back as it twists and then starts to roll. It is bringing its head back around, it wants to snap again, but then it is too late. First Cayman pulls out his legs so they are out of range, and then he is out of range even if his feet are dangling beneath him and his arm is straight. The water stirs beneath him—the ammits are angry, but there is nothing more they can do to him.

He looks up, and he expects to see at least some of the others, cheering him on or maybe happy that he managed to survived, but he cannot see any of them.

"Hey!" he yells. "Anybody up there?"

There is no reply. But he hears voices. In the true way of the idle, they are arguing about something that in truth does not matter much.

The first voice he hears is Groovetooth's. "I'm telling you, this isn't how ammits operate. They don't hang out near shore, and they don't move in packs. There's something weird about that group."

"They kept having food slide down to them," Akuchi says. "Any animal gathers where there's food."

"Ammits never have trouble finding food," Groovetooth says. "When you have no predators, you can go anywhere you want and find what you need. They wouldn't be here just for food. There's something else."

Then X-Prime speaks. "Like that?"

There is a pause.

"Holy shit," Groovetooth says.

"What? What? What's going on!" Cayman says, but he has his answer before anyone speaks.

He turns as the rope twists, and he is looking out into the lagoon. There is a wall, a blue-green wall of water, at least fifteen meters tall.

It is coming straight at them.

CHAPTER ELEVEN

ONE WEEK BEFORE THE BRIDGE

When Cayman first saw the lagoon, it seemed harmless. Yes, the color of it was not right, it was darker than the nearby ocean and greener, but such is the way of many inland bodies of water, they are not the same as the great nearby oceans. It was just a body of water, as far as Cayman could see, and he had nothing against bodies of water, as there tended to be fewer humans on the water than on the land. This is not to say that Cayman had anything against humanity, but he had been a runner a long time, and when that is the case, you cannot help but notice that it is people who are trying to kill you most of the time, and thus when there is a place where there are fewer people, you conclude that it must be safer, because the number of times you must turn and look to see if someone is sneaking up in back of you is reduced.

The lagoon certainly looked safer than the airport Cayman flew into. He had plenty of time to look at it as his plane kept circling, one, two, three, more times. He wondered what was going on, but the sparse crowd on the rest of the plane seemed to be well-well with what was happening, so Cayman did not let it bother him.

With each pass, with each look he was able to get at the airport, his confidence in its safety decreased. Details emerged, each more troubling than the last. The potholes on the runway, they did not bother him. He had always thought that the worse the runway's condition, the better, because pilots that landed on such runways tended to be more alert, more aware, and better able to improvise than any other pilots. In the rare occasions when he must put himself in someone else's hands, those are the kind of people he wanted to be in charge. So the sadly neglected runways were not a problem, but the many, many people who stood around and killed on the airfield were. Some of them were in jeeps, some of them were on foot; a few of them were in uniform, most of them were not. They disembarked from planes that stopped in the middle of some runway, taking whatever piece of tarmac seemed convenient and out of the way, and they grabbed bags that may not have been theirs and ran as fast as they could. Some of them were armed, others—the ones who ran faster—had firearms out, and they were pointing guns here and they were pointing guns there, and many people were trying to look threatening, but Cayman could not tell from his high-up perch how well they were succeeding. They landed in chaos, which is not the best way to start a mission into a foreign city, but what else did Cayman expect? He did his homework, he'd known what he was getting into when he was going to Lagos; he just didn't want to get the full immersion in the chaos this quickly.

Then the plane straightened out and started to go down. The reactions of the people around him were rapid—as soon as the descent started, they were on their feet, moving around, grabbing their things and putting packs on their backs and pushing their way to the door. If there had been a flight attendant, perhaps he or she would have tried to instill some sort of order in the plane, but there wasn't, so they didn't. Cayman faced toward X-Prime, so he could give him a look that said, *"We should get up, too,"* but the boy was already on his feet and walking to the hatch. Cayman then felt regrettably slow, so he stood and straightened his shoulders and took up as much space as he could so that no one could move by him until he let them.

The plane shook, but Cayman was ready. He had stood in too many moving vehicles to let this one throw him. People around him stumbled this way and that, but most of them looked like they had done this before, too. A few of them stepped past the unfortunate ones who stumbled.

There was a bump, a *thump*, and many rumbles, and then another solid *thump* that Cayman guessed was a pothole. There was the roaring, slowing rushing sound of the engines braking the plane, and then the plane stopped, and almost as soon as it wasn't moving (there was no taxiing anywhere, the plane landed, then stopped, then was done) the hatch was tossed open.

There was nowhere to go, of course, but the two or three people in front poked their heads out and looked here and looked there and one of them stuck his hand out the hatch and waved at someone, and it looked like someone responded, because soon a staircase drove up to the side of the plane.

The first person was out of the plane before the staircase was firmly in place; he jumped across a meter-wide gap and hit the top of the stairs and ran down, three steps at a time, and then was off to whatever place it was that required such speed and urgency. Cayman hoped he made it wherever he was going, but he never liked to bet on a man who was pitted against jeeps full of people with guns.

Cayman walked off the plane when it was his turn, and that put him about five people behind X-Prime. He hated to admit it, but he was impressed with the way the boy moved. The skittishness, the look here and look there that Alex did a few years back, was gone. He couldn't intimidate people, he never would, but he had learned to walk like he was comfortable wherever he was, and to slip through crowds at whatever speed he desired. Cayman decided he should take credit for the way he moved and seemed comfortable in the street. He walked quickly and caught up to X-Prime.

"I taught you how to walk, you know."

"Yeah. Thanks, Mom."

"One day you'll thank me. Genuinely."

"Yeah. You brought me to one of the absolute shitholes in the world so we can do a run we don't know anything about. Thanks."

"Would you have rather stayed in Seattle?"

Now, let me say that I truly wish that I had time to detail all the reasons why Cayman and X-Prime did not feel like this was a good time to be in Seattle, because it is a good story, but I cannot stop and take time and tell every good story that comes to mind, so I will stick with the one I have already started, and perhaps afterward you can stay later and we will follow one or more of these digressions. Now. Cayman and X-Prime do not, of course, know the layout of the Mohammed International Airport, and it is not the sort of facility that has convenient signs telling you where to go. There are buildings here and buildings there, and some of them are clearly airplane hangars and some are not, and the purposes of the ones that are not hangars were often unclear. The people who exited the plane were not helpful, as they were heading in a myriad number of directions, and so Cayman made a simple call, and that was to head toward the closest thing that looked like it would be a way out. There is a break in the fence not too far away, and while it is guarded, there are people passing through it, so it seemed as likely an egress as any. Cayman angled toward it and X-Prime, as independent-minded as he may have become, still had the instinct to follow Cayman, and so he did.

It did not take long for them to reach the gate, and when they did there was a tall, thin ork with mirrored sunglasses who smiled at them, and it was not a welcoming smile. It was a smile that reflected the amusement and sense of contentment possessed by an ork holding a gun who is surrounded by friends who also hold guns.

"This is a restricted exit," the ork said. "You have to go through the building."

"Which one?" Cayman said.

"That one," the man said, and pointed to a building entirely across the airport.

Cayman looked at the building, then looked back at the man. "That building is a long way away."

The ork's smile broadened. "Then perhaps you should have walked that way as soon as you got off the plane."

Two people edged their way past Cayman, nodded at the guards, and walked out of the airport.

"See, those people just left. So this is an exit, right?" Cayman said.

The guard shook his head. "They are special. They are from here, and they have made the proper arrangements. You—" and here he smiled again "—are not from here, and have not made the proper arrangements."

Cayman did not bother to ask how the guard knew that, since he had little use for obvious questions. He swallowed, took a deep breath, and did the thing he hated most. He stepped back, looked at X-Prime, and nodded.

"Do your thing."

X-Prime smiled and stepped forward. "Look. We know we're *oyibos*. We know we're not going to get the same treatment that natives get."

The ork sniggered and looked back at some of his fellow guards. "Look at that. He knows a word."

"Here's another one I know. *Hawala*."

The ork pointed to the same building he'd indicated before. "You can find one there."

X-Prime did not turn around. "I'm sure I could. If I wanted to." He reached into his pocket and pulled out a white plastic disk. He rotated it slowly in his hand so that the ork could see the picture on it, which was a woman who had a snake wrapped around her neck. "But I don't need a *Hawala*."

The ork barely glanced at the chip. "You got good money. Good for you. But you don't have very much of it."

"Yeah, you're right. Assuming I have only one of these."

"You could have five, ten of them, and it still wouldn't do you much good."

"You're right again. But look, I'd like you to have this chip anyway. Just for you."

The other guards had paid a little attention to the conversation once X-Prime had gone digging for money, but the handover of a single white *Hawala* token did not cause much interest to stir in them. Most of them went back to looking at the people walking toward them and sizing them up.

But the ork had heard something. He had noticed the careful inflection of the last three words X-Prime had said. When X-Prime reached out the hand holding the white chip, the ork grasped it, shook it. When he pulled his hand back, he opened it long enough to verify that the chip that had actually been passed to him was grey. He pocketed the chip.

That was all X-Prime needed. The bribe had been accepted, and since he got to keep it all for himself, the ork should now be quite willing to help X-Prime and Cayman get through. There would have to be more conversation, but it was just to establish a pretext, so that appearances matched the actions that were about to take place.

"You know a single white *Hawala* chip is not going to do anything for you," the ork said, perhaps too loudly.

"All I want it to do is buy us a little time to talk," X-Prime said, and the pretext building began.

Ten minutes later, there was something bothering Cayman, and it was not the fact that he was squeezing through narrow gaps on the city streets while sitting on the back of a bike that had a plastic rear seat for him that cracked and bent alarmingly every time he put the smallest little bit of pressure on it. It was not the dust that seemed like it might be red from its heat as he breathed it in and it scratched and seared his nose and lungs. There were plenty of things that could bother Cayman, but none of them were the thing that was making him feel annoyed. Or maybe they were, because he could not put his finger precisely on what it was that was wrong. But he would figure it out.

Sometimes he was ahead of the *okada* that was carrying X-Prime, sometimes behind it. Twice, as they moved through the always-shifting street, the two *okada*s nearly crashed into each other, and the drivers yelled at each other and shook fists at each other, and once even pushed each other, and then they smiled at each other, and squeezed the throttle and drove much faster than safety would recommend. They were on the way to a bar, which was so normal to Cayman that he was firmly convinced that he could tell the entire story of his life as a journey between bars, with stops and places of less importance along the way.

Cayman believed that the traffic in Lagos moved on the right, but he could not be sure because his driver moved freely on either side of the street—to the driver, the only wrong side of the street was the one not currently moving. Cayman worried he was throwing off the balance of the bike, that the driver would make a miscalculation in one of his turns because he was not used to carrying so much weight in the back, but the driver remained quite sure handed. It all seemed like extended improvisation, no planning, just reacting, and it probably was, but it worked. It got the *okada* from point A to point B, and when Cayman finally arrived at point B he was grateful both to be there and to be moving in a way that did not risk his life each second.

Point B was a place called the Three Friends, and Cayman could almost see the whitewash actively peeling in the afternoon sun. It seemed popular enough, though, and there were many young people who walked in and walked out, with most of them carrying or consuming some sort of food substance, and Cayman figured that meant that whatever was served inside likely would not kill him, which he viewed as a plus. But he was working, so he could not view this place like he would a customer. He would have to look for dark corners, for people who might be watching him too closely, and for anything else that might not run smoothly and that he might be able to fix with the simple, precise application of force.

He walked into the building ahead of X-Prime and found his contact immediately. Hippo was described to him as "the biggest fixer in Lagos," and there was a table in the Three Friends designed just for him. It was a corner booth underneath peeling, faded posters of Lisbon, Buenos Aries, and Portland, and the tabletop sat on top of a single post that was bolted tightly to the ground. That meant it could not move, which would be a problem for someone of Hippo's build because he could not fit behind the table unless he placed a significant portion of his bulk on top of the table, which would present an unusual and somewhat unappetizing sight to all in the restaurant. So someone, maybe the restaurant owners, maybe Hippo himself, cut out a nice, large arc from the table, giving him the perfect place to sit. It was possible, Cayman thought, that Hippo was the only person who ever used that table. It was also possible that he only left that spot to sleep, and maybe not even then.

Hippo was at his table, a huge ork with perhaps the roundest, jolliest ork face Cayman has ever seen, though the cheerful effect was set off a bit by the teeth. His eyes lit up when he saw Cayman and X-Prime, and he smiled and waved them over, but of course he did not stand to greet them.

Cayman wondered briefly how Hippo recognized them so quickly, but then he remembered his *oyibos*-ness. He would have to get used to sticking out on this mission.

"Sit down, sit down," Hippo said, waving them over with great sausage arms that continued to shake long after he had stopped moving them. "You are Halim's out-of-town friends! Come, come, have some good Nigerian food! You look like you could use it!"

Cayman may have been new in town, but he'd be damned if he'll look like he doesn't know his food. "Pepper soup, *fufu*, and palm wine," he said to the first server he saw. X-Prime ordered some roast goat, then got down to business with Hippo.

"How's business?" he said.

Hippo beamed. "The city is lawless, the oil pipeline is rich. How bad could business be?"

"I wouldn't think there's enough to go around," X-Prime said.

"Of course there's not. There are many people who struggle. Many people who fight over scraps. But for the best—for us, there is plenty. Plenty for me. Plenty for you. Plenty for your friend Halim."

"Not my friend," X-Prime said. "I've never had the pleasure of meeting the gentleman. He knows Cayman, though, and Cayman doesn't say bad things about him, which is good, because usually Cayman has bad things to say about anyone."

"Halim must like your friend as well, to fly you all the way out here."

Cayman's eyes narrowed as he chewed a piece of goat meat (the food was not exceptional, but it was delivered very fast). Hippo was fishing. He may not even have known why he was fishing, or what he hoped to catch, but it's reflex. When there's something you don't know in this business, you try to know it. You may not know how you will use it, you may never use it, but it is always better to know than not know.

Cayman, though, would not be trusting X-Prime to talk if he didn't think the boy had learned his way around a conversation with a fixer. X-Prime did not disappoint him.

"Oh, I can't speak for what Halim was thinking when he asked us to come out. If you want to know that, you should ask him."

"Then I will! I will!" Hippo said. "And I suppose you would like to know where to find him?"

"That might be a good thing to know, at some point. But we're in no hurry. Especially when we have good quality palm wine to sample."

That wasn't strictly true—Cayman at this point would much rather be talking to Halim and planning the mission than sitting in some little *buka*, and also the palm wine was too young, too sweet for him to consider it top quality. But he had learned long ago that he was too blunt and direct in these matters, which is why his mouth was not moving except to chew and drink.

"Wonderful!" Hippo said. "Then we have plenty of time to talk! I can tell you about the city, about all that is happening, about anything you want to know! And when you are ready, we can talk about what you want to know, and how grateful you will be to me when I tell it to you."

What followed was a half-hour of indirect bartering. Rather than directly haggle over what Hippo would charge to direct them to Halim, X-Prime tried to be entertaining enough so that Hippo would consider him a friend and, when it came to it, lower the price for his services. Cayman spent that time balancing the spiciness of the pepper soup with the mild *fufu* and the sweet palm wine, keeping an eye on everything around him in case someone decided to do something interesting.

They did not. But then, before he knew it, X-Prime was standing and shaking Hippo's hand, and some data was, he hoped, flowing from Hippo's PAN to X-Prime's, and they were done. X-Prime may have been the first to stand, but Cayman was out the door before him.

"Where do we have to go?" he asked as soon as they were outside. "Can we go on foot?"

"I think so," X-Prime said. "It's only three kilometers or so."

Cayman nodded. "Okay. We'll walk. Have you sent me the data?"

"Yep."

Cayman looked in front of him, and sure enough there was a floating green arrow pointing east. "Let's go."

He had hoped, when he set out on foot, that walking would be easier than riding the *okada*. That he would be able to slip through gaps easier, that the crowds and throngs would not be a problem. The masses of people turned out not to be a life-threatening problem, as they were when he was on the cycle, but they were still unpredictable and annoying. They surged here, they pushed there, they followed no logic or order. They pushed and fought each other, they tripped and stepped over and on each other, they ground each other into the dust, but they also refused to stay down when stepped on.

Cayman grew progressively irritated as he walked, and he started relying less on his glare to move people out of his way and more on his arms. He swung them freely, throwing an elbow or a forearm when he needed to, not worrying whom he knocked down, because most of them were being hit from so many sides that they would not know which one had actually knocked them over. He followed the green arrow as it led him through twisty streets, through narrow streets, and through streets that once were narrow but now had only demolished buildings on either side in which squatters sat, as if they hoped that someday the building might heal itself and again provide them with shelter. He followed the green arrow until it led him to a whitewashed brick wall, a dead end of a small alley.

X-Prime smiled at the wall. "That wouldn't happen to be Halim, would it?"

"Damn map's out of date," Cayman snapped. He looked at

the wall—it was a good five meters high, and Cayman had no faith that there would be anything passable on the other side of it. "Reprogram the maps."

"You got it." X-Prime fiddled here and there, and then the floating green arrow abruptly changed, helpfully indicated that maybe Cayman wanted to travel away from the wall and leave the alley.

Cayman kept up a steady stream of curses as he followed the arrows, and no one seemed to care, because most of them were talking to themselves too, and only a few of them were more coherent than him. They were so loud that Cayman cursed louder just so he could hear himself, until he was almost yelling his curses into the crowded street.

Then he felt a hand on his elbow. He whirled. It was X-Prime.

"What the hell is the matter with you? Late onset Tourette's?"

"Shut up," he said. Then he scowled. "I don't like this place. First thing you do when you go someplace new is figure out the rules. Figure out how it works. There aren't any rules here. We can't predict a damn thing."

"Yeah, I know. Neat, isn't it? You get the feeling that you never know what's going to happen next, and it could be anything." He smiled, a smile so young and happy that Cayman wanted to punch all his teeth out. "I like it."

"That's because you're an idiot," Cayman snapped. "This—all this here?" He waved his arm wildly, in the process knocking over a tall, thin man who happened to stumble into his way. "This is no way to do business."

CHAPTER TWELVE

But that sentiment did not carry the day, as Cayman obviously found a way to do business in this city, as the only reason he has taken himself to the bridge is because of a damned job. And the bridge is where we left him as he looks at the grappling hook, thinking maybe it could be an anchor and perhaps would keep him on the bridge when the large wave that is bearing down on him hits. But how will it hold all six of them? There is not time to get them all tied down.

He can keep himself on the bridge, though, then worry about finding the others later. Cayman secures the gun on his hip, then lies down, holding the cable in his hands. He gives the rope an experimental tug, and it holds. He takes a look to see how much time he has before the wave hits—

Water wallops his face. Then he is tumbling and desperately trying to float.

He has enough sense to push up, up, up, because he does not want to hit the other railing or anything solid. He reaches for the cable, hoping it can pull him somewhere safe, hoping it is still attached. But it probably is not. It is likely loose and tumbling, like everything else in the world now seems to be. He thinks he is moving up, but he cannot tell. He cannot see the sky, the sun, or anything. He closes his eyes so that no more lagoon water gets in them.

He keeps hoping he will feel a pull of magic, that Agbele Oku will do something to get him out of this. But he does not know where she is, what she is doing. Before the wave hit, he was trying to take care of himself and only himself, and it is very possible that she was doing the same.

He feels wind on his face and knows he has a moment to take

a breath, so he takes advantage of it, an explosion of air out and a whoosh in, but the end of the whoosh is water and he is back under, his lungs wanting to cough, but his brain firmly saying no, no, you cannot. His legs move when he tumbles, because he knows that the lagoon is not very deep, and despite the size of the wall of water, he should eventually be able to find the ground. It cannot go on forever. He has to find land eventually.

But the ground remains elusive. His lungs are burning, they want to heave, he swears he can feel the liquid inside him, he swears it is poisoning his blood, but there is nothing he can do. He holds his breath and holds it and holds it, he keeps his eyes firmly shut as if that will help his mouth remain sealed, he holds and holds and holds until this small red knot that is building in his head gets bigger and bigger and then it explodes into yellow and white, burning white that overwhelms everything, takes away everything he can see and hear and feel, everything is that white explosion, and then he is gone.

And then he is back. But slowly. For a while he just concentrates on the simple pleasure of breathing, of feeling air in his lungs and nothing else. His mouth doesn't feel right, so he reaches up and touches it and there is something dry and crusty around it. He wipes that layer off and it is damp underneath. He does not want to know what it is, but he has a guess, as there is only one natural reaction to swallowing a large quantity of filthy water.

When he is done wiping his mouth, his hand drops to the ground and it is sandy. Or dusty. Or both. There are some plants there, too, long, rough-edged blades of something. He does not rub them too carefully. He has not been in Lagos very long, but even a few days are enough to teach you that most plants in the area do not respond well to being touched, and your skin tends not to like it either, especially when your skin is pasty and weak.

He decides it is time to open his eyes. They sting. He blinks a few times, then he moves his head because he is looking almost directly at the sun. He sees that what he is lying on is not exactly a beach—it's an empty lot, the base of some building or another, that had the ground erode out from under it, and then collapsed down into the lagoon. It happened long enough ago for sand and dust to pile up on top of the concrete, which at least made it a more comfortable place for him. It was mostly enclosed—there were buildings to the north and south, the lagoon to the east. The only way out, assuming he did not want to go back into the polluted water that may already be poisoning his system, was west.

There is someone not too far away, legs slightly spread apart, his back to Cayman. Cayman's eyes cannot quite focus yet, but he knows it is Halim.

The sight of another member of his team gets his mind moving. Where are the others? Where are the boxes? Did they lose any of the boxes? If some of the boxes are floating in the lagoon, how will they recover them?

But before he gets to those questions there are perhaps more immediate things he should address. Such as, what is Halim looking at?

Cayman pushes up, tries to get to his feet, and finds his legs surprisingly wobbly. His knees even bonk together once, but they don't cave. They firm, then he pushes with his arms again and he is standing entirely on his own.

His steps toward Halim are cautious and halting, and he considers calling out his name, but since he doesn't know much about what is going on around him, it probably is not a good idea to draw attention to himself.

He coughs. There must still be water in his lungs. He coughs again. Halim does not turn around.

He walks slowly toward him, still feeling a tickle in his lungs. The water is persistent. But then he smells the air, and he decides that maybe it is not water that is bothering him. And now that he can see Halim better, he sees that one hand is over his mouth and nose, and it looks like he is holding some sort of cloth.

Cayman straightens up and finally follows Halim's gaze. There is a haze over the city, a grey haze, and it has an orange glow to it, like the sun is setting on the horizon underneath it. But it is the afternoon, the sun is not setting, so the glow is coming from something else.

"The city is burning," Halim says, in the same way that he might tell a waiter that his goat is a bit stringy.

"Oh," Cayman says. He looks at Halim to try to find a trace of emotion. "I'm...sorry?"

"It will make our journey south more difficult."

"Yeah, fires do that."

Halim briefly turns to him to shoot him a look of complete contempt, and Cayman is thankful that it does not last long.

"Downtown is clearing out," Halim says, "so even more people are in the streets, coming north. Once we get by them, the streets will be empty."

"And full of fire and smoke."

"We can find a way through."

"You're crazy!"

But Halim is moving forward.

Cayman walks quickly to keep up. "Look, I want to get downtown as bad as anybody, but first of all, we don't have any of the packages. Second, there's a reason all of these people are coming out of the city. It's because the burning parts of a city are not good to be in. I don't care how determined you are, you can't just plow through a bunch of smoke and fire just because you're stubborn!"

But the only effect Cayman's words have is to make Halim walk faster. That will stop soon, though. The small alley leading to the beach where Cayman washed up is ending, and ahead of him is the throng. The same crowds who had greeted him when he arrived in Lagos are there, only there are more of them, and they are angrier and more panicked. But they are just people, and they can be moved through.

Halim is trying to part them with the stare, but the crowd is too occupied with each other to notice. Many of them take a few steps down the alley before realizing it was a dead end, then they step back and try to rejoin the flowing stream of people.

Halim takes a step into the crowd and was immediately rebuffed, pushed back into the alley. Cayman blinked in surprise for a moment, but while Halim is an ork and a fairly strong one at that, he is still only a finite amount of biological material, and material can always be moved when enough force is applied.

Halim's eyes narrow, and he steps into the crowd again. He is jostled, but he holds his ground. He is pushed, and he pushes back and sends someone down on his hoop. In a crowd packed this tight, a person cannot fall without hitting others, and many others around the hapless victim stumble and nearly go down themselves, and some of them do, in fact, fall to the dust.

This, then, results in a large number of unhappy people in the street, people who are unhappy they are being bumped, people who are unhappy they are on the ground, and people who are unhappy that they live in a diseased hellhole that has the unfortunate habit of having large portions of it go up in smoke. They start lashing out at whatever is convenient, and in some of these cases that thing is Halim, and in other cases it is Cayman, but both of them must fight off blows while delivering some of their own.

Halim, turning a bit after jabbing an elbow into someone's gut, takes a forearm swipe across his cheek, jarring his head. It hurts only a little, but it is tremendously annoying. Halim has had enough. His forearm blade unfolds, and he stabs. He thinks he got the person who hit him, but he cannot be sure. A dozen people around him see his blade, they see blood, and they react in a dozen different ways. One drops to help the bleeding man, another draws a knife of his own, another screams, another tries to run away, and so on. But Halim is going to get through this crowd no matter what it takes, and he moves his arm blade in a way that he hopes convincingly delivers this message.

There are gaps that appear, as they always do for someone who is armed, but there are also obstacles that pop up, people reaching for his arm, trying to knock it out of the way, and there are limbs flailing around him, some of them lightly bumping into him, some of them hitting him quite solidly, even one fist impacting the back of his neck.

None of this angers him. His breathing is slowing. His focus is shortening. It will be a unique fight, this struggle against this single crowd entity, and all the pieces of it who think they are individuals, but are really just a part of this larger organism, this enemy that must be beaten. The corners of Halim's mouth pull back, and he steps forward more aggressively.

Only to have a hand on his shoulder yank him back.

He whirls, armblade slashing while his other hand reaches for a gun. But his slash misses, and the person behind him already has a gun pointed at his head. Halim sees red, furious that he could have so badly miscalculated so soon in the fight, but then he realizes his mistake—the person who is now pointing a gun at him is one he did not consider carefully in this fight because it is a person who is supposed to be an ally.

Cayman is shaking his head. "No," he says. "We're not doing it this way."

Those who might have wanted to attack Halim are backing off, making a wise decision to leave the matter in the hands of the big man with the shiny gun.

"That way is the Island," Halim says without turning around or even gesturing in the correct direction. "That is the direction we want to go. You know that. You want to go there, too."

"Not this way," Cayman says. "Not by killing anyone who gets in our way just so we can walk through a furnace. Not without the people who have the actual goods we're supposed to be bringing. We're not going to accomplish much heading that way right now."

Halim thinks about fighting Cayman. He bears no ill will toward Cayman, and he cannot even dispute the logic the other shadowrunner just laid out. But he cannot easily leave the state he is in. He has never built the temperament that can walk away from a fight.

There is a scream, one among many, but louder. And from a different direction. This one comes from behind Cayman. It is not from the direction most people are walking away from—it is where most of them are going.

Then the crowd is moving in two directions, as people continue streaming from the south while others are now coming from the north, and there is an impossibly dense collection of people gathering in the street, and Cayman and Halim know they need to find some other way to move. Even the small alley leading to the lagoon that they came out of is becoming crowded.

Cayman looks up. There are plenty of buildings in this section of town, which is unfortunate—a nice collection of vacant lots would widen their travel options. But most of the buildings here are three or four stories tall, which provides an alternate path—assuming the grapple gun can still fire.

"Come on," Cayman says, and leads Halim back into the snub-nosed alley where there is a little more room to operate. He walks up to the wall, fires the gun, makes sure the hook has purchase, then gestures at Halim to get moving, but he does not need to. Halim is already a few meters up the wall.

Cayman follows him quickly, reeling the rope in as he goes. He does not want anyone following him. If there is anybody in the crowd who was angry with Halim for his attacks and who is carrying a gun, they are in trouble. But Cayman guesses that if any such person had a gun they would have fired it already, so he is not overly worried. But he hurries up the building nonetheless.

They arrive on the roof to find that it is less crowded than the street, but not empty. People have found their way to the rooftops through staircases in other buildings, and most of them are milling around, simply relieved to be out of the crowd and apparently not convinced that they can journey far on the rooftops. In a city that is a grid, they might be right, but in a loosely planned, casually constructed city like Lagos, there are more possibilities. There are narrow alleys, thin streets, where the distance from one roof to another is not great. If you are quick enough and strong enough, you can make it across many of these gaps. Halim is already running forward toward the first such gap, and his relief at being able to move freely is evident in every step.

More screams stream up from the street below. On city streets, sound carries better up than it does across, so these screams sound very clearly in Cayman's ears, clearly enough that he can begin to tell what kind of screams they are. It is perhaps unfortunate that there are people who hear enough screams in their lifetime that they are able to discern between the different types of screams, but while it was a painful ability to develop, it is a skill that has often been useful to Cayman. What he is hearing are not just screams of pain or anger. There is fear in them, terror. There is something worse than the pressing mob in the streets ahead.

Cayman would just as soon avoid whatever it is, but their path across the rooftops does not give him much choice. They hop over the small walls that divide one roof from another, they dance around the broken skylights over rotten wood floors, and their path takes them closer to the screams. There are more of them, and then there are ripping, tearing noises, and even Cayman, with all he has seen and heard, has not heard that particular noise very often, which is a good thing.

Chaos is useful for many, many purposes, including several that are destructive. Chaos allows borders to be crossed. And so some of the shedim that are often content to remain in Alimosho have ventured out because too many people are too busy to do anything to stop them. There is, in fact, at this point a long, scattered line of shedim, stretching from Lagos Mainland to Alimosho. They came out in several groups at different times, and when one group found a spot that provided the food they were seeking, they stopped and fed and encouraged any other shedim who came along to move on and find their own damn food. Now they are feeding at many points, including on the street below Cayman and Halim, and of course the many, many people could overwhelm the small number of shedim if they wanted to, and while some of them would undoubtedly die, the threat would be ended, but mobs are not good at concerted action, so they continue to panic and scream and run here and there and back and forth while the shedim enjoy a very messy feast and blood and innards quickly rot in the streets.

Cayman is transfixed by the shedim for only a brief moment, but it is enough for Halim to disappear from view. Cayman looks around quickly for the samurai, then he sees another broken skylight. He runs to it and gets there just in time to hear a distant door slam.

He is not going down there. There is no reason to be in the street now. That scene down there, that mess, will not help them do what they want to do in any way.

But Halim sees it differently. He is moving at full speed when he emerges from the building, every bit of him a blur, and he comes at the shedim like a blinding light. A few blocks ago Halim was going to be the scourge of Lagos, killing and killing citizens as needed so that he could get to where he wanted to go. Now he is the savior, bursting out into the streets to save those confronted by the shedim. He does not think about either role, scourge or savior, for neither means anything to him. What is important is that he will get his fight. He will return to the calm Cayman almost took from him. And like the shedim, he will take the opportunity to feed.

CHAPTER THIRTEEN

SIX DAYS BEFORE THE BRIDGE

Perhaps the most remarkable thing about a group dynamic is how quickly it forms. Yes, it will evolve over time as group members start to know each other better and as relationships shift, but the basic ground rules are established quickly. Whether the group is supportive or competitive, humorous or dead serious, sincere or full of shit, comes out soon. Once the initial small talk is over and people start letting their real selves show, you know what kind of group you have, and you know what you will be stuck with.

The first thing that struck Cayman about this new group he was now a part of was the mistrust.

They were not in anyone's house. They were not in anyone's favorite hangout. No one was willing to give away where they lived or where they often spent time to anyone else. So they met in a neutral location, a nightclub that turned the bass up terribly loud in the hopes that patrons would get blinding headaches and therefore would not be able to see that they were in a rickety wooden structure that might fall in on them if a termite happened to set its teeth into the wrong beam.

Agbele Oku had filtered the noise so they could talk, and Halim, as the person who had brought them all together, had bought a round of palm wine for everyone. The place was a dump, but at least the palm wine had been aged a bit, souring it, encouraging sipping rather than drinking.

They were not supposed to be working right now. The planning and all that could start tomorrow, Halim had said. This was just to get to know each other, feel each other out, which, of course, is also work, just of a different nature. So all six of them looked casual while remaining quite poised. Cayman already had several conversational openings jump into his head, but all of them were along the lines of, "So, this is quite a shithole you live in," so he remained silent and left the job of starting talk to others.

X-Prime was quite happy to take up the baton. There once was a time, when he'd lived a life that was routine and relatively safe, that he watched what he said very carefully and measured his words like a desert traveler measures his daily ration of water. But he had lost that entire existence and yet still survived, and over time that had built of a certain lack of caution in him—not carelessness, or even recklessness, but an idea that there were some things, like the common courtesy of social conversation, that were not worth worrying about.

"So, this is quite a shithole you live in," X-Prime said.

The reactions of the Lagosians were as follows: The corner of Halim's mouth twitched, Akuchi smiled and raised his plastic cup in acknowledgement, Groovetooth nodded, and Agbele Oku frowned and offered the first reply.

"If what you say is true, it is only because there are people who gain from it being that way," she said, her eyes flashing. "They are the ones who keep it as it is."

"Of course they are," X-Prime said. "Just like almost every place else in the world. It's just been going on here a little longer, is all."

Some of the anger left Agbele Oku's face. "Yes. That is very much the case."

"That's right," Akuchi said, still smiling. "We're not the problem, we're the solution. Sure, we exploit people for our own ends, we cause occasional suffering, but we do it for the *right* reasons. Unlike those wealthy and powerful bastards, who just do it to become rich and powerful."

Groovetooth looked around, and her nose twitched. "I'm not trying to become rich and powerful." Another twitch. "At least, not powerful."

"Of course," Akuchi said. "We're all just trying to earn a living. Just happens that we're in a business that the only way we get paid is if someone else loses something—some information, some money, their job, their life, whatever."

The curious thing, at least from Cayman's perspective, was that Akuchi delivered these words in a casual, off-hand manner. He was indicting the whole group, himself included, but he did not seem to care in the least.

"We're providing services," Groovetooth said. "Something we can do that other people can pay for. That's what a job is."

"And we didn't have too many choices about it, either, right?" X-Prime added.

"There are always choices," Agbele Oku said. "And there are always people who deserve to lose the things we take."

"You're saying you only take from the guilty, and you've *never* hurt anyone innocent?" Groovetooth said.

"Are *you* saying there aren't enough guilty people here to keep us all busy for the rest of our lives?" Agbele Oku said.

"This is one of those conversations that does not matter," Halim said. His voice was even and mild, but Cayman noticed that the others, they immediately became quiet and did not speak again until they were certain that Halim did not have any more to say. "Anyone who wants to make this a better city can work on that when the job is done. This job is not about anything besides this job. That's all."

"That's never all," Agbele Oku insisted.

"Maybe," Akuchi said. "But that's all we can worry about."

Cayman had not said anything during this brief exchange, but he was almost ready to make his journey back to the airport, pay whatever bribes he had to make, fly back to Seattle, and write off any expenses he had incurred as an unfortunate loss. The disagreement, it is true, was not severe, and no one seemed to be on the verge of escalating it. But he did not like the sound of people going in different directions the first time they spoke together as a group. He was not confident about his ability to maneuver in a city with few rules, and he was even less confident about how he would do with these other people around him. The only mitigating factor, to him, was the deference given Halim. He trusted Halim, and if the others did too, than perhaps that would be enough.

As the evening continued, though, he began to think that he was worrying too much. Drinks came to their table, Agbele Oku let a little extra external noise slip in, and conversations broke into groups of two or three and turned to the topic that often comes up when runners got together—war stories.

Everyone loosened up a bit as they talked, and even Groovetooth became less nervous. The more animated she became, the more her head bobbed and weaved on top of her neck, keeping time to some rhythm that did not quite match the music in the club.

"So, when you in a van you not supposed to be in, when you in a place you not supposed to be in, you cannot just go and flash to everyone that you're there, *abi*? So I am looking, I am monitoring, I am checking anything with a PAN that gets in range and seeing what it is. And of course I am linked into everything the vehicle has, sensors and microphones and whatever, and so anything that gets near enough, living or not, I see.

"I am waiting for the right signal, waiting to find who we want to see so that we can finish the job, and I finally see something, but I know right away it is not who we are waiting to see. There is no PAN, no nodes, but there is life. Something living is approaching our van. The sensors, they are not specific. They just tell me something is approaching that is warm enough to be alive. That is all I know.

"If it is not who we want to meet, then we can just lock down. Make sure whoever it is, whatever it is, they leave us alone, and then we wait more.

"I wait, and the sensors show much warm temperature, maybe enough for three or four people—or one or two trolls. They are coming for us, they are moving quickly, and I hope that they pass by and move away just as quickly.

"Then they are close enough that I can see what it is, and it is not two trolls, it is not four people, it is about a dozen things, they are low to the ground, they are shiny, and they are not happy to be in the light. The run quickly, they come under my van, and then they stop."

"What were they?" X-Prime asked.

"Bedroom bugs," Groovetooth says. "Bedbugs, but larger. Which means they are hungrier, and they need more blood than bedbugs. So I know why they are under my van, with their sense of smell that can smell through anything.

"They are on the bottom of the van, and then they are somehow shaking it, and I do not know if it is only because of their weight as they walk here and there, or if it is because they are doing it on purpose, but the van is moving, and I know it is moving because of the dozens of bug legs that are on it. I want to tell the driver to move, to drive somewhere, anywhere so that we can shake the bugs off, but we are under orders to be where we are and I feel lucky to be on this job, and I don't think I can say anything.

"But I do not need to, because the driver was more in tune

with the vehicle than I am, and he knew what was on it, and he was as horrified as if they had been on his skin. He hits the accelerator, and then we are rocketing through empty streets with big potholes, and instead of avoiding them he is driving toward them so he can get the vehicle low and scrape off what is underneath. He did not tell me to fasten myself in before he drove, so I am in the back, bouncing all over, falling almost every time we hit a bump.

"Then there are the two bad things that happen. One of them is that I fall against one of the van compartments and the lid breaks and the container inside breaks and my hand is covered in the things the bugs are after. The other bad thing is that a latch breaks, and one of the back doors flies open.

"This becomes very bad because there were two wiggling antennas at the base of the door, and they moved higher, and they were on the head of a bug that had made it up from underneath and could smell or sense what it was after, and part of what it was after was on me.

"It raised up to the level of the van's floor, and it got its footing, and then it could skitter forward too too fast. I didn't have anything that could stop it, no gun, no knife, I only had my own weight, and that bug was so big that I did not know if it would be enough.

"I jumped when it came near, jumped into a flat-bellied flop, and as it ran toward me I plunged toward it, and I landed on top of it, hard, and I was the very large shoe, and it was, of course, the bug. So it did what it was supposed to do, and it squished, and the noise was like hitting a sponge full of gelatin, and it was horrible and it was all over me, along with the other things that had made it come after me in the first place.

"It turned out that the driver had taken us in a large circle, and we were back where we started, and he stopped, and the next thing I knew the people who we had to meet were there. And I stood in front of them, covered in bug remains and other muck, and I did my business. And they tipped me a little extra so I could buy myself a shower."

Cayman laughed along with Akuchi at the story, but in the back of his mind he couldn't help notice how smoothly Groovetooth left out telling details. Like, just what was it she was transporting that would attract bedroom bugs? What was the name of her driver? What part of the city was she in? It was, he thought, the perfect shadowrun story—entertaining without giving away anything crucial about the teller.

Yes, it showed that Groovetooth had secrets, but Cayman had worked long enough that he did not trust any runner who was completely open. His worries about this group did not disappear, but he was at least willing to stay in the city for a time longer.

CHAPTER FOURTEEN

There are many worse things in the world than being wet and covered in dust that the water on your skin has turned into a red mud, and one of those worse things is being dead, which seemed like a distinct possibility as Groovetooth rode the wave that swept her off the bridge. So, while she is damp and dirty, she is alive, and that fact is enough to please her.

She also knows, once she has her feet on dry ground, and has some time to attempt to decide where she has landed, that there are many people in the city who are having a worse day than she is. It is one of Those Days in Lagos, and anyone who has lived in the city long enough learns to recognize the feel of Those Days. On a normal day, the city is chaos, millions of individual currents and breezes flowing and drifting in millions of different directions, colliding into each other, swirling around each other, and generally finding some way to exist in the chaos. On one of Those Days, on the other hand, the currents and breezes of the city overlap too much, they reinforce each other too much, and they become too large, too powerful for the people who are not caught up in that growing storm to navigate, so you hope to find shelter and let the storm, whatever it may be, play itself out.

Unless you have things to do, or no shelter nearby, or both.

Groovetooth knows some of the things that might be bothering the city, like VITAS and that smell of smoke in the air, and knows there are probably other things besides that, but she is not going to bother finding out what those things are. You do not need to know the height of the clouds to steer far clear of the lightning.

There is a throng of people moving in a street ahead of her, and she approaches them and then shrinks back. She quickly wishes that Halim or someone was with her, then just as quickly is angry at herself at wishing that. She has made it for a very long time in this city on her own, and there is no reason to start relying on anyone else now.

There is a tangible heat coming from the people in front of her, the warmth of their bodies and the anger on their breath adding to the air all around. There are people in the crowd, she can pick them out one by one, who are looking for prey; their eyes glow with a red tint that may or may not be the dust in the air, and their heads swivel back and forth, slowly, looking for any excuse to lash out. They will strike, they will be violent, and they will not care much for their own well-being. They are the mines in the city's battlefield.

She has one advantage, and that is that her entire PAN is still working. She learned long ago that waterproofing is not just a mere luxury, even if you spend the vast majority of your time on dry land and cannot conceive how you would ever be submerged in water. You never know what could hit you, and you always want that PAN working.

There is no structure to the AR Groovetooth can see, no overarching framework to give it order. On a normal day, there would be a few merchants, here and there, displaying something in front of their stores, but this is one of Those Days, and so they have turned the AR off and gone into hiding, likely lurking in the back of their shops in case the crowds decide to turn their energy to looting. So it is a jumble, a mass of many people without any PAN at all and a few people with one, some broadcasting a little more information about themselves than they probably should, others not giving away anything. She takes in as much as she could, because everything she knows about this crowd, every bit of information she takes in, might help her get through it. There are words and images flying around, many of them middle fingers or upraised thumbs. The public messages people are sending are not pleasant, but some of them—like "There's a piece of shit UE behind me with a too-big gun"—are very helpful.

Groovetooth has a faint moment of hope that the "UE—"useless element"—nearby might be the *oyibos*, Cayman, but she does not think he is dumb enough to wave a gun around in a crowd. From what she has seen, he does not draw a gun until it is time to fire it.

So she avoids this UE and moves into the crowd. It already seems clear that she will not be able to find a clear route south, and she wonders if it might not be best to move back to the north end of the Third Mainland Bridge. She saw a trideo once where there was a family, and the parents told their child that if they got separated the child should return to the last place where they were all together. That seems like sound enough advice to Groovetooth, so she resolves to head north.

She merges into the crowd and no one pays her attention, because what does some not-even-1.2-meter-tall dwarf matter in this throng? She makes progress, and it is not slow, but it is also not fast. It is movement, which in any circumstance is better than stasis, even if it is movement in the wrong direction. Groovetooth, though, can only enjoy the movement for a moment before ideas leap all over her mind like army ants swarming over a Goliath beetle, and those thoughts tell her all the things that could go wrong if she does not meet up with her team. The packages have to make it to Lagos Island; she has to be with them. She is not carrying any of them. She does not know where they are. And the others, she cannot be confident that their communications equipment is watertight.

She quickly attempts to call each of them, hoping some miracle of jerry-rigged technology brings her message to their ears. There is nothing from Agbele Oku. Nothing from Cayman. She thinks maybe X-Prime has a connection open, but he is not responding to anything at the moment. And nothing from Halim, though that is par for the course.

But Akuchi is out there. She cannot locate him, the Matrix infrastructure is not detailed enough for her to pinpoint him. But she can tell he is there, and he does not seem to be far off.

She calls him on her comm, and he answers quickly.

"So the mouse can swim," he says. "Good job."

"Thanks. Where are you?"

"Just a little east of the go-slow. Wave carried me in a ways, people carried me farther. Looking for a way to make up some speed."

Groovetooth looked up, hoping to see some signs of the freeway near her. But she had never been able to see much when she was in a crowd, and the buildings on the next block, let alone the concrete pillars of the freeway, are far beyond what she can see.

"I'm going to head to the north end of the bridge," she says. "What about you?"

"Makes as much sense as any place else," he says. "I'll try to see you before then."

That's good, then. She's connected with one person, the one who can move the fastest. Her odds of not being cut out of anything are now better.

When she thinks this, there is not a moment where she stops and considers that perhaps one of the team members will try to do something on their part to make sure that she is not cut out of the job, that she will get her cut no matter what happens from this point on. That is not a thought that occurs to her.

She slips and worms her way through the crowd, grateful for those brief moments when she has a clear path and can walk normally, shoulders squared, steps fast. Those openings close too fast, and she is back to moving like a viper, or perhaps more appropriately, like a mongoose chasing a distant viper, wriggling and twisting.

There is one twist when she is facing west and a gap in the crowd opens and she thinks she sees the white-grey of the go-slow a few blocks away. That does not mean she is near Akuchi, there are lots of places that are near the go-slow, but she hopes that since they rode here in the same wave, maybe they are about in the same place.

Then she hears a buzz, a whine like a very big mosquito. It rises, falls, rises. She knows the sound. She activates her comm.

"Akuchi?" she says.

"I've gotten a little faster," he says.

"Rev your engine."

"You got it," he says. She hears a whining over the comm that rises and falls, but the whining near her does not change.

"That's not you," she says.

"What's not me?"

"Never mind," she says. The whining is coming closer and will require her attention. Then it takes a certain bend and curves toward her. It still has to rise and fall, because he cannot keep up any regular speed, but soon enough Groovetooth sees the crowd jumping and bumping, moving out of the way of an object she still cannot see.

She sees the tire first, narrow and dark and quite smooth with age. The cycle is primitive, without so much as racing lines in its AR overlay to make it look fast. But it does not seem complicated, and it has a functioning engine. That is all that concerns her.

She wishes she had a pipe, or even a stick, but all she has is the crowd and a hope that the rider has a basic sense of decency. This being Lagos, there is perhaps a one in three chance that this is the case.

The bike comes closer, and Groovetooth grabs the arms of people near her and first pulls them toward her, then leans forward. They are stumbling with her, cursing and yelling, and then they see the cycle and that they are in its path and they scream and jump. Groovetooth lets them go. The cyclist's eyes widen, and he sends his bike into a skid to avoid this sudden logjam. Groovetooth is already running, moving toward the back of the cycle, so that when its wheel swings by her she is able to give it a swift, sweeping kick. The lean of the cycle becomes more drastic, and the cycle goes down.

The slip catches the driver off guard, and he lets go of the bike. He stops on the pavement, and the bike scoots a meter away from him. He is on his side, Groovetooth is on her feet, so she has the advantage. She leaps forward, bending, grabs the cycle, picks it up, and runs ahead with it. The cyclist is getting to his feet behind her, but the engine is still running and Groovetooth leaps on it quickly. She pulls the throttle and the cyclist yells, but he is left behind.

She still does not feel like she is moving fast enough, but there is an undeniable charge when she sees an opening and is able to leap half a block forward in a single lunge. She also enjoys seeing people leap out of her way, diving, scurrying for cover, scared. She has never seen people avoid her—at least, the meat-space her—out of fear before. It's a sensation that she assumes she should not be enjoying as much as she is.

Then she reaches a block that is a mess. The blocks where people were mostly moving one way were hard to get through, but this one, here the people are moving two ways, there is one group trying to get north, and another group that seems to be trying harder to get south. The ones coming south, their mouths and eyes are wide, their limbs are flailing, they are pushing people out of the way or down to the ground to get to where they want to go. Whatever is happening ahead is bad, but Groovetooth has no other place to go.

She makes her way forward and comes to an especially broad intersection, a plaza where three four-lane roads come together. There is lots of space here, and most of it is in use. People are coming into this square and then trying to get out, most of them doubling back to avoid it but a few thinking that they can rush through the chaos and get to the other side. In the middle of the plaza are the things trying to stop them, people that look mostly like people but with a certain slackness about the jaw and eyes, along with a tendency to have messy hair and dirty clothes. These things might be enough to identify them for what they are, but the fact that a few of them are sitting on the ground and feasting on body parts they have claimed from people who have been trampled by the crowd make it clear who has taken over the plaza. This is now shedim territory.

There are shots echoing around the square. Someone is firing something. A shedim falls, so that means someone is firing at the right party. When the shedim goes down, Groovetooth briefly sees someone standing over the body, holding a gun, until the crowd closes and takes him from her view. But she saw the graying hair, the camouflage vest, and she knows that Cayman is ahead.

The gap in the crowd closes and the people shift, pushing Cayman away from her. But she knows the right direction to travel, so she goes there, avoiding the swipe of an arm with ropy muscles and long, sharp fingernails, and the arm might belong to a shedim or it might not. But it misses her, she dodges around it, then leans right to turn back toward where she thinks Cayman is.

She does not find Cayman, but there is Halim, his loose, light robe flowing around him as his sword blurs, creating a sphere of light silver around him that Groovetooth knows she should not approach. She waves to Halim, tries to get his attention, but he is absorbed in what he is doing. He makes a series of moves—a downward sweep to the right, a step with the left foot and a pivot, a wheeling motion with both hands that sends the sword into a circular motion and raises it, then a chopping motion then brings it down into the chest of a shedim with blood around his mouth. He leaps, flipping over the shedim and driving the sword deeper into him, then pulls the sword out after he lands, creating a grievous, tragic rip in the creature's chest while bringing the sword over his head and down to meet another foe. All his motions are of a piece, and they are graceful and hypnotic.

Groovetooth keeps herself from staring at him. She tries to get closer so that she can signal him, but the shedim recognize a threat when they see one, so they are closing in on him. He does not seem to mind.

There are more coming into the block. Some of them seem to be shedim, but there are too many metahumans of various types in the square, and Groovetooth cannot be sure who is what. Whatever they are, many of them are heading toward Halim, and many of them are spoiling for a fight.

She has to get them out of there, but the cycle is not big enough. She could make a pass by them, buzz them, but that wouldn't accomplish much. The cycle is far too small to pick up one of them, let alone both.

Cayman is turning to Halim, yelling something, but Groovetooth cannot make it out. There is something about ammo in what he says. Perhaps that is why Halim is relying on his blades, and Cayman is firing his handgun only sparingly—they do not have unlimited supplies of ammunition, and they cannot afford to waste much on a side battle with shedim.

But this is turning into more than a side battle, as more shedim pour into the square and some of the few living humans left find a way out. This is now the largest gathering of shedim Groovetooth has ever seen, and the sight of them puts a twist in a part of her gut that she did not know could move like that. It is not a pleasant thing to learn.

She knows she has to get out of there. She could make it on her own, but she has been helped enough by Halim that she owes it to him to try to bring him with her. She knows that he might refuse any offer of assistance and stay in the square and keep fighting shedim as long as they keep coming, but if he does that then it will at least be his decision to stay. He deserves that choice.

She guns the engine, dodging a shedim on the left, then one on the right who resides in a corpse whose left arm was mauled into hamburger meat before it died, and it swings this arm at Groovetooth, and she pivots so it hits her leg as she darts by, and she takes a piece of the arm off as she passes. The shedim screams, and she knows it is yelling in frustration, not pain.

She is clear for a moment, so she starts looking around without knowing what she is looking for. Something, anything, that might help, whatever that might be.

There is an alley that is full of things, but they are broken and useless. They are rusted metal tubs, they are broken planks and shattered crates, and they are bottles and wax paper and other refuse that blew for kilometers before comfortably settling in the dead air of this alley.

She goes to another alley and it looks as unpromising as the first. She looks over her shoulder every few seconds, waiting for some shedim to emerge at the other end of the alley, but they do not appear. Cayman and Halim seem to be sport enough, for now. There is more garbage here, more junk that has been picked over several times by scavengers desperate for anything of even the most remote value. Her only hope is that Lagos, with its great strength in producing new junk, may have dumped something here recently before the scavengers had a chance to find it.

And then, lo and behold, there it is. A large paper blows to one side as she passes, and underneath it is a thick plank of wood, and it is connected to another, and there are four altogether, and they are on four casters. It is a furniture dolly, and if it is intact it will hold the weight of both Cayman and Halim—though how they will both sit on it is a thing that she does not much want to ponder at this moment.

She leans over, grabs it, and guns out of the alley, back toward the square. She is fortunate, for Cayman looks at her when she approaches the square and makes eye contact, and she lifts the dolly up to show him. He nods. Then shedim close on him, and she cannot see him.

She guns the engine and races toward the melee. Shedim hear her coming and turn to her, and some of them bare their teeth and snarl, and one of them has quite nice teeth, in fact, white and even and well maintained, and they simply do not look right in the mouth of a creature who is growling for the taste of flesh. She has the dolly in her left hand, and she swings it up, and it cracks soundly into one of the shedim, who falls as she goes by. She runs toward another, then turns at the last minute and gives it a kick, and it falls backward. She guns the engine, turns again, and she can see Cayman again. He is waiting for her.

She pushes the bike forward, dropping her left arm toward the ground, getting the casters level and then letting the dolly go. It rolls alongside her only briefly before it starts to slow. Then Cayman is near her, and he is holding something practically in front of her face, and instinctively she grabs it as she whizzes by. It isn't until she is ten meters or so past that she realizes she has his grapple gun. She nods. He had known what to do the moment she showed him the dolly.

The gun is letting out cord as she drives—and a quick look over her shoulder tells her than Cayman is tying the hook end around the dolly while Halim holds the shedim at bay. She looks in front of her to make sure she has room to drive, then looks back. The dolly is secure.

She wraps the grapple gun around the bike's handlebars, yanking on it three times to make sure it is set, then she presses the button that stops the cord from unwinding. There is a small tug behind her, and the dolly is on the move.

She slows the cycle, and now she is looking almost entirely behind her, hoping nothing suddenly pops up in front of her. She sees Cayman and Halim break into a run as the dolly starts rolling, Halim's blade moving in a flash, Cayman's gun finally firing and opening a path for the dolly. Then he runs and dives, belly-flopping onto the dolly. The sudden addition of a hundred kilos or so to the dolly could have put an abrupt strain on the cycle, but Groovetooth is ready. She lets out some slack on the grapple gun, in fits and starts, so the bike keeps hitting a brief wall but then moving again, jerking forward. The dolly starts moving, its inertia is overcome, so each jerk on it becomes easier.

Bracing his arms on the sides of the dolly, Cayman pushes his torso up, then slings his legs underneath him. His feet hit the front of the dolly, and he sits his ass on the back. Now he is sitting up, able to both look around and move his arm to fire at anything he needed to.

Halim is running beside the dolly, blade flashing, waiting, and once Cayman is sitting, he moves. His strides become faster, and then he leaps, and one foot lands on the side of the dolly. Cayman quickly grabs his leg, holding him, as Halim stands, knees bent, balanced, like a terribly outsized and misplaced hood ornament. Then he lifts his other leg over Cayman's head and drops it on the other side of the dolly. He squats and leans forward, almost sitting on Cayman's chest, his sword at the front of the dolly. They may be terribly awkward, but they are also mobile.

Groovetooth starts winching some of the cord back in. There is a jerk on the handlebars, bucking them under her hands, but it is not bad, and she does nothing more than trace an awkward swivel on the pavement before getting straightened up. She accelerates, knowing she will have to push it over thirty to get away from the shedim, wondering how fast the dolly will be able to go. She hopes she can stay straight as long as possible.

When she has a moment to look back, she is impressed at the coordinated balance of Cayman and Halim as the dolly carries them along. When she has to move to one side of the street, they lean and drift with her. They lift two wheels off the ground when they do it, but only slightly, enough to make the turn they want to make. At one point, as they are shifting, another shedim emerges, looking for the feast that escaped its nearby brothers, and Halim slashes it with his sword as he passes and does not disturb his balance for a moment.

They pass a block, two, three, and more, and the shedim are gone. There is plenty of slower prey in the city, so there is no reason to expend effort on the prey that knows how to flee.

The streets have cleared greatly, and Groovetooth decides it is time to get her bearings so she can stop heading in the approximate direction of the bridge and start being more exact.

Unfortunately, this act of thinking makes her somewhat distracted, so while she recognizes that the street she is on is ending and she will have to make a turn, she forgets that she is not alone on the cycle, but rather is carrying cargo. So when she makes the turn as she normally would, she feels the tug on the handlebars too late, and she realizes what she has done. She reduces her speed, but she is already pointing east instead of north, and the men on the dolly behind her are desperately trying to match her change in direction. The dolly swings out wide, they are leaning to their right as much as they can, but the casters were not built to be used this way. The strain is too much for one of them, and it snaps, and a corner of the dolly hits the street. The balance of the two men is interrupted. They roll into the street, on top of and beneath each other, skidding and tumbling and finally stopping in a messy heap.

Groovetooth, eyes wide, turns the cycle while unwrapping the grapple gun. Her mind is full of the apologies she is prepared to deliver, but then the two men get to their feet and their expressions tell her they are not ready to listen to anything she has to say.

She quickly turns the cycle back around, drops the gun, and accelerates forward.

"Remember that I got you out of there!" she calls, but she hears their footfalls running behind her, and she knows they are not trying to catch her to thank her. Fortunately, she is faster.

She does not know how far she will have to go until the two of them calm down, but then, abruptly, she stops. The smell of rotten seaweed hits her. And there are three people waving to her at the end of a ramp that turns over sparkling water and points south. This is the bridge, and the three people waiting are Agbele Oku, Akuchi, and X-Prime. She has found the bridge. She has found her group. She feels relief spread throughout her body. She stops the cycle, steps off, breathes deeply, and smiles.

Then her head jerks forward, there is a sharp *thud* on the back of it, and her vision is replaced by stars. When the stars start to fade, she sees Halim walking by with a broken piece of the furniture dolly in his hand. She is certain some of her hairs are caught in the splintered board.

"Thank you for the rescue," he says without turning around. She follows, and continues seeing stars in her vision, here and there, for a good number of minutes afterward.

CHAPTER FIFTEEN

ONE HOUR AND FIFTEEN MINUTES BEFORE THE BRIDGE

Any two people develop certain ways of dealing with each other, and each time they are together, they build on and refine those ways, which tells us that if we want to understand why Halim hit Groovetooth on the head, we might benefit by looking at how these two have related to each other at a time a bit earlier in the day, and it would be best if we started with Groovetooth speaking.

"You're going to have company in a few minutes," she said.

Halim nodded. That was fine with him. He had been walking through the city for a good amount of time now, and while there was plenty of chaos around him, no one had challenged him directly, and so he had not been compelled to fight anyone. Seeing all this disturbance but not partaking in it was, for Halim, somewhat like being invited to a pickup game of football, only to be asked to be the equipment manager, which is quite unsatisfactory—when one takes the field, one wants to be part of the action, not stuck on the sidelines. He hoped that soon, someone would give him the gesture that told him it was his turn to play, and Groovetooth's message indicated that the time had come.

"There are four of them," she continued. "All of them have blades, two of them have guns. They won't be too anxious to use the guns, probably."

Halim waited. Groovetooth didn't say anything else.

"Anything else?" he finally asked.

"No," she replied. "Wasn't that enough?"

"It was more than enough," he said. "But I thought perhaps you would continue, and provide their eye colors, or some other pertinent details."

Groovetooth did not bother to reply to that. Halim supposed he should be thankful—he was quite aware that, generally speaking, more information was better than less, and it was kind of the dwarf to want to help—but he did not regularly need assistance with street fights. And besides, Groovetooth's assistance was variable, sometimes quite detailed, other times very lacking. She clearly had good sources of information, whatever these may be, but they were not comprehensive.

He thought about making quick work of this fight—the quickest way to deal with people who were reluctant to shoot is, of course, to shoot them first. There was the problem that gunfire on open streets sometimes brought down bystanders, and Halim liked to avoid that when possible. He viewed shooting the wrong person the way an artist would view an accidental brush stroke on the canvas, as an annoyance that could mar what otherwise might be a masterpiece. So he kept the guns put away for the time being, which allowed him to rely on the more graceful and elegant close combat methods he preferred.

There was no mistaking the four when they came into view, mainly because they already had their weapons out. All of them had knives, double-edged blades that were twelve or so centimeters long. Two of them also had guns, charming little pieces that they might have stolen from the display cases of a museum of antiques. If it were not for the sad fact that Halim was going to have to dispatch them, he would have liked to ask them how they acquired ammunition for such old pieces.

One of the other two thugs only had a dagger, but since he was an ork that was okay—he could do a fair amount of damage simply by virtue of being himself. The final member of this group carried a long, curved blade, and Halim could see the nocks and pits in it from where he was standing. He was not happy about that, because he knew that a decent swordsman would not let his blade slip into such a shape. This would be too easy.

They came at him in an arc, the two gunmen in the middle, the ork and the swordsman on the flanks. The gunmen had not fired, which Halim believed was an all too common tendency among younger brawlers. He firmly believed that you shouldn't draw a gun until you were ready to use it. If it was out and not firing, that plainly meant you weren't ready to shoot. That whole idea some people had, the idea where you could get people to do something because you had a gun pointed at them, held no weight with Halim, because most of the people he knew were, like himself, nonplussed to be looking into the barrel of a gun.

If they were not going to fire, they were hoping for the flankers to do most of the work for them, and of the two flankers, Halim had the most respect for the ork. So the ork would have to be first.

He made a quick, underhanded move with his right hand, and a metal ball went flying at the ork's throat. The ork bared his teeth and swatted the ball away with his free hand—which was not fast enough to catch the second ball Halim had thrown at the same time. It hit the ork in the gut, not hard enough to take the wind out of him, but hard enough to at least make him reflexively bend forward.

Which put his forehead in perfect line for a third ball. It hit him, and he went down.

The gunmen still hadn't fired. This, then, was not a real attack, which put Halim in a quandary. He tried not to kill people unless they were trying to kill him—it was important to keep a line between himself and those he thought were truly evil—but these four were deliberately wasting his time with a fight that did not have any real consequence, and there was a part of him that felt like maybe he should kill them to teach them a lesson.

But as soon as he had the thought, he knew he wouldn't do anything about it. If they were not truly trying to kill him, then they were not really demanding that he kill them first. And killing someone who is not asking for it is much like having sex with someone who is not fully engaged in the act—the motions are the same, but the moment of fulfillment is significantly less.

So his sword went away, and he faced them unarmed. He did not even flip out the blade of his cyberarm. He stood ready.

The eyes of the gunmen narrowed, and they stretched out the arms carrying the guns. Halim was at this point quite sick of their nonsense, so he ended it. He made a feint at them and they dropped into a defensive stance, while the swordsman on the side made an advance. But Halim was already moving toward him, and he pulled his midsection back so that the blade barely missed him, and he kept moving toward the swordsman and grabbed his arm. Then he swung the swordsman around, and the thug's balance was terrible, and Halim shoved him, stumbling, into the gunmen.

They became a tangle of legs and arms, and Halim added his limbs to the fray. They were down low, which meant he could use his feet, and he stayed clear of the heads and guts so that he could enjoy himself before putting them out of commission. A few kicks to kneecaps kept two of them from immediately jumping to their feet, and stomps on the hands made the gunmen let go of their weapons so they no longer had to pretend that they might use them. At this point the three of them were all still conscious, and Halim thought about asking them why they were pretending to attack him and who sent them, but information was not his job, and he did not have the patience for that sort of interrogation anyway. So he let them squirm on the ground awhile, like three miserable little grubs, and then a kick here, a punch there, and a chop in a third place shut all of them down for a time. The ork, by this point, was trying to push himself up to his hands and his knees, and so Halim, as he was walking away, gave him a swift kick to his crotch. A crude move, but it remained a classic for a reason.

The ork was prone again when Halim walked away.

Halim punched up Groovetooth on the comm as he continued toward the bridge.

"Is there anything else I need to worry about?"

"What happened to the four people who were approaching you?" she asked.

"They were nothing."

"They didn't do anything to you?"

"No. They attacked. But they were not serious."

"Oh." Groovetooth was silent for a moment. "Did you kill them?"

"What does it matter?" Halim asked. While he was truly curious to know the answer to that question, a response from Groovetooth was not immediately forthcoming, and he did not have any particular ideas about how to pursue that line of questioning. So he let it drop.

"Is there anything else I need to worry about?" he asked again.

"Not that I know of," she said. "You're not far off. Hopefully you'll make it without incident."

Over time, Halim had come to understand the fact that to some people, it was desirable for a run to proceed without incident. He could understand it, but he could not come close to agreeing with it. From a practical standpoint, it meant much less work for him. When he was involved in a run, it was because there was likely to be some sort of incident, and the people who hired him wanted to be sure that incident would go their way. And putting the practical standpoint aside, having a run that went without incident was like having a story about a group of people who all got along. Such stories may be simpler to tell, even more pleasant than other stories, but they are also far less interesting.

By the time he had mulled through these thoughts, enough time had passed that it would have been awkward to reply to Groovetooth, so he said nothing. He was fairly certain that she knew more about the four people who had just attacked him, but he was also fairly certain that he would never know what it was she was keeping from him. There were people he had run with who became all bothered and high-strung when they discovered that the people on their team had secrets that they were keeping from other members of the group, and on those occasions Halim always wondered just what kind of people they had run with in the past. Everyone had secrets, and of course everyone was not willing to share them. This was not a surprise. This was normal life. And he was not going to spend much time worrying that things were going, in a general sense, as they always did.

CHAPTER SIXTEEN

The good news is that they all survived the ammits and the wave and the city, and they even managed to keep hold of all the packages they are supposed to deliver. The bad news is that they have had to go to the easiest and closest entry point of the bridge, which is the point where their boat exploded hours ago. They have been through much in the past few hours, and as they approach the bridge, they are forced to realize that they have gotten exactly nowhere.

There is a small debate at the head of the bridge about whether the cycles should be taken along to speed their journey, but the gaps in the bridge that they know are ahead make the cycles of limited use, even if they could find a way to put the six of them on two cycles. So the vehicles are left behind, and once again they are making rapid progress south, on foot, over the Third Mainland Bridge.

They cross the first kilometer, then the second, and then they are approaching the gap with the ferry, and at first Cayman feels good about this, because there are no people waiting on the bridge. There are no lines. They will be able to get on the ferry without a problem.

The raft is on the other side of the gap, and five people are sitting on it. There is a nearby fishing boat, and another two people are on it. There are no other people on the other side, either.

Cayman walks in front of the group, taking long strides, and he comes to the gap and waves the ferry over. The people on the ferry, they are in no hurry. They look at Cayman, and they don't move. Cayman keeps his patience. He knows how gangs work, he understands their need to keep a certain aura of cool, and he knows that aura involves not immediately responding to demanding people. Then finally one of them, a dwarf, stands, and she walks to the rope, and with strong pulls she starts the ferry moving back to their side of the gap. Cayman hears the putt-putt of the fishing boat's engine, and it slowly moves closer to the ferry while also crossing the gap.

Then there is a shift in the breeze, and a flag that had been almost invisible because they were looking at its edge rotates, and they can see it from the side, and it is not a black flag. It is red. And it has a picture of a curved sword on it.

"Oh shit," Cayman says, and he takes a few steps back.

"Looks like the Razor Cutlasses came back," he says to the others without turning to look at them. "And it looks like this time, they won."

"They were easy enough to take out before," Halim says. "They will be easy enough now."

Cayman turns on him. "Weren't we just worrying about ammunition back with all the shedim? If we can talk to them, let's talk. For all we know, they have no idea who we are. And even if they do, what they want is the ferry, not us. And they've got it. So why should we cause them any trouble?"

"No reason," Halim says, and he smiles a bright, white, completely insincere smile.

Cayman, he is not always happy that he has spent as much time with X-Prime as he has, but there are certain advantages to it, and one of those advantages are that some things between them do not need to be said. So he gives X-Prime a certain look, a look with a raised eyebrow and a twisted mouth, and he knows that X-Prime understands the intent, and that intent is "Keep an eye on him while I am talking, and let me know if he makes a move." X-Prime does not even nod in reply, because there is no point to subtle communication if you then go ahead and are obvious about it. He stays at the top of the stairs, on bridge level.

The Razor Cutlasses slowly make their way across the gap, then stop when the raft is a few meters from the lower platform. With the runners still at the top of the stairs, the Razor Cutlasses will have no problem moving the ferry out of range before any of them could get to it.

"You want a ride," one of the Cutlasses calls, putting the words in the space squarely between a statement and a question.

"Yes," Cayman says.

"We'll give you a ride," the Cutlass says. "Except for the Igbomen. They want to get across, they can swim."

"No," Cayman says without turning around. "We're all coming across."

"Not as long as this is our ferry," the Cutlass says.

Cayman hears a very familiar *click-clack* sound behind him, and then Halim speaks. "Those are very nice words," he says, "from someone who is below us like a sitting duck."

And Cayman knows what is happening, because he knows Halim does not draw his gun idly. And sure enough, the Cutlasses are drawing their weapons, and there is a *pop* behind Cayman, and the head of the Cutlasses' spokesman twists, and there is blood pouring from his jaw. His hand reaches up to grab it, but it is his non-gun hand, and his gun hand is firing.

All six runners drop to the bridge, and the Cutlasses have no shot. The runners do not either, of course, but Cayman believes that situation will not last long.

Behind him, Halim speaks. "Get me down there."

Cayman is about to reply, wondering just what Halim expects him to do to get him to water level, but then he realizes that Halim is not talking to him.

"I'll protect you the best I can," Agbele Oku says. "But the movement part is up to you."

Halim does not say anything, but there are footsteps behind Cayman, moving quickly, and Halim hits the top of the staircase. There is a glow around him, white with touches of pink, and he is moving quickly, taking three steps at a time, grabbing the handrail and using it to propel him around corners.

Cayman moves quickly too, scuttling to the edge, pulling out his rifle, and laying down cover fire. The fishing boat has moved away from the ferry, so he has to move back and forth, back and forth, keeping fire on both of them as much as possible, but they are still getting shots off, and once Cayman sees a bullet that bounces off the glow around Halim and embeds itself in the staircase, and he swears there was a small spark when it hit the shield.

The ferry has moved backward by the time Halim reaches the bottom of the staircase, and the gap is too large for him to leap. There is no hesitation, though, as he runs to the end of the platform, firing his handgun at the Cutlasses on the ferry, hitting one in the arm, then he is at the edge of the platform and he leaps and dives into the water, and the Cutlasses are running forward, looking to spray to water with bullets and hit Halim while he is under. Cayman focuses his efforts on the ferry, laying down a whole row of bullets across the front of it, hitting the same Cutlass that Halim hit and driving the others back.

These odds, they are not good. There are seven of them down there and only one Halim, and Cayman cannot keep enough cover fire to occupy all of them. He takes a handgun and throws it to the boy.

"You need something more powerful than the damn holdout," he says. "Help me keep them occupied."

X-Prime nods and drops to the ground, leaning over the edge of the bridge to fire down on the Cutlasses. To Cayman's eyes, it looks like most of his shots are hitting water, but even inaccurate gunfire will do something to keep them occupied. Now he had to hope that they didn't have a mage down there that could mess with Halim's protections.

"Spell's gone," Agbele Oku said.

"What?"

"Protection spell's gone," she said. "Someone down there blew it away."

"So put a new one on!"

"I can't see him," she said with a shrug. "I won't be able to do something to him until I see him."

Cayman grits his teeth and wishes for the hundredth time in his life that mages could somehow be required to carry signs that said *"MAGE"* in big letters so they would be easy to identify. While he was at it, he also wished that they all would have bull's-eyes on their foreheads.

But then he remembers he has his own mage.

"Which one is it?"

"In the boat. The one near the front."

Cayman is not entirely surprised, because there were a few shots at that one, a squat man with no shirt and a white skull painted on his chest and generous belly, shots that he had felt very good about when they were fired but had turned out to be very far off target.

There is no fire coming from the Cutlasses below. They know Halim has been under the water for a good amount of time, and they are waiting for him to come up for air. They probably have a small hope that one of their bullets found him while he was swimming, but if that were the case his body would likely have come to the surface already. When he comes up, they will be ready with a barrage that will drown him right there.

"Forget protecting Halim," Cayman says. "We need to keep them busy. Annoy the mage."

Cayman does not know much about magic, but he knows enough to understand that it is like most other kinds of fighting. There are times when you know you are stronger than your opponent and you can just overpower them. But there are other times when you must be more patient, when you must find the way to get the right blow in, and the way to get the right blow in is to do something your opponent does not expect. One of the keys to success, then, is to have a fine array of weapons and moves that most people would not be looking out for.

He concentrates his fire on the boat, and the boy does the same. The Cutlasses on the ferry immediately see what is happening and all but one of them stop looking in the water and concentrate their fire on the bridge above. They kick up plenty of concrete dust with their bullets, but that is about all they are able to do, and the fire from above keeps raining down on the boat.

Then there is a whining in Cayman's ear, an annoying high-pitched sound, and his non-trigger hand moves quickly and slaps his cheek. He brushes something large, and he sees a blurred shape move past him. He reflexively jerks back as buzzing wings skim his cheek. It is a mosquito, but it is ungodly large, longer than his hand, and his hand, as hands go, is quite big. He can clearly see its proboscis as the big bug flies away, a long thin tube that tapers to invisible sharpness, a needle that could draw plenty of blood, or even stop a man's heart if it hits the wrong place.

He looks, and sees more of these bugs descending from every direction. They are going to the same place, and that place is the fishing boat. They are ghede flies, and there is not a moment, not one, in the entire lives of the females when they are not hungry.

They descend on the mage, who frowns both with his real mouth and the skeletal mouth on his belly, and he swats them away. Some of them freeze in the air, drop to the boat, and shatter where they land. But there are more of them, maybe a dozen, and they smell the blood under the mage's ample skin and they want some of it.

At that moment there is an eruption behind the boat. Water explodes upward, and it is pushed by a head, and that head clears the water level and so does a hand, and the hand grabs the gunwale of the boat and heaves, so the boat bobs down and the head and the body that is under it shoots further up, and another hand emerges from the water and it has a knife, and that hand moves forward, and the knife enters the body of the man in the back of the boat between his shoulder blade and spine, and the hand holding the knife starts to fall back to the water, so it moves down the entire length of the man in the back of the boat and opens him from shoulder to waist.

To his credit, the chubby mage does not worry about the bugs or the fact that his fellow Cutlass is dead. He turns and makes a small hand motion, because, necessary or not, hand motions just seem to make a spell feel *right*, and the air waves and wobbles like it has become extra hot, and something is coming toward Halim there in the water, but without astral perception Cayman cannot be sure what it is.

Halim is already back under the water, but Cayman is not sure that will offer enough protection. He is firing at the mage, but the mage's protection is holding, the bullets still are not finding a landing place. But there is only so much a mage can do at once, and with the bullets, Halim, and the ghede flies, this particular mage seems to have found his limit. So when another wave of air flies out from Agbele Oku, it penetrates whatever defenses he has and connects with the back of his skull. He drops.

He is down, but not out. He scrambles quickly to his feet. Cayman fires once, twice, three times, and he thinks he made contact, but not enough to stop the mage. The mage is turning, getting something special ready, but then the boat tips, the bow raising high out of the water, and the mage stumbles, falling back toward the engine. And just like that, Halim is there, his hand makes a fast motion, and the butt of his gun hits the mage in the back of the head. And once again the mage's knees buckle.

Perhaps the mage was strong enough to have gotten up again, but that will never be known, as Halim is not one to take a chance. As the mage falls, Halim's gun muzzle finds its way under the mage's chin, and he fires. That results in such a terrible mess that it is, for once, possible for someone such as Halim to enter the waters of Lagos Lagoon and actually become cleaner.

The rest is just clean-up. When your mage goes down, if you're good, you adapt, you move to new tactics. If you're not so good, you pause, you feel panic in your throat, and you start firing wildly as if the very high amount of lead in the air will make up for the lack of mana on your side. But it doesn't. There are fewer shots coming from on top of the bridge, but they are more accurate. And there is Halim, who has climbed back into the boat and assumed a prone position, and is doing damage of his own.

It does not take long, and then Cayman is on his feet, moving down the stairs, while Halim motors over to the ferry. The sight of the boat, that wonderful boat, sends Cayman's heart soaring, until it sinks just as Halim pulls next to the ferry.

"Did you do that?" Cayman screams.

"Do what?" Halim asks, in level tones that still easily cross the distance between the ferry and the stairs.

"Sink that boat! Did you sink that boat?"

Halim looks at the slow procession of bubbles moving to the surface to mark where the boat went down. Then he looks up.

"The boat was hit. A few times. It wasn't too sound to begin with."

"Yeah, yeah," Cayman says. "Lucky none of them got through to you." Then he looks closer, and he sees there is red on Halim's robe where there had not been red before. "Oh, shit," he says. "How bad is it?"

Halim looks at himself, as if just realizing that second that he had wounds on him. "They are not bad. I do not think."

Cayman turns to X-Prime. "You get to play street doc." Then he turns back to Halim. "Good thing we didn't try to negotiate, huh?" he says with an amount of sarcasm that could undoubtedly be detected by satellites hovering far overhead.

On Lagos Island, Sir is not happy.

He saw the wave. It came out of the clear blue, blue water and blue sky, no visible cause, no visible anything, and suddenly there is a towering wave in a lagoon that for the most part is not deep enough to go over an average person's head. He doesn't know where the water got sucked in from, he doesn't know what or who is causing it, but whatever or whoever it is, he hates it or them. Because his packages, they were supposed to be on the way, but they are not here yet, and he has good reason to believe that the wave is the reason. Or, at least, one reason.

He has many eyes in many places, and none of these eyes can tell him where the runners are. He knows that keeping track of six people in this city is no easy task, but he had put so much effort into this, and it had worked, and then this *wave* comes out of *nothing*...

He is standing at one of his windows, his hands balled into fists, both raised and leaning on the window above his head. It wouldn't take much to pound the window with them and shatter the glass. Not much effort, and certainly not much thought.

He backed away from the window. He had used others' anger against them so many times that it would not do to display his own.

Besides, anger is not necessary. His eyes, all those eyes on the street, are not necessary. They were a luxury, one he didn't need. He had put together a professional team, and he had offered them enough money to make sure the job was done. They would want to collect the fee for finishing. They would find a way to get the money. They would find their way south. He was firm in his belief that six of them would make it to the checkpoint to Lagos Island.

And five of them would move on.

CHAPTER SEVENTEEN

THREE AND A HALF HOURS BEFORE THE BRIDGE

It is possible that Cayman would not have been thinking so much about talking to the Razor Cutlasses instead of killing them if it were not for what happened earlier in the day. There was a part of the day when Cayman and X-Prime were able to enjoy the luxury of being driven by Akuchi. And it was not just on a cycle, or an *okada*, or anything else without a roof. It was an honest-to-god car, a Citroën Ztana, with the popular rust-colored paint job that makes the actual rust spots virtually invisible.

The interior of the car would not be recognized by the manufacturers, as all the controls and dials and everything else they had put in were gone. There was other equipment, better equipment in there now, but to anyone who was not Akuchi it looked like plain metal cases. To Akuchi, of course, it was the body of the car and the world around it, and he was so absorbed in his driving that he never would have noticed anything Cayman and X-Prime said, even if they were commenting on his mother's propensity to engage in sexual relations with wildebeests. So they talked freely, and they seemed to have been continuing a conversation, though whether it was a conversation that had started five minutes ago, five weeks ago, or five years ago was not clear.

"We don't have different jobs, really," X-Prime said. "I mean, I know, I know, that's your thing, you like to talk about how we've all got our jobs to do, and we all have to do our part and that, but some of the things you think are separate really aren't. Your thing and my thing really aren't that different."

"You're flattering yourself," Cayman said. He did not look at X-Prime when he was talking to him, instead looking out the window and watching the city, counting the number of ways it could kill him. Here, the most likely fatal element seemed to be the air, which had a brown-and-green haze that reminded Cayman of a very thin split-pea soup. He was very accustomed, of course, to seeing industrial areas that contribute plenty of smoke to the air, but he could not recall seeing such a variety of colors coming from the various smokestacks in the factories around him. There were the normal shades of grey, black, and brown, of course, but he also saw greens, dark reds, and hints of blue. From some angles, the plumes lined up next to each other like the end of a muted, dirty rainbow.

"No, I'm not. Look, we're both in the persuasion business. The main reason we do things is to help people understand that it would be better for them to do things the way we want them to than some other way. Except for those times you're just pointing guns at people and shooting them because it's fun."

"It's not *not* fun."

"But you don't just go around randomly shooting people. I mean, it pains me to say this to your face, but you're not a psychopath."

"Thanks."

"To begin with, you're not charming enough," X-Prime said, then grinned broadly in a way that was far more annoying than the actual joke. "Anyway, you usually have a purpose when you point a gun at someone, and that purpose is to get them to do what you want them to."

"Okay."

"And it's the same with me. I talk to people so that they'll see things my way and go along with what I want them to do. Same goal as you, just different weapons."

"Your voice is a weapon now?"

X-Prime smiled. "Damn straight. In fact, in some ways it's better than your weapons, because I can use it to make everyone happy. I can convince people that doing what I ask them to do is actually what they want, so when they do it, we will all be happy."

"I do the same thing," Cayman said. "When I point a gun at people, they think they are going to be shot. So when they find out a way they can avoid being shot, then they're happy to take it, and I'm happy they're taking it, too."

"I suppose. But it's nice to, you know, have the lighter touch. To get to the point where everyone gets what they want without someone having to think they're about to die."

Cayman finally turned from his window. "You're slipping back into old X-Prime. Worrying about other people and shit."

X-Prime frowned. "I guess."

Cayman looked out the window again and didn't say anything.

"But it's not just being nice," X-Prime said. "It's walking lightly. The smaller the weapon you have to use, the smaller the impact. You don't leave as big a trail behind you."

"Why are we talking about this?"

At that moment, as if on cue, the Ztana slowed to a stop. Coming out of his driving daze, Akuchi turned to them.

"We're just a few blocks away," he said. "It's probably better to approach on foot."

X-Prime straightened his collar, since he had gone to great trouble to wear a shirt that looked as presentable and nondescript as possible. "We're talking about this," he said, "because I want you to fully appreciate the value of what I'm about to do."

He got out of the car and led the way, while Akuchi and Cayman followed, and X-Prime seemed to enjoy walking in front.

Their walk took them a few blocks down a crumbling street, then they turned into an alley and pushed open a fence door that was no more than a sheet of corrugated metal. On the other side of the door was a dusty piece of land that, judging by the various kinds of footprints and the flecks of blood, fur, and feathers on it, was often used as a combat arena for animals of many different types. There were people in there, sitting on many things, none of them chairs. They sat on tree stumps, sideways garbage cans, cinder blocks, or anything else that was horizontal and more than a third of a meter off the ground.

There was a shack in the back of the lot, and the people there gathered in a way to clearly communicate that if you approached the shack and were not supposed to, you would meet with a host of consequences that could very well cause future nightmares, assuming your mind was left in a condition well enough to allow for dreaming.

There were seven of them in the yard right now, and Cayman estimated their ages as being between fourteen and twenty. They had the expression common to all people who have learned to strongly dislike anything that is not themselves. Cayman had seen hundreds, or maybe thousands of people just like this, and there was one crucial thing about the first moments in dealing with them—you have to know that you cannot win. If you try to be tough, they will refuse to be intimidated. If you try to be low-key or friendly, they'll mock you for being weak. Whatever you do will not be enough. The only thing to do is ride it out and hope you'll get beyond the initial chest thumping before violence breaks out. This was what X-Prime was bragging about, that he could handle this kind of situation without the always-useful threat of violence, so now he had to put his words where his mouth had been.

"You *oyibos* in the wrong place," one of the men inside said, an older one who wore his sheen of sweat like a bodybuilder wears mineral oil.

"No, we want to be here," X-Prime said. Simple and direct.

"You want to be here?" the ganger said. "You want you ass kicked?"

"We're here on business."

"What business you got here? You got no business with us. You got no business in this city, 'cept letting your white skin burn up and crumble away."

"There's something we'd like to buy. Something we heard you just got."

The man who had been talking stood up. His left hand was metal, and it was not well integrated into the rest of his arm—the attachment scars were rough and ugly.

"You know what I got? Biggest damn dick in all Africa. You know what I'm going to do with it?"

And here came the moment that showed why X-Prime was speaking instead of Cayman. It was the point where Cayman would almost be jumping out of his skin to take this son of a bitch down a peg, and plenty of good answers to the ganger's question leaped to his mind, like "Beat off into a hole in the ground, since no woman will touch you?" or "Keep looking down at it, and hope maybe you'll get it up someday?" But he stayed quiet. X-Prime was the one who got to talk, and he didn't rise to the bait.

"I wouldn't have walked in here unless I could make it worth your time," he said.

"Make what worth our time?"

"My proposal to you. The business offer I'm bringing you."

The ganger looked around at his friends. "Look at the white boy, all marching in here and talking business-like and shit. He got good manners, *abi*?" There was a low rumble that moved around the group that might have been a kind of chuckle.

Then the ganger looked at Akuchi. "You know what happen you spend too much time with white boys? You get soft. You start wearing perfume, getting you nails done. You get out now, if you smart."

"I don't want to make this into a thing or anything, but I think Akuchi there can choose who he associates with on his own."

Cayman smiled tightly. On the surface, it was the most confrontational thing X-Prime had said, but it was also the thing most likely to make the gangers a little more willing to listen.

"Akuchi?" the lead ganger said. "Akuchi hanging out with white boys now? God*damn*, times must be bad for that." He pointed. "You really Akuchi?"

"Really," Akuchi said.

The ganger shook his head. "So Akuchi walk in here with a couple of white boys to do business. Well, white boys, you give me a good story to tell. So I can listen to you business."

"We just want to make some of your vulture work pay off. A few of your boys happened to be there when the body of a woman pretty much fell at their feet. And like any smart thief, they didn't wait long to grab anything that looked at all valuable. Like the string the body had in its hair."

"You think a string in someone's hair look valuable to us?"

"If it's set with turquoise and pearls, yeah, I think it would."

"If it's so valuable, then how valuable is it to you? How much would you pay?"

"Are you saying you have it?"

The ganger smiled. There was sharp-looking metal in his mouth, and Cayman was pretty sure it was not just decoration. "I'm saying we might have it in the back."

"All right, then. We have something to talk about. I don't suppose you'd be willing to let it go for, say, Akuchi's autograph?"

Again, the ganger smiled and displayed the extra shine on his teeth. "His scribble on paper don't have value. At least not 'til he dead."

X-Prime smiled too, and he put one hand in his pocket and stood with his right leg kicked out in front of him, toes up, heel down. When he talked about this to Cayman, he called it his "Casual Hick" pose. "Okay, then how about some in-kind contributions? I'm pretty sure there's got to be a few people out there that you'd like to have a few things smoothed over with. That's what I do. And I'm not talking about how I'll owe you a favor or anything if you give me the hair string—I'm talking about real work, immediate, whatever you want me to do."

"Not that impressed by you," the ganger said. "Not sure I'd hire you for free, so really not sure I'm giving you anything so you can fuck things up for us."

"How about ammo?" Cayman's ears perked up when he heard X-Prime say that—he hadn't been aware that ammo was on the table as a bargaining chip. "My friend here, he's got all kinds of ammo. We could get you a case or two."

At least the ganger didn't immediately reject that idea. He sat still for a moment, then shook his head. "Nah," he said. "Like to get weapons and shit from people I know."

X-Prime took a deep breath. "Okay. How about—"

The ganger interrupted him "Why you dicking around? You trying to be trickish? You talk about everything except what people use to buy things. Offer me money."

X-Prime's posture didn't change, but if there was someone there who was watching him closely, they would see that his left leg had stiffened beneath him. His light smile, though, remained in place. "I'm afraid I'm not carrying much cash with me. You know how it is in this city."

One of the other gangers, a wiry woman with crosshatch scars around the base of her neck, guffawed. "We know how it is. We the ones who take cash from people like you." The other gangers laughed, louder and longer than Cayman thought was necessary.

"But there you have it, then," X-Prime said. "You can see why I don't have much on me."

"You full of shit," the lead ganger said.

"I am?"

"Yeah, you am. What kind of shit-brained *oyibos* goes to buy something from people like me without cash? You got cash, only you don't want to give it to us. That won't work. You give us cash, we can buy all the shit you want to sell us—ammo, talk-talk shit, whatever. You want the string, you give us cash."

"I'm not sure that we've really discussed all the possibilities—"

"Cash," the ganger said.

After that, it was just haggling. X-Prime named one price, the ganger rejected it outright, then there was another price, then back and forth, and finally cash changed hands and Cayman had the hair string, which he tucked safely away.

He walked out of the yard carefully with Akuchi and X-Prime, ready for the gangers to turn double-faced, to decide they wanted the cash and the hair string both, to think that a little cash gain is worth possibly losing the lives of some of them, because this is the way they live, that is the bargain they always make. But either Cayman's look, or Akuchi's rep, or just their mood that day kept them quiet, and the three visitors left in peace.

As they were walking, Cayman looked over at X-Prime and saw a look he knew too well—the look that was smug and, to Cayman, completely insufferable.

"Shut up," he said, though the younger man had, in truth, not said a word. "You bought yourself a hair string. No big deal."

X-Prime shook his head. "It's a shame you don't see it. I hate to work in front of an audience that doesn't appreciate the full depth of what I'm doing."

"The full depth...? You tried to rip them off, they didn't bite, so you bought the damn thing. What the hell are you patting yourself on the back for?"

"It's what we were talking about before. About letting people think they're winning. Do you think I would have gotten the same price if I walked in there, whipped out a load of cash, and said 'Okay, how much?' They thought they were getting one over on me just by getting a cash offer—so once they had that victory, they weren't as concerned about price as they would have been otherwise. We got the item, and they got to think they talked me out of giving them cash that I didn't want to part with. Everyone is happy. Everyone got what they wanted. Or at least, what they *thought* they wanted."

Cayman shook his head and turned to Akuchi. "Have you ever seen anyone so desperate for a compliment?"

"Many times," Akuchi said. "Look, give me the hair string, I'll take it where it needs to go, and you guys can keep over-analyzing everything."

Cayman passed over the hair string while X-Prime smiled. "It's what we do."

"Okay," Akuchi said. "Did you ever think it was okay to stop poking at everything and just react for a while?"

"Yes," both said, and then both of them wondered why the other one had answered so quickly.

CHAPTER EIGHTEEN

After they had made their way across the first gap in the bridge, the six travelers arrive in the crowded area they had traversed before, and Cayman is fully prepared for events to repeat themselves. They were set upon in this area once before, and that was when one of their boxes broke open so that they could see its grisly contents, and now they are here again, and Cayman does not want to have to fight again, and he especially does not want to see what is in the other boxes. Not that he is faint of heart, but there are some human body parts that are best left where they are and not removed, and there are some pieces of knowledge about a mission that should, likewise, stay where they are and not be exposed to the rude light of day.

They wind their way through the people on the bridge, all amazed that the panic rampant on the mainland has not seen fit to infect the people on the bridge. That could change at any moment of course; there could be some event, any event, that would snap the collective sanity of the people on the bridge, and they would turn on each other and go feral like the rest of the city. But though there are many events that might bring this state of things to pass, none of them have happened yet, and for that reason small thanks are offered to whatever supernatural powers the runners happen to give a moment's thought.

Then comes the moment when the crowds start to thin and the runners can move faster, and Cayman once again allows himself to find hope that there might come a time when this journey will be over, the destination will be reached, and the nuyen will be distributed to the hands that deserve it.

But then they come to that spot where some of the bridge has crumbled, and it is only half as wide as it normally is, and once again there are eight robed women standing in their way. Cayman believes this might be a different group of women than was present the first time, but he is basing this belief on a brief impression of women who have covered many of their features, so he is not certain how reliable his opinion is. Whether they are the same people or not, though, it is clear that they belong to the same organization, and that they share the same purpose as the previous group, which is to slow their progress.

An impulse stirs deep in Cayman, and that is to give Halim the go-ahead to just move them out of the way, to get rid of them all, but he manages to override it, if only for practical reasons. Since they are Daughters of Yemaja, it is likely that more than one, if not all, of the women before him are Awakened, which would make the combat exceedingly unpleasant. At best. So he takes a deep breath and turns to X-Prime instead of Halim.

"All right, Alex," he says. "Time to be worthwhile. Go talk to them. Make everyone happy. Get us *through* here."

X-Prime gives him a smile and a thumbs-up that makes him look exactly like the corp-exiled rookie Cayman had met six or seven years ago. Then he goes to work, walking quickly until he is several meters ahead of the others.

"Hi!" he says. "Are you here on the same job that some of your other people were here on, or are you doing something new?"

One of the women steps forward, and the wind blows her robe against her, making it cling to what looks like a skeletal frame underneath. Her eyes are sunken, her chin is sharp, and she speaks every word with a flat finality.

"Discussions with you need to be re-opened," she says.

Agbele Oku is close enough to hear this. "Why?" she says. "We had an agreement! You could at least give us enough time to fulfill our part."

"Your part of the agreement is no longer needed," the Daughter of Yemaja says.

"What?" Agbele Oku shouts.

X-Prime holds up a hand, hoping that here, in this different culture than his own, the gesture is still understood to mean what he wants it to mean. "Please, let me handle this."

"You're saying you don't want us to assense the boxes and forward the information on to you?" he asks.

"No," the Daughter says. "We already know more than you can tell us."

"Really? Care to share any of that information?"

The Daughter makes no speech or movement in reply.

"Well, it was worth a shot. But let me ask you this—when we talked before, you were worried that if you didn't get your hands on this stuff now, you wouldn't be able to learn what you wanted to about it. But you've learned more in just a few hours—doesn't that mean you could dig up more information somewhere else? You don't need these boxes."

"Perhaps not. But these objects are the most direct way to find out what we want to know."

"Except that we have them. So taking them from us might be *direct*, but that doesn't make it *easy*."

"If that is what it must come to, then we are ready to take care of you."

Cayman does not bother to look to see if Halim is reaching for his weapons, because he is too busy getting ready to grab his. But X-Prime holds up both his hands now, a signal to both groups. "Whoa, whoa, no reason to get aggressive. Not yet. We're just establishing our positions, right? Now, you want a look at the items. We can probably work that out. Take a look at them, cast a spell, do whatever you need to. That's fine. My big friend in the inappropriate camouflage will not like it, but I'm betting at this point he's willing to live with it. So if you want a look, take a look."

"We will need more than a look," the Daughter says.

"Fine. Take a long look! Whatever you need! As long as we have the items intact and ready to be delivered, we're fine."

"No. We need more than a look. We will take them."

X-Prime smiles, and while Cayman is forced to admit that the expression on his round, innocent-looking face might be found charming by someone, or even by a fair number of people, it does not have any effect on the Daughter.

"You're not giving us much negotiating space here," he says. "But I think we can still work something out. After all, if you weren't going to talk, if you weren't willing to negotiate at all, you would have just attacked us when we were in sight, right?"

"It would be easier for us if you gave the items to us than if we took them by force. It would also be considerably easier for you. That is the only reason we are talking."

And now I would like to break from this conversation and talk to you for a moment about muzzle velocity, and if you do not believe the things I am about to tell you, than you have my sympathy, because that means you are not capable of understanding the full range of wonders that are in the world, and I will call them wonders even when they are things that are capable of producing extremely dire and fatal effects.

The muzzle velocity of a long-barreled gun is significantly greater than that of a handgun, though to many people it does not make much of a difference, because even a slow handgun fires a round at approximately 900 kilometers per hour, which means that all bullets, no matter their speed relative to each other, fall into the category of "things that are traveling much, much faster than any material things around them." Yet to those who are experts, these differences do matter, and knowing that the bullet they fire from a handgun may travel at half the speed of a bullet from a machine gun is a vital piece of information. That speed does not, of course, make a significant difference in time over a short distance, such as the distance between Halim and the leader of the Daughters. But there is *some* difference, and that is a fact that must be known.

From the moment that X-Prime held up his hands in order to signal that he did not want a fight to break out, Halim had been preparing for a fight. It does not take long for Halim to prepare for such things, so that by the time the leader delivered the statement that made it clear that negotiation and compromise were not possible, he was quite ready. He had an Ares Predator in one hand, and a Shiawase Armaments Taipan FMG in the other. The FMG is a fine little demon that folds up into an innocuous-looking metal box, and then unfolds back into a machine gun in mere seconds. It has a specialized customer base, of course, because for most people in the world who want to hide the fact that they are carrying something that could kill you, a handgun is sufficient. But there are those who need weapons that function on a larger scale but are also concealable, and Halim is a person of that nature.

And so we reach a moment where Halim's two weapons suddenly emerge, and he fires both of them, and because the machine-gun round travels at twice the speed of the handgun round, it arrives first, though only a fraction of a second before the second round. But that is more than enough time. The round hits with impact and an explosion, a lightning-quick flash that weakens the magic armor at the Daughter's forehead. And then the second round hits, an armor-piercing round moving through already-weakened mana armor around the Daughter, and that armor is insufficient. The bullet passes through it, then through skin, then through skull, and then it is finished for the Daughter, and her stern face does not have a moment in which it can look surprised. She is obviously the head mage of this group, and she has been well and truly geeked.

This is a turn of events that does not sit well with the other Daughters, and they are momentarily confused and flustered, which are not good things to be when there are people around you with their weapons out and firing. There is damage done by the rounds, but not as much as Cayman would have expected, as some of them deflect off in odd directions. The Daughters may be in a bit of panic, but it seems at least one of them managed to cast something defensive.

The Daughters' confusion, sadly, does not last long, and they are soon spreading apart, all drawing on mana, all looking at the source of their anger. They are all looking at Halim.

Halim is well armored under his robe, of course, but Cayman cannot be certain that he will hold off all that the Daughters are about to throw at him. So he turns to Agbele Oku to request her assistance, and he sees a curious thing. She is not looking at the Daughters, but rather is focused on Halim, and her expression is much the same as the other Daughters that are working their magic. This is quite bad, Cayman thinks, because many mages against no mages is a situation Cayman has seldom been in and, in those times when he has experienced it, never enjoyed. There is not much he can do but react and hope his instincts take him to a good place.

He is running forward as magic erupts around him in many forms, some visible, some not. There are bolts of power and electricity flying through the air, there are punches of pure force passing by here and there, there is pavement erupting under his feet. And ahead, Halim is reeling. He has stopped firing his guns, because the blows he is receiving have him flailing his arms, and he knows better than to shoot wildly. His knees are buckling, and he is going down.

Cayman is right on top of him. He falls, and as he goes down he sees new holes and scorchmarks in Halim's robes. He is shielding Halim with his body, and there are things happening that he cannot describe; they are not quite fire, not quite shock, not quite nausea, but they are not far from any of these. And there are also sensations he knows, the pummeling that he has felt from too many sources over many years.

He is still acting from instinct, his right arm is moving out from under him, and his mouth is moving, yelling, and he hopes to God that he can be heard.

"If you destroy me," he yells as his arm becomes outstretched, "you harm this!"

And it stops.

The first thing he hears is the wind, which had been drowned out when there was so much other noise going on, but is now free to reassert itself. Then he hears many people around him, breathing hard. He is relieved that one of these people is Halim. He looks up, and sees that every single person at this part of the bridge is looking at the object he holds in his hand. It is cold, his fingers are growing numb under it. A light coating of frost on it is sublimating into mist. It is dark red and grey, and it is quickly growing softer in Cayman's hand.

It is a heart, and from all appearances it recently had a place in a human chest.

A Daughter takes a step forward, and Cayman squeezes his hand lightly. She stops. Then he brings out his other hand, and it is holding a grenade. The pin has been pulled, and he is holding down the striking lever. He places the hand holding the heart next to the hand holding the grenade. When he talks again, his tone is level and is easily heard by everyone.

"Let's see how badly you want this thing to remain intact."

He slithers backward, gets on his knees, then stands. The grenade and the heart stay next to each other. The Daughters look at each other, confused, as if waiting for someone, anyone, to make a decision, but no one is forthcoming with anything. Cayman, however, is not in a mood to wait. As far as he is concerned, all decisions have been made. He walks forward, toward the Daughters, next to the Daughters, and past the Daughters. He does not look back at them once he is past.

He assumes the others are with him. He knows that Halim is breathing, and he believes that a Halim that is breathing is one that is also capable of moving. He hopes Agbele Oku is with them, but he is not at all convinced that she is.

There is one thing he is fairly certain of, though, and that is that X-Prime is with him, and is, in fact, not too far away. He speaks, firmly believing that X-Prime will hear him.

"Halim wanted a quick and dirty fight. The Daughters wanted the heart. And Agbele Oku wanted to be the Daughters' new best friend. And we're walking away, and no one got what they wanted. Sometimes, that's what it takes."

CHAPTER NINETEEN

THREE HOURS BEFORE THE BRIDGE

There are holes here that we can fill in now. We have seen Cayman, X-Prime, and Akuchi acquire the hair string from the gangers that had quite accidentally come into possession of it, and we have seen Agbele Oku turn that hair string over to the Daughters of Yemaja while doing much talking to convince them that she saw the world in a fashion similar to them. But we have not seen the hair string make its journey from the gangers to the Daughters, and that is an area that deserves a moment of our focus.

Akuchi was not displeased to leave Cayman and X-Prime behind. Their combativeness could be entertaining, but they had a problem just living life. It was a common problem, Akuchi noticed, one he had once shared. People try to force the currents of life until they finally realize just what a vast river that son-of-a-bitch is. Akuchi no longer tried to force that current, and he found that life had become much more relaxing as a result. He understood that there were many people who did not share his perspective on life, and that generally was perfectly fine with him. But there were people, such as these two *oyibos*, who were so insistent on not only trying to force life's current, but on studying the movement of each little leaf floating in that river in an effort to support their futile efforts, that they drove Akuchi a bit mad. The silence of his car was a blessing as he drove to find Agbele Oku.

The silence continued once she was in the car. He studied the road, enjoying the various inputs his car gave him, and she kept to herself. She sat in the passenger seat, with the box on her lap, staring at it.

"I should probably look at this thing," she said, and since Akuchi could not be sure if she was talking to him or not, he decided not to respond.

Agbele Oku, for her part, was in fact talking more to herself than she was the person next to her, so the fact that Akuchi did not talk back was immaterial. As soon as she had touched the box, a strange sense of trepidation came over her, and she both did and did not want to find out what was bothering her. She knew, of course, that on a run more information was always preferable, but she also knew that there had been plenty of things in her life that she would have been quite happy not to know.

But this was a job that could not be avoided, and so she opened the box that was supposed to contain a hair string, and was not at all surprised to see that it contained a hair string. It was actually two parallel black strings, and they had beads of turquoise and pearl strung between them. It was simple and elegant, but also not extraordinary. To most people, it would be a pleasant-looking hair string and nothing more, if they noticed it at all. But the moment Agbele Oku looked at it, she saw the aura around it, and she knew that it was not just an ornament. She also knew that the gangers that had this very likely did not know its value, and that whatever Cayman and X-Prime had paid for it had probably been quite low.

There was more information she could get about it, and she had time, so she focused on it, both deepening and widening her focus, letting the aura grow into her consciousness and tell her whatever it can about the hair string. She received a fair amount of information, including some of the purposes it served, but all of that was overwhelmed by a single piece of information—the hair string belonged to a woman named Atinuke. Agbele Oku knew her, and she owed a debt to her, and the account she had heard about this hair string was that it had been taken off a dead body, meaning Atinuke was dead. A coldness seeped into Agbele Oku at this realization, and it expanded the more she thought about the task she had to perform.

She had met Atinuke three years ago. Agbele Oku was already on her own at that time, because options in life are not broad for an Awakened Igbo woman. Agbele Oku worked jobs when she could, but most of her time was spent avoiding the various people who had use for Awakened people with no traceable roots.

She had a friend, a girl named Squeek, and they made their way through their marshy corner of Shomolu, learning a fine array of offensive spells and other ways to scare off or otherwise take care of anyone who came after them. The people who were coming after them were slavers, and so they did not feel guilt about anything they did to them.

But there was a morning when Agbele Oku woke up, lying on a raft tied to a stilt holding up a rickety house, and Squeek was next to her, and she was dead. There were no visible wounds, no sign of why Squeek had been alive the night before, but dead in the morning, but just because Agbele Oku did not know what happened did not mean it did not happen. There were many diseases sitting calmly in every corner of Shomolu, and one of them may have claimed Squeek. Or she could have been poisoned, or she could have been found by those people who know how to kill without leaving a trace, though why those people would kill Squeek and leave her alone was a mystery. Agbele Oku was neither more nor less important than Squeek, so if someone was going to kill one, why not just kill the other?

Agbele Oku wanted to find out what happened to Squeek, but she did not really know how to go about it. There was no doctor she knew who would do an autopsy, and divining was not her specialty. She tried her hand at playing detective, asking questions here and there, but anyone she talked to either ignored her or laughed at her, and she did not get anywhere for a long time.

She remembered Squeek often, and felt guilty every time she did, trying to tell herself that she had done her best for her friend while also knowing that if that had been her best, then her best was quite pathetic. When the thought came up, she would try again to find out what had happened, asking questions of anyone who might maybe know something, and then once again she would receive no useful answers, and her efforts would fade.

Until one time when she was talking to someone, a little man who paddled a canoe through the swamps looking for flowers for both perfume labs and drug labs. He cocked his head and thought for a moment, and then said, "Squeek? You say her name is Squeek? I heard that name recently. Where did I hear that name?" He cocked his head the other way. "Was it the Daughters? I think it might have been the Daughters. You should talk to one of the Daughters."

He paddled off, but Agbele Oku sat right where she was, on a skiff that seemed to be flaking apart beneath her, and did not move for a time. She had talked to many people about Squeek, but never one of the Daughters. She loved the Daughters, she admired them, she spent much time wishing she could be one of them. And she avoided them regularly.

When she finally moved out of the swamp, she did not immediately find one of the Daughters. She did not find one the next day. She told herself that she did not know how to find them, that it was not as if they had a large headquarters where they all could be found and it had a sign that read *Daughters of Yemaja here!* And she used that for a time as an excuse to not track them down at all.

But the passage of time failed her, in that it did not make her memories of her friend fade or her loss grow less painful, so eventually Agbele Oku applied her meager detective skills to locating some Daughters that she could talk to. As it turned out, people were far more willing to talk about a group of people that were known to be helpful than they were about an unresolved death. There were people who answered her, and eventually that led her to a small shack not far from where Squeek had died. She was able to walk right in, and she found a simple interior, with five women sitting on floor mats. They looked neither comfortable nor uncomfortable.

"Agbele Oku," one of them said. "You make more noise than a drunken hippo."

Agbele Oku looked at her feet, then back at the door. "I didn't think—"

"Not your walk! Your questions! The entire district knows you are looking for us! You are clumsy and unsubtle!"

"I'm sorry. I just didn't know who to talk to."

"So you thought you should talk to everyone," the Daughter said.

"I just wanted to help. I wanted to do something for Squeek."

"Yes. By randomly talking to people and hoping they know something. Well done. We will find out what happened, and perhaps once we do, we will find a way to let you know. Until then, it is probably best that we stay out of each other's way."

All five Daughters then stood. "You should go. You will not find us here again."

Agbele Oku could not leave. She stood in the hut, and she was right on the verge of yelling at the Daughters, and condemning them for judging her, and telling them that she would be happy to leave, because she did not want to have anything to do with them. And she was also on the verge of asking them if she could join, if she could become a Daughter. But a few moments passed, and she said nothing, and so then there was not much to do but leave.

She walked out slowly, because she wanted them to see her move with dignity, but her pace grew quicker as soon as she was outside, and it was not long before she was almost running, though she was not confident of what her destination was going to be. But before she could get herself into a full run, a hand fell on her shoulder, and it was gentle, but it stopped her. She quickly turned around, ready to shout at and perhaps slap whoever was behind her.

But the expression on the woman's face was so gentle that a small portion of her hostility melted away, and when the woman spoke, it calmed her even further.

"That was not fair. Back there," the woman said.

"No," Agbele Oku tried to say, but the word would not come smoothly out of her throat.

"We all have to learn how to act," the woman said. "We are not born knowing."

Agbele Oku nodded.

"We have high expectations of people, and there are reasons we act the way we do," the woman continued. "But sometimes those reasons do not excuse our behavior. We cannot always expect people to know more than they do."

"I would have done better if I could," Agbele Oku said.

"You *can* do better," the woman said. "You just need help. You're not going to figure out how to make your way through this world on your own. Or with a friend like Squeek. You need more help than that."

Agbele Oku had been ready to attack the woman a few moments ago, but the kind words had done their work. "Then let me in! Let me in to the Daughters! Teach me anything you want to teach me, and I'll listen! Tell me what to do, and I'll do it! Just let me in!"

The woman smiled softly, and the expression sent Agbele Oku's hopes into the grimy sky. "You would do whatever you say, would you?"

"Yes!"

"Why?"

"Because...because you said I needed to learn. You said I needed someone to teach me."

"And you do. But we are not a school. We have a mission."

"Then teach me about the mission!"

The woman shook her head. "That needs to come first. We cannot take on just anyone. The people that join us, they are people that understand our cause and have put it first. They have a purpose beyond themselves."

Agbele Oku wanted to protest, she wanted to say that she was like that, too, but she looked at this woman and her straight back and her stillness and she could not say what she wanted to say. So once again she was silent.

"There will come a time when you are ready," the woman said. "I hope it will not be long. When it comes, I look forward to being one of your sisters. My name is Atinuke."

The woman stretched out her hand, and Agbele Oku was not sure if she should shake it or kiss it. She went with the more conventional shake, which Atinuke accepted gracefully.

"Goodbye, Agbele Oku," Atinuke said. "Be safe."

And Agbele Oku had, it seemed, paid attention to that advice better than Atinuke herself, because Atinuke was dead and Agbele Oku was not.

As she sat in Akuchi's car, her stomach did everything it could to squeeze itself into nothing, to form a small black hole in her gut. She was not a Daughter of Yemaja yet, it had been three years, and now she would never be Atinuke's sister. There had been reasons she had not been able to join yet, many things that occupied her, but all of those reasons could perhaps be exemplified by one simple thing: While she sat and looked at Atinuke's hair string, a part of her mourned and wished to avenge the woman who had once been lost to her, but a larger part of her wondered how this might complicate her mission and interfere with the reward she hoped to collect from this job.

She was still not ready.

CHAPTER TWENTY

So, as it turns out, Agbele Oku is in fact with the team of runners, she has not abandoned them, because she knows she is still not ready to be part of the Daughters. But that does not mean she is willing to be a part of this.

She knows that she must wait until the Daughters are out of sight, but she does not wait for long past that. She keeps looking over her shoulder, and when they are out of sight, she stops.

"I am done," she says.

"Lord help me," Cayman says.

"This one," Agbele Oku says, pointing at Halim. "This one is a cold-blooded killer. And now we know that we, all of us, are organ traffickers. Organ traffickers! There are lower forms of scum than that, but not many."

If anyone had been looking at Groovetooth at that moment, they would have noticed that the muscles beneath her left eye were twitching unmercifully, but no one happens to be looking at her, and she is grateful.

"Little late to be coming up with objections now," Akuchi says in calm tones.

Agbele Oku turns on him, and her eyes seem as red as the ever-present dust. "Forgive me," she says. "But I only just now found out what we were doing."

"You only now found out the specifics," Akuchi says. "But you had to know it wasn't good. Whenever Mr. Johnson withholds information—like, say, what's in the packages you're carrying—you've got to assume it was something bad. This isn't your first run, is it?"

Agbele Oku, she does not dignify that with a response.

"If you had some brainpower and some experience, you

knew whatever it was, wasn't good. So, to act all surprised about it now—well, that means either you're a rookie or an idiot." Akuchi's words are hard, but his tone is so soft it somehow sounds almost like a compliment.

But Agbele Oku is listening to the words, not the tone. "A rookie or an idiot," she repeats. "Fine then. I am sure you do not want someone like that with you. Then I will leave. I am done."

Halim turns away from her. He does not say anything, but it is clear that he does not see the mage's departure as a tremendous loss.

Cayman, though, feels the deep stab of fear that comes from trying to face magic without magic of your own, and he is not about to let the only spell-slinger in the group just walk away.

"Wait, wait, wait. Hold on. You have a job to do. A commitment to fulfill. Sure, Mr. Johnson didn't say we'd be delivering body parts, but he didn't *not* say we'd be delivering body parts either. So he didn't do anything to cancel our deal. You've got a job to do, and you don't just walk away from a job."

"And that's the highest good you can think of?" Agbele Oku says. "That's how you make your decisions? Your job?"

"The job," Cayman says, "is the only thing that has consistently fed me. So yeah, it's the highest good I know."

"Then I will pity you, but I will not travel with you." Again, she turns to walk away.

"All right, fine, let's look at some other kind of good. Maybe, maybe this heart's for someone who wants a transplant. I mean, they put a lot of care into keeping it cold and fresh, didn't they? Maybe we've got a heart that's about to save someone's life."

"You are an idiot," Agbele Oku says. "No heart could be viable after this much time outside a body."

"I thought you magic people were all about redrawing the lines of what's possible," Cayman drawls, and Agbele Oku frowns in a way that allows Cayman to chalk up a point for himself in his head.

"I do not believe we are on a mercy mission," Agbele Oku says.

X-Prime jumps in. "Then that's your choice. You can believe what you want to believe, but we're saying if you want to believe we're good guys, you can. There's plenty of ways to do it. Like, maybe the heart and the scalp belonged to someone who really needed to have their heart and scalp taken away. Someone who's been hurting women across the city. And we're about to deliver proof that the bastard is dead."

Again, Agbele Oku must pause. When she speaks again, it is with the extra vehemence of a wavering soul. "I do not believe that!"

"Fine. But it's *your* choice not to believe. So don't act like you *have* to leave the group. You just want to."

And that is the button to push. X-Prime has not known Agbele Oku long, but he makes it a point to watch whoever he is with to see what they respond to and what they do not, because he knows that for a person that does what he does, that is the most valuable information in the world. Agbele Oku would leave a job for moral grounds, but she would not just quit. And he and Cayman have taken away her moral grounds.

She cannot just give in, though. Not after making her stand. So, there is more talking that must take place.

"You say this could be from someone bad. But we do not know who it is. Maybe we should," she says.

"That would be good," X-Prime says. "But we don't have much to go on. You saw—we all saw—the scalp. Anyone recognize the person from that?" He pauses, there is only silence, then he talks again. "And while the heart's got plenty of DNA, I don't think anyone's carrying a portable DNA lab. Are they?" Silence again. "All right. So for the time being, we're a little stuck."

"What's in the third box?" Agbele Oku says.

Cayman saw where this line of questioning was going right from the start, he was waiting and ready, and a roar starts to emerge from his lungs, only to be stopped be an abrupt, palm-forward gesture from X-Prime. The fact that this gesture actually silences him surprises Cayman more than anyone.

"I don't know," X-Prime says. "But I can't imagine there's much point to keeping it closed. We already know what's in two of them—why not open a third?" And Cayman has trouble disagreeing with that.

The third package is being held by Groovetooth, and the group moves toward her like her gravitational pull has suddenly increased a thousandfold. It is not accurate to say they are ready for anything to be in the box, but they are certainly prepared, based on the other boxes, to see just about any type of body part. They have all seen various body parts in all kinds of conditions in their time, so there is more curiosity than squeamishness as they lean forward.

Groovetooth does not feel comfortable in the spotlight, so through a quick and subtle gesture she manages to put the box in Agbele Oku's hands, who shows little hesitation before opening it.

There is a brief puff of mist as the lid of the metal box is removed. The box is insulated, but not actively refrigerated like the container with the heart. The mist clears, and no one is surprised to see something the color of brown skin in the box. It resolves itself into a shape quickly, a rough oval with five tendrils. It is a hand.

There is a moment of relief that it isn't something quite as visceral as the heart, and then a moment of collective guilt that they all felt relieved that they had just laid their eyes on a severed human hand.

X-Prime is the first to speak. "So," he says in an inappropriately jovial tone, "anyone recognize this hand?"

Most of the others say "No," except for Agbele Oku, who glares at him.

"Okay then," X-Prime says. "The good news is we can ID this sucker. Even if the hand came from a different body than the other parts, we can learn something that we didn't know before. Go get 'em, Groovetooth."

Groovetooth is quick enough to know what X-Prime wants her to do, and she has equipment with a sharp enough resolution to pull it off. She reaches out, she grabs the hand, she does not flinch—and there are a couple people watching who note the lack of a flinch—and she takes a nice detailed picture of one of the fingers. Then the software goes to work, flattening the image, finding the highlights, looking for what makes it special and unique, and then trundling off with the information to break into a large number of databases and see if a match for the print can be found.

There is a quiet moment while the team stands in a small circle, all of them staring at Groovetooth's commlink as if it is about to do something. But no matter how good the agents are, databases take time to penetrate, and so there is nothing immediately forthcoming, and even if there was, it would only be visible to Groovetooth, so there is very little point to them standing around and staring.

"Let's get moving," Cayman says, and the team, all of them, move forward. For a few more moments, at least, they are still a team.

There is a high whine in the distance, and Cayman immediately tenses himself. He does not stop walking, but he wary,
poised, ready for anything as the whine gets louder and closer
and separates into two or three distinct whines. The sounds are
coming from the south, and the fact that they have continued on
for a good few moments is encouraging to Cayman, as he takes
it to mean that there are few breaks ahead that will cause trouble.
So they will make progress quickly, assuming the whines that are
approaching are not going to cause them trouble.

The whines are fast, they come into view and they are black
blurs, moving quickly, and Cayman sees the twitch from Halim
that means that the samurai is considering a pre-emptive strike,
but they are moving too fast for him to take them all out at once,
and killing one of them would likely only serve to make the other ones mad. So he remains ready, but he does not yet draw a
weapon.

Cayman can see now that there are three of them, hunched
black figures over the silver and black blurs of bullet bikes, and
they drive them with weaving, serpentine movements that are
never straight lines. Some of the bikes have two people on them,
and the people sitting in back are looking ahead carefully, watching for something, and Cayman firmly believes that when they see
it, things will get significantly more complicated.

He does not want to wait for that to happen. He tosses the
box with the heart in it to X-Prime so his hands can be free, and
he pulls out a sword in his right hand and a gun in his left so he'll
be prepared for any circumstance.

But as soon as he made the toss, the people on the back of
the bikes saw what they wanted. They swung their legs over the
cycles and dropped to the ground, but they barely slowed. There
are wheels on their feet, and they are shooting forward, moving
their legs only to keep their balance, not to propel themselves.
Cayman sees where they are headed, and he immediately understands his mistake.

"Throw it back!" Cayman yells.

"What?" X-Prime says.

"Throw it *back*!" he screams. And X-Prime hears. He was
about to drop the box in a backpack, but he stops and prepares to
toss it back to him.

But the people on skates, they are coming fast. Too fast. With
his gun, Cayman fires, and he is pretty sure he hits his target, but

nothing happens. The black clothing they are wearing is very possibly boiling them alive in the Lagos heat, but it is also keeping bullets from having much impact on their bodies. Cayman aims for the face, takes another shot, but it flies wide.

And X-Prime is listening. The one time he listens, the one time he does not decide to fight about what Cayman says, is the wrong time. The package is moving out of his hand, and to his credit he tried a high path, a lofting arc that might go over the heads of the approaching skaters, but these are people who can climb off a bullet bike and then skate at speeds that must be over fifty kilometers per hour, and jumping on skates is not going to be too difficult for them. And one of them jumps, and he has a wonderful angle, he flies in the air like the ground beneath his feet is elastic, his arms stretch, and the box lands gently in his hands.

He is close to Cayman, close enough for him to take a swing with his sword, and he does, a sweeping but quick swing, heading right for the skater's belly, but the skater's arm moves down and connects solidly with the sword, and the arm is armored and likely metal, so it does not take much if any damage, and the sword is bounced aside. The skater does not seem hurt, and most importantly he is not stopped, and the box is in his hand, and he is going away.

The only consolation is that he is taking the box in the direction it is supposed to go, toward Lagos Island.

CHAPTER TWENTY-ONE

THREE HOURS AND FIFTEEN MINUTES
BEFORE THE BRIDGE

Akuchi has always loved being a rigger, loved almost everything about the job, except for this one thing, and that is that when you are a rigger you are expected to give a ride to everyone. When you are part of a team and the other members need to go somewhere, they don't even bother to stop and think about how they are going to get there. They just think, *the rigger will take us!* And that is that.

Having other people in a vehicle with you is annoying for any number of reasons, the primary one being they generally are telling you where it is you need to go, and more often than not it is a place you would not choose to go if you were on your own. Which you are not.

Another annoyance is that other people in the vehicle cannot help but react to the way Akuchi drives, and try as he might he cannot help but notice the way they are reacting. Usually this does not stop him, and he just drives as he pleases, but still he notices that people are nervous or even disapproving, and he does not like it. It prevents him from feeling the full immersion with his vehicle, the feeling of oneness that is the chief joy of his occupation.

All this is to say that when Akuchi dropped Cayman and X-Prime off in Ikeja, he felt a certain relief and freedom and pleasure that comes from doing his job the way he wanted. He could take any street he selected, come as close to pedestrians as he pleased, kiss any vehicle whose driving he did not like with a tap of his fender, and no one would say a word. At least, no one in his vehicle would say a word, and since that vehicle was at the moment his entire world, that was all that mattered.

He wished he could take his time, go to the destination of his choosing, but he had another passenger to pick up. Even in his brief freedom, he was constrained.

When this was all over, he resolved, he would go for a nice, long drive around the city. He would challenge any Yoruba he saw driving a vehicle, and he would beat their ass. Then he would ram them.

He had hit a populated section of the city, which meant the streets were crowded. He was planning on switching to his cycle shortly, and the crowds made him anxious for it. The cycle was a challenge in crowds, but it was also faster—he knew all sorts of maneuvers to get him past and through people. And there were plenty of them. With the heat and the discomfort and the unrest, no one was inside today. Everyone was out, but no one had anyplace to go, so they were standing and walking aimlessly, which made traffic slow for those who did not know what they were doing. For Akuchi, the people with their white-with-splashes-of-bright-red-and-yellow clothing were bright pylons, marking an obstacle course he felt more than saw. He navigated it quite successfully, with pivots and spins that cut through layers of loose dust to grab the hard road underneath. He avoided most of the pylons, he hit a few of them, but he didn't think he inflicted any serious damage. He was not terribly worried about it, as there were a million risks that came with walking the streets of Lagos, and if people could not be bothered to pay enough attention to avoid them, that was not his affair.

But then he sensed something that was bad. Pylons without a path through them. People had lined up, maybe three or four deep, across the road, and there was no path through them. He saw them not long after he sensed them, and it was clear that this was no random pattern. They were standing there for a purpose.

Akuchi could run right through them, but some of them looked heavy and would do some damage to his car. Besides, glancing blows were one thing—cold-bloodedly driving the car directly into people was something else. Akuchi did not spend a lot of time worrying about things like ethics and absolutes, but he knew what it meant to be a monster, and to know that a monster was not something he wanted to be.

So he blared his horn, having little confidence it would work, and when it didn't he did a trickish move where he skidded around and came to a stop right in front of the group and parallel to them. Then he blared his horn again.

That was when he heard the one thing he was not anxious to hear. His name.

"Akuchi," someone in the group said. "We would have a word with you."

Akuchi sighed. The silence in his car since he had dropped off the chatting *oyibos* had been a welcome relief, and now there were more people who wanted to talk. The world, he firmly believed, was dying from too much talking and not enough doing. But they had not yet annoyed him enough to make him run them over, so he slowly climbed out and got ready to listen until they were ready to let him go.

Once he was standing on the road, he leaned against the door in the time-honored way that people who are proud of their vehicles have been leaning against their doors since vehicles were invented.

"You are Akuchi," a man in the middle of the group said. He wore the *fila* of a Yoruba Olorisha, which was not a good sign.

Akuchi nodded, but did not speak. The fewer words he said, the fewer overall words would be added to this conversation, and the sooner it would end.

"Eshu has led us to you. Eshu has revealed your path to us. Eshu serves us because we serve him. Glory to Eshu," the Olorisha said, and the crowd around him echoed the last three words.

Akuchi made no movement or reply. The words were a show for the Yorubas around him, not for him.

"Akuchi," the Olorisha said. "You have been warned."

"Yes," Akuchi said. He did not have the smallest idea to what the Olorisha was referring, but agreement seemed to be the best way to go at the moment.

"You have been warned many times," the Olorisha said.

"Sure," Akuchi said.

"You have been warned, and the consequences of ignoring the warning have been clearly explained to you."

"Right," Akuchi said.

"And yet you are going to meet the Igbo Halim. You are working with him against the Yoruba. You have ignored the warning."

"I'm working with an Igbo," Akuchi said. "But that doesn't mean I'm doing anything against you people. I know all these tribal squabbles are important to you, but not every Igbo spends every waking moment plotting against the Yoruba. Sometimes they just do things for themselves."

"This is not one of those times," the Olorisha said.

"Really? Did Eshu tell you that? Because frankly, we don't know what the hell we're doing."

The Olorisha's mouth curled in a very unpleasant smile. "It would not be the first time that runners were the last to know their own business."

"Touché."

"And you are not a fool. You know something of what has been happening in the city. You know that the Igbo have attempted to gain control of oil fields and been stopped, and that they are now full of fake outrage at being denied what they feel they deserve. You know what is happening in the streets."

"I've heard a few things. But I thought maybe everyone would just relax a little and not turn the whole thing into another foolish war."

The Olorisha's eyes narrowed. "Avenging honor is never foolish."

"Seeing as how honor ain't worth a thing, yeah, fighting over it usually is pretty stupid. But that's not the point. The little oil field spat went the way it went, but it's all over. I don't know what the Igbo are planning to do to strike back at you, or what you're doing to strike back at them, and I don't care. I'm doing a job, not fighting a war."

"Ignorance will not save you. This job you are doing is part of the war, and you are on the wrong side of it."

"Fine. Look, I'll stipulate that I was warned and that I was told the consequences for ignoring the warning. In fact, I remember the warning quite well, and it included promises of death in any one of a number of horrible ways, but what it didn't promise was that I would have to endure a conversation before I was killed."

"Justice demands that the condemned understand the reasons for his punishment. If you believe the demands of justice have now been met, then I am satisfied as well."

The Olorisha turned to his people and prepared to give some sort of an order. Akuchi moved, hoping he could be inside his vehicle before any guns fired, and hoping all the Yorubas had were weak weapons that wouldn't penetrate the vehicle's exterior.

But he would not be fast enough. It is difficult to do much in the time it takes for a man to utter the words "Kill him." He knew he never should have left his car, and he decided that, in retrospect, being a live monster was better than being a dead human.

The fatal sentence, however, did not come out of the Olorisha's mouth. Akuchi scrambled toward the door, waiting to hear words, or gunfire, or anything that indicated his death was on the way, but he didn't hear anything. He looked up, and he saw that the Olorisha was not moving. His hand was poised in mid-air, frozen. His face had a blank expression. There was not much that Akuchi knew about magic, but he knew what it looked like when someone was receiving a message through a mindlink. It looked like the Olorisha looked—eyes unfocused and distant, face somewhat slack because the mind is somewhere else.

Akuchi was not stupid enough to stand and do nothing. He moved, into the car, and started the engine. He felt much safer when he was inside.

He looked at the road, ready to gun through them, but the Olorisha was parting his people. There was a path opening for him. Part of Akuchi said screw it, run them over anyway, but there was no point to damaging his vehicle unnecessarily.

He made a thought, and his car moved. The acceleration was perfect.

He did not hit a soul as he moved through the crowd, but what mattered was that he was past. He was free again, at least for a short time.

If he were inclined to analyze the situation, he would ponder just who it was on the other end of the mindlink. The Olorisha was ready to kill him, but someone decided to keep him alive. Akuchi found that a bit surprising—he, like most runners he knew, could name several people off the top of his head who wanted him dead, but very few who would go out of their way to make sure he stayed alive. It would be an interesting puzzle, and it might even make him think about just what larger mechanisms were moving in the city at this time.

But he was not so inclined to think along those lines, so he did not.

CHAPTER TWENTY-TWO

I have told you before that there are stories about Akuchi and there are stories about Halim. There is at least one story about Agbele Oku, and you know that this is so because I have told it to you. I am not as familiar with the stories of *oyibos*, but I am led to believe that there are some stories about Cayman and X-Prime that have been told, though since I do not have firsthand knowledge of them I cannot vouch for their quality.

So that leaves us with Groovetooth. Some people believe that there are no stories about Groovetooth, that she is a quiet mouse who avoids noise and trouble, but they would be wrong. There are stories about her, but they do not have her name attached to them. While Groovetooth acknowledges that getting one's name out there can have a positive effect when it comes to building a reputation and bringing yourself business, she believes those benefits are far outweighed by the benefits of anonymity. There are many stories in the world where it is better that no names are attached to the actions those stories describe.

And so, when the fast-moving people on their skates came through and stole the heart that had been flying from X-Prime to Cayman, she was confronted with a dilemma, because, you see, there were things she knew about the people that had just passed through, there were things she could say that might help the other people she was working with, but if she shared that knowledge, that could very well result in her name being attached to stories that had heretofore allowed her to stay anonymous and unknown.

It is a difficult decision for her, and so she takes some time to think about it. It helps that she, along with all the other runners, is running at top speed and does not have breath for much conversation.

The runners, they did not have to think or talk about what they were going to do once the heart was taken. They know they want to go south; they know they want the heart. Both goals require the same direction of travel, and so they are moving as fast as they can, and doing all they can to ensure that the skaters are slowed up.

Some of this involves long-range weaponry. Halim had a rifle out—Groovetooth remains stunned at the size of the arsenal the man has hidden under his robe—and he has taken a few shots as he squints ahead of them. Possibly he sees something, possibly he just intuits it, but whatever the case he has fired, and seems convinced that his actions have had the effect of slowing the skaters down for a time.

Cayman has followed his example and fired what weapons he has available, but to Groovetooth he does not seem to have the same confidence in his work, the same certainty that what he is doing will make a difference. But he does it, and Groovetooth can only assume that means that he believes some good may come of it.

But what Groovetooth is happiest about is the expression of concentration on Agbele Oku's face. She is running easily, with the smooth grace of someone who is not thinking about her movement but is just doing it. Her mind is elsewhere, and Groovetooth is certain it is on the skaters ahead, and on slowing them down. There was no hesitation from Agbele Oku about this—the theft of the heart is a clear case of right and wrong, and Agbele Oku believes she is on the side of the right, so she will help get the heart back. Groovetooth cannot sense the astral plane, so she could not tell when Agbele Oku started working her mojo, but simply from the way the mage looked, Groovetooth believed it did not take her long to send magic after the fleeing skaters.

The skaters have been left on their own. When they passed and stole the heart, they were on one side of the runners and the bikes on the other, and the bikes made larger targets. Halim had quickly disabled a bike with a handgun, and the surviving bikers took that as a sign to depart. They drove off to the north, and since they did not have anything anyone wanted, were left unmolested as the runners headed south after the skaters.

As they continue south, Agbele Oku, with a smooth glide of a run, moves next to Halim.

"They like to run around obstacles," she tells him. "They do not just bull their way through. You can make them go out of their way if they think they will keep their speed."

Halim nodded. "Cayman and I will keep fire in the center, with a few shots to the side. Keep them weaving."

"Okay," Agbele Oku said, and glided away.

And there it was, the reason why Groovetooth might have to tell what she knew. Any information she had about these people, it might help. Especially to someone like Halim, who had fought almost every group in the city, and knew how they fought. He knew how to prepare for them, and knew how to strike. The sooner she tells him what she knows, the sooner he will be able to make specific plans.

She takes a breath. She opens her mouth to talk, then pretends she was just gulping in air. Her mouth closes. She swallows. Then she opens her mouth again.

"The people ahead of us?" she says. Then she pauses. "The people on skates," she says, as if clarification was needed. "They belong to a group."

Halim does not look at her. She has seen this from him before, where when he is not interested in what has been said, he does not acknowledge that words have been uttered. She has not yet said anything of interest.

She swallows again, and feels like she has just gulped a mouthful of fetid bay water.

"These skaters," she says. "They are Tamanous."

And her words are acknowledged. Halim looks at her, a quick movement, and she has his interest, which is terrible to her.

"How do you—" he starts, but then he stops. Just like that, he knows.

Just like that, they all know.

A silence falls over the group, a quiet so profound that Groovetooth cannot hear the individual footfalls of the runners around her. Her revelation has exploded in the air, absorbing all the noise around her. Or maybe it is that the blood pounding in her ears has covered every other sound.

She is pleased that no one has been sufficiently shocked that they have stopped running. She hopes the fact that they are out of breath will prevent them from speaking the condemnations she is certain are on their lips.

At first she is relieved by the silence, but the longer it continues, the tenser she becomes. Her imagination goes to work, dreaming up all manner of things they will do to her because she has associated with some rather unsavory characters, characters generally more unsavory than the ones running beside her at this moment. She wishes they would stop making her wait, that they would just decide what they wanted to do and do it. Shoot her, tell her to go home, whatever. Just do it.

That is when something extraordinary happens. Halim speaks, and it is not about her.

"Tamanous almost never stands and fights," he says. "We don't have to worry about them setting an ambush or anything—they'll just keep running until they get away."

"What if we give them no choices?" Cayman says. "What if they run out of places to run to?"

"Any cornered animal fights," Halim says. "But they will fight to get past us, not to kill us."

"I'd rather they try to take us head on. Then we'd kill them, and it'd be over," Cayman says.

"That's why they will not do it."

Cayman thinks for a time while the running, the spells, the occasional gunfire continues. "And we don't really have anything they want. Not anymore."

Halim remains silent, as he believes Cayman's statement is obvious enough to stand on its own without confirmation.

But then Cayman sees it. "If we corner them, we know what they'll do. Which is a good thing."

Halim nods.

"Then how do we get them to turn around?" Cayman asks.

Halim looks at Groovetooth, and she flinches, ready for the conversation to turn back to her, and for Halim to deliver whatever punishment she deserves.

"Tell me where the next break is," he says.

Groovetooth had not, of course, started the day with a detailed map or photos of the Third Mainland Bridge, since she had not expected to have to deal with it. She had tried to find one while they were marching across it, but Matrix traffic has been so spotty that she was not able to find anything that she judged helpful. When she was washed ashore, though, she had Matrix access, and while she could not know for sure what the rest of the day held, she had an idea that up-to-date information about the bridge would be a good thing to have, so she sent some agents after it, and as it happened they returned, before she traveled to the north end of the bridge, with usable data that she has not yet had an opportunity to examine. Now, though, seems like the right opportunity.

She looks at the data the same way she looks at any data, barely seeing it, but having the information bury itself deep into her brain so that she knows things without being exactly sure how she knows them.

"There are no more complete gaps until Lagos Island," she says. "But there is a spot a few hundred meters away where there's only about a three-meter wide piece of bridge intact."

"How far ahead? Exactly?" Halim says, his voice crisp.

"326," Groovetooth says, then she takes two running strides. "325."

Halim turns to Agbele Oku. "Can you see it?"

She nods. "I believe so."

"Put something in their way," he tells her. "Make it good."

Agbele Oku nods. Something happens, and the effect is immediate. There is a rumbling, a cracking ahead. They feel it where they are as a slight tremor that passes through their feet. The beleaguered skaters, who had been slowed by regular gunfire, are now coming back toward them, and the runners see what made them turn around.

The bridge has come alive in that narrow section, heaving to life, blocks of rough concrete cracking out of the surface and rising up in a shapeless mass where each block can be a limb, each chunk of concrete can deliver a punishing blow. It is a spirit of earth, and the bridge, for a short time, will be its home.

The people from Tamanous, they want no part of it.

They must know they are heading into danger, but they are moving quickly, likely hoping their speed will save at least some of their lives. One of them finds that hope in vain, as a shot from Halim's rifle catches her in the cheek and does many unpleasant things to the inside of her skull. She falls, but she is not the one with the heart, so she is ignored by both groups.

Cayman pumps a few rounds into another skater, but he hits him below the shoulders, and it seems the skater has enough armor to either keep him from being wounded or to prevent the wounds from being serious enough to stop him.

Halim and Cayman could be firing more, but they are not. There was a plan made without speaking, a plan made as soon as Cayman mentioned that they would know what the skaters would do. They are to put up a token resistance. And then they are to let them pass.

The skaters, they think they are doing a tremendous job weaving between the bullets the runners are firing, they see daylight between Cayman and Halim, and they go for it, moving forward quickly. They do not hesitate, they hit the gap accelerating, for they want nothing more than to be gone and free.

So when a sheet of ice appears at their feet, it is an unfortunate and inconvenient thing.

They flounder. They are from Lagos, they have skated on many surfaces, they have made their way across rubble and dirt, but they have never had to deal with ice. Both of the surviving skaters keep their footing, but they are unsteady, slipping and sliding, flailing arms over the blinding mirror under their feet. But there is still daylight ahead, this piece of ice is not so long, they can cross it and still get free.

That is why a second spell pours out of Agbele Oku, and this one creates a glowing wall that the out-of-control skaters abruptly bump into. There are two bumps, then two *thumps*, then there are two skaters on the ground. There are several guns pointed at them.

Groovetooth is not anxious to approach the fallen skaters. She had recognized them as Tamanous quickly, but she had not yet recognized them as individuals—she does not know who these people are, and she is quite willing to keep it that way. But the skaters react as many people who believe they might be at the end of their life react. They uncover their faces, both so that they could face death openly, and so that their possible attackers would have to look them in the face as they kill them.

Groovetooth is relieved not to recognize them, but she wonders how different it might be for her if she did recognize one. She did not have many—any—close acquaintances in that organization, very much on purpose. She did not like any of them. But could she make the jump from not liking them to seeing them die?

She thinks she could.

She believes she is about to see them dead, as Halim appears ready to kill them where they lay. She cannot argue with this decision—they have caused trouble, they are in the way, and there is little reason to waste time with negotiation.

But Cayman speaks before bullets fly.

"You're dead as soon as we want you to be. Give me the box, get out quick, and maybe you can stay alive. Don't turn around.

The minute any of us sees your face again, we'll shoot it off."

There are causes that people die for, but organlegging generally is not one of them. There is little hesitation as the skaters toss the box to Cayman, get to their feet, and skate off, thanks to the disappearance of the now-dispelled barrier.

Halim may not be happy, but Groovetooth has not yet fully learned the subtleties of his narrow range of expressions. He looks at Cayman steadily and does not speak for a time. But then Cayman walks by him, and Halim speaks.

"I thought you wanted to move quickly. My way was faster."

Cayman does not respond. He walks south, and the others follow.

A few moments later, Groovetooth finds herself next to Cayman, and she is not certain how that happened. She glances over—her eyes are just higher than his waist—then looks ahead.

"Halim put this team together," Cayman says with no lead-in or context.

Not knowing what he's getting at, Groovetooth can do little but agree. "Yes."

"But he didn't have total freedom. Some people were recommended to him—strongly recommended."

"That's what I hear," Groovetooth says.

"You were strongly recommended," Cayman says.

"Maybe," Groovetooth says, and she starts to assemble a remark about how she has cultivated a reputation, and Mr. Johnson must have heard of her, but Cayman cuts through that before she can speak.

"You were picked because you know about Tamanous. That's why you're here. I'm not sure why they picked you for that, or who did it, but that's why. At least, that's what I think."

"All right," Groovetooth said.

Cayman turns his head to look at her. She can almost hear his neck creak as he turns his face down.

"I'm telling you this because you should know that someone knows. I'm guessing you want it to be a secret. It's not. Not totally."

At that point, Groovetooth lets Cayman pull away from her. It's not hard—his legs are long, hers are short. She fades away from him, and he lets her.

CHAPTER TWENTY-THREE

THREE HOURS AND FIFTEEN MINUTES BEFORE THE BRIDGE

There are quieter moments. Not every part of a run is chasing or fighting or doing loud or violent things. Sometimes a run involves walking, sometimes it involves waiting, sometimes it involves talking. If you have been running long enough, you know that you ignore these moments—or forget about them—at your peril.

When Akuchi left them, Cayman and X-Prime had, of course, hoped to be right where they needed to be to pick up what they needed to pick up. But they had two things working against them—they didn't know the exact location where they were supposed to be, and Akuchi did not have time to help them figure out where they were supposed to be. Once they were at a reasonably promising yet empty part of Ikeja, Cayman and X-Prime were exiled from the vehicle and left on their own.

They surveyed a few nearby dumpsters to see if any were the one they were looking for, then quickly determined that none matched the vague description they had been given. In fact, most of the buildings and dumpsters in the immediate vicinity did not match the description they had been given, so they were left to walk through the district, occasionally glancing at brick buildings and dirty streets to see if their surroundings were starting to look like where they were supposed to be.

As they walked, X-Prime talked, because, as Cayman had noticed, his feet and mouth seemed to be directly connected.

"Do you want to play Who's On Top?" he asked brightly, almost skipping as his feet skidded on the dusty streets.

"No," said Cayman.

"Come on!"

"No."

"You never want to play!"

"That's because it's stupid!"

"No it isn't!" X-Prime said. "It's information. A long time ago, you told me that was the most precious thing we had. So how can it be bad?"

"Because it's not information! It's just guessing!"

"But we could guess our way to the truth!"

Cayman scowled. "How would you know when you get there, though?"

X-Prime tapped his stomach. "You feel it. You feel it right here, when you get it right."

"Bullshit," Cayman said.

"Okay, maybe *you* don't feel it, but that's not my problem. *I* do. So I'm going to figure this out, and you can help as little or as much as you want."

"Thanks," said Cayman. He turned a corner and felt a faint breeze that was welcome on his sweat-damp skin. Then it faded and was gone.

"Okay. So it's someone with cash, because Halim could afford to bring us out. We may be pretty much acting like couriers, but the job's being treated as more than that. So we know that."

Cayman studiously refused to reply.

"And there's more than just money. If they're bringing us in instead of using somebody local, it's because they think it's not a bad idea to have some people in the group without local entanglements."

"Then why not make the group all outsiders?" Cayman said, then immediately hated himself for contributing to the conversation.

"Good question!" X-Prime said. "That's the spirit! I don't know—maybe it's that all conflicts aren't created equal—some they want to avoid, some they're willing to embrace."

"Why would they embrace local conflicts?"

"Ah, they're always good for something," X-Prime said. He looked one way and then another, back and forth rapidly, the way he did when he was excited or happy or both. "Tensions exist to be exploited."

"How?"

"Hell if I know. Can't say I'm up on all the local politics and stuff. I'm still learning the names of the tribes. But they don't seem to like each other much, do they?"

"Of course not," Cayman snorted. "Any time you've got people divided into groups, one group always find reasons to not like another group."

"The question is, what tribe are the people in our group from? Maybe that's why they were chosen."

"Halim's Igbo. I think he said Akuchi's Igbo, too. Don't know about the rest."

"Maybe they're all Igbo?"

"Maybe."

"Maybe whoever's on top here figured an all-Igbo team would be the best, Most likely to be loyal, right?"

"So you think whoever hired us is Igbo?"

"Could be," X-Prime said. "Makes sense."

"Then why bring us in? Igbo got no faces?"

"Good point. Maybe it's organized crime, then. Maybe these other four are all known mobsters or gangers or whatever, and everyone else in the city knows this and refused to work with them, so they had to bring us in."

"What kind of mobster lets everyone in the city know what they do for a living? And what kind of runner flat-out refuses to work with mobsters?"

"See, this is why you should play this more often," X-Prime said. "You always ask about things I forget."

"Being smarter than you is not much of an accomplishment," Cayman muttered.

"Pardon?" X-Prime said.

"Nothing," Cayman said in a normal voice. "So, it could be mobsters. Hell, let's say it is. We're working for mobsters. Does that work for you?"

X-Prime frowned and stood still for a moment. "Nope," he finally said. "The gut's not telling me this is right. Have to move on to another theory."

"Oh good," Cayman said, carefully scrubbing his voice of any inflection.

"Corps have enough money to pay for whatever it is we're doing. And we all know what corps use out-of-towners for."

"Deniable assets," Cayman said. "Out-of-towners either die or go home. Either way, they don't spread stories around."

"And we're heading for Lagos Island, which is corp central."

"Not just corps. Anyone with money is there. Just because we're going there doesn't mean it's a corp."

"That's a point. But who else is there?"

"Don't ask me," Cayman said. "This is your game, not mine."

"You're no help at all. All right, well, let's be radical. Let's say they brought in outsiders because they're dealing with some shit that's scary or secret or both. Who deals in shit like that?"

"Everyone," Cayman said.

"You know, the more I think about it, the more I think it's *not* a tribe hiring us. I mean, if you're doing tribal work, you'd keep it in the tribe, right? You get more loyalty from your runners then, anyway. Tribal pride and all. So I'll bet it's something else. And if we want a scary or secret something else..." He stopped.

Cayman almost stopped too, but then remembered he didn't want to spend any more time in the smelly alleys behind abandoned warehouses than he had to, so he kept walking and waited for X-Prime to catch up.

There was a quick scuff of footsteps, and then X-Prime was next to him again.

"Do you know who it is?"

Cayman didn't say anything.

"Do you want to know? I can tell you. I can tell you who hired us."

"Good for you."

"Don't you want to hear it?"

"No."

"Why not?"

And he lost it. He knew the boy didn't deserve it, but he had a long habit of blowing up at X-Prime whenever he felt like it, and it was not a habit he was of a mind to change.

"Because it's a silly game!" he said, yelling so loud that dust on the ground a meter in front of him stirred into small eddies. "Because it's a lot of talk at the kind of thing that gets people killed!"

"What are you talking about?"

"What you're saying, all this stuff, it isn't real, but it gets out, and people think it is, and they act on it, not because it's true or anything, but because it *feels* right. It feels right down here." He mimicked X-Prime's tap to the stomach. "And so you spout nonsense, and then other people spout it, and it hits the wrong ears, ears belonging to people who don't know if it's true or not but don't care, because if they're tied to the wrong info it's bad. So they don't bother with verification, they kill, all because you *talk too goddamned much!*"

X-Prime didn't respond for a time. They walked quietly for a while, and Cayman listened to the dust flying past his ears and his feet scraping on the ground. He looked straight ahead, and he did not glance once toward X-Prime.

Finally, X-Prime spoke.

"Man, you *really* don't like this game."

"You're an idiot."

"Right, but you still think the idiotic things I might talk about to keep myself entertained are enough to get someone killed. I don't know if I should be flattered because you think what I say is so influential, or worried because you think the world is dumb enough to be so easily manipulated."

"The second one," Cayman said.

"Well, you're wrong. It's like in the old days, back when the Matrix was new."

"How would you know anything about those days?"

"I read stuff. There were people who thought the Matrix would make it easier to find the truth, because information would be out there, and people would be able to find whatever it was they might be looking for. But there were others who said the signal-to-noise ratio would be so low that things would be more confusing than ever—there'd be all sorts of crap out there, all disguised as something real, and most people would have no idea how to tell shit from gold. Those people in the second group were right."

Cayman didn't say anything.

"So if I add a little noise to the world, don't worry about it. Just a little more confusion out there to throw people off."

"Fine," Cayman said. "You can talk all you want. Just don't expect me to listen."

X-Prime grinned. "Same as always, then."

They kept walking for a while. X-Prime opened up his mouth two or three times like he was about to say something, then he closed it. Cayman didn't ask what he wanted to say.

Finally, X-Prime said it.

"The new queen of Asamondo. You never asked, but I think it's her. She's the one who hired us."

"Now I'm sure you're an idiot. Why would you say that?"

"You bring in outsiders when you can't find anyone local to work with. The queen was lucky enough to find four people here willing to hang with the ghouls, but not six. So we were imported."

"You've got no evidence."

"No, but it's what I believe."

"Why?"

"Because it's cool!"

"That's a reason?"

X-Prime smiled. "Best reason I've got," he said.

CHAPTER TWENTY-FOUR

On a run, you cannot help but picture how you think things will go. Positive visualization, people call it, the practice where you picture yourself succeeding, so that when you actually do succeed, you're not so surprised. In reality, though, you are lucky if you have two, maybe three moments that exactly match what you had pictured. The rest is all about gaps between ideal and reality, and the improvisations runners use to fill in those gaps.

There have been plenty of gaps for Halim, Cayman, and the others on this run, but now that they have cleared the Tamanous skaters and are moving south, everything is just as Cayman pictured it what they first started on the bridge. Of course, this is tainted by the regrettable fact that had the mission lived up to its original design, they never would have been on the bridge in the first place, but still, the point is that Cayman had an idea of what travel across the bridge should be like, and for the first time their actual travel was somewhat close to this picture.

And the better thing for him was that the mission in reality was finally catching up to where the mission in planning was going to be. There had been a plan, a plan that existed only a couple hours ago, but to Cayman feels like days or perhaps weeks, and that plan involved taking a boat to a point just ahead, docking it, and then entering Lagos Island through the security checkpoint that was now just ahead of them. A few more steps, and they would be where they were supposed to be, albeit a few hours later. But they had all the packages, they seemed to be intact, and no one had suffered any ill effects that a night's rest could not cure. There are mishaps on a run, but if you manage to work around them and get yourselves to the point at which Halim and Cayman and the others now found themselves, then you have done well for yourself, *abi*?

The checkpoint, it was not expected to be any sort of problem for the team, since if someone is demanding that you meet them on Lagos Island, then it is only appropriate and fitting that they provide a way for you to meet them there. So the runners had been provided with the necessary IDs and clearances, and Cayman was firm in his belief that they would walk through security, have those clearances scanned, and not have to hesitate. And then they would be on the Island, and it may be the case that the streets of Lagos Island are not paved with gold, but they are, in fact, *paved*, which gives an immediate veneer of civilization superior to anything the runners have experienced in the past few days, and that veneer is accompanied by security forces and money and all those things that often make runners nervous except for those times when they have the appropriate clearances, and then those things, the people in uniform and the omnipresent cameras and the men and women in unstained suits, they are reassuring rather than threatening.

Cayman wasn't looking forward to being on the Island, as having things around him that are reassuring tended to make him nervous.

The towers ahead are beautiful. Tall and shiny, sparkling, looking like new, even if they are a decade or two or more older. They have a look that is different from the rest of the sprawl, and it is different for the simple reason that the buildings here are regularly cleaned. The red dust that is everywhere in the sprawl is on the Island, too, and you can find it in the cracks and crevices, but it is removed from there far faster than from most locations, since at most locations it is never removed at all.

The security point ahead is not beautiful, because such things were never meant to be appealing. It is a series of open gateways, a few big enough for a vehicle, most for pedestrians since that is who will be coming here along the bridge. A few people are here, but most people are not, because those who travel the bridge are not the same as those who travel the Island, plus the fire on the mainland has made the Islanders even more nervous than usual, so access to the Island has been even more restricted than normal.

The gate has visible guards with guns purchased for the central purpose of looking threatening, and then there are unseen things that are even more deadly, because security everywhere is nothing more than an ongoing game of poker where most players are very careful to hide their strength. By now someone has seen Agbele Oku's aura, knows she is glowing with power and with righteous anger, and they are prepared in case any of that anger is directed at them.

But it will not be, Cayman believes, because they have the clearances, and it is in the best interests of the person who hired them that the clearances work. He does not know if the others share his confidence on this issue, but they seem to be keeping up with him and walking with the same confidence he has, confidence with a touch of weariness. No one has weapons drawn. It should be easy.

But then the voice of Groovetooth stops him.

"They are looking for us."

They all turn, and Cayman is the first to speak. "What?"

"There's been a notification going around. They're looking for us. They have our names."

"So what?" Halim says. "We're not giving them our names. We're giving them what we got on the IDs Mr. Johnson gave us."

"Those are the names they're looking for," Groovetooth says. "Well, one name." She looks at Akuchi. "Yours."

Akuchi shrugs. "Okay."

"Cover him up," Cayman says. "Make him invisible as we go through. We walk through in a group, they won't compare IDs to heads, he'll pass through fine."

"That's a risk," Halim says. "One we don't really need to take. We have no vehicle on the Island. We don't really need him there. He can meet us later."

"After the rest of you have been paid?" Akuchi says. "Yeah, that sounds like a good idea."

"They have your account information," Cayman says. "You were paid once, they know how to pay you again. You don't need to be there."

"And you'll tell them why I'm not there? That I deserve a full payment?" There is a brief pause. "You won't say I took off, or am dead, or did something so that my payment shouldn't go to me?"

Agbele Oku speaks first. "Of course not!" she says, and her words are immediately echoed by the others.

"Yeah, yeah, very reassuring," Akuchi says. "You know what? I'm going through the gate."

"I can't guarantee that I'll have you covered," Groovetooth says.

"No such thing as a guarantee anyway," Akuchi says. "I'm walking through, and what happens, happens."

"Since when did you get suicidal?" Cayman says.

"Since never. Look, Agbele Oku can do her thing, Groovetooth can do her thing, and between the two of them I'm sure they'll do enough to get me through."

The others, of course, nod so that they show their faith in Groovetooth and Agbele Oku, though all of them, including Groovetooth and Agbele Oku, feel a twinge of doubt that they do not feel it would be right to express in this time. But Akuchi is leading the way, and in some ways he is the most defenseless of all of them, since most of his vehicles and drones are elsewhere, and the runners, especially Halim and Cayman, will not be shamed by a rigger going where they are not willing to walk.

They do not, of course, draw weapons, because they are not amateurs, and they know there is no better way to look suspicious than to walk somewhere looking like you might have to kill someone, or like someone might want to kill you.

They walk through the gate, and nothing happens, but then most of them would not notice if anything happened because if it did happen it would not happen to them. There might be astral flares, there might be alarms blinking in the AR displays of the people who are supposed to be alarmed, but those are things that for the most part would stay safely out of sight.

Groovetooth has agents everywhere, and it feels good to have them, to be surrounded by electronic life and to be sending her programs and tools out into the world to be active. They will tell her if they see anything of note, but she has not heard anything from them yet.

And Agbele Oku is assensing, waiting for a spell to flare up from any direction, or for the aura of someone, anyone nearby to spike with anger, panic, or just adrenaline, but while some guards look borderline psychotic and others look like they crossed that border long ago and have misplaced the directions detailing the way back.

And they are through. They are past the checkpoint and on Lagos Island, where everything is bright and shiny, and you can decrease the percentage of people who would be willing to kill you with little provocation to three percent, down from approximately twenty.

Unfortunately for the runners, one of the reasons Lagos Island is as safe as it is, is because the security personnel are generally are of a high caliber. The people on the ground are often low level, of course, because that is the way of the world, but there are others who are possibly the best at what they do, and that means that if they have a shot to take, they can take it without feeling anger or aggression or really very much of anything. They can pull a trigger, and their aura will not change at all.

And that is what happens. There is a shot, and it kicks into the road just behind Akuchi. The runners react quickly, because there is only one possible reaction to have. They run, moving quickly away from the gate. There is another shot, it seems like it comes from the same place as the first, though it is difficult to tell with the echoing noise of the Island's skyscrapers, but this bullet does not come close to Akuchi or anyone else, because there is a glowing wall that has just appeared behind them, and the bullet hits that wall and clinks to the ground. Cayman turns to see if guards besides the sniper are running after them, or doing anything, but they are going about their normal business, watching more people pass through the gates, apparently not caring about the shots behind them or the wall Agbele Oku had abruptly erected. Pedestrians and vehicles are passing through the gate, and if the wall was in their way they move around it, smoothly and easily. It has remarkably little effect—aside, of course, from protecting the runners from a shot that might have killed one of them.

Cayman decides he will wonder more about what was happening when they are safe, but that moment had not yet arrived. He looks ahead of him and sees the type of businesses that would serve people who were about to go out into the uncivilized wilds or those who had just returned from them—carry-out food, med supplies, commlink tuning-up and repair, and other things of that sort. They offered the same tradeoff you always face when you are on the run from someone who would like to kill you—the gain of shelter and a modicum of protection, the loss of moving from an open space to a confined space.

"Is anyone following us?" Cayman says.

"Not that I see," Groovetooth and Agbele Oku say at the same time.

"I say we stay outside then," he says, and no one disagrees.

They keep up a very fast pace for about half a kilometer, and then, without a signal or spoken word, all of them slow to a jog. There are people on the street, and they are staring, but Cayman cares very little about anything any of them do, so long as none of them have a weapon drawn.

"Anything?" he says.

"Not yet," a number of voices say—possibly every member of the group but him.

"Okay." He shakes his head. "We'll figure out what that was all about later. Let's drop the package off, get paid, and get out."

No one disagrees.

They are on the sidewalk, and vehicle traffic has picked up, since they are in a place that people want to be. There are helicopters and other small aircraft darting here and there overhead, touching down on the top of buildings and dropping off or picking up those who will indulge themselves with the luxury of visiting the city without setting a foot on the ground of Lagos. There is even AR, mostly commercial signage, making the street look lively and shiny.

They are moving quickly and attracting the occasional stare, but that matters not at all to them. They feel the pressure of the gate behind them, of the shots that were fired, and the farther they get from those bullets, the better. They, whoever they are, might try to kill Akuchi again on the way out of Lagos Island, but that will be later, at a time when they all should be a bit richer. Perhaps they will take a taxi, since they are in one of the few parts of the sprawl that has ready access to them.

There is a taxi right now, in front of them, parked on the side of the road, waiting for a passenger, or disgorging a passenger. In fact, it seems to be the latter, as the rear door is opening and someone is stepping out. The person is not dressed in business wear, but rather in full traditional Yoruba outfit, with a lovely blue *buba* and a yellow *gele* wrapped around her head. It is difficult to see the woman in the middle of all the fabric, but she seems round-faced and cheerful. She smiles as she emerges from the cab and nods at the strangers walking by her, and most of them walk quickly by her except for Akuchi, who is blocked, so he tries to step around her but she moves with him, and she smiles again, this time awkwardly.

He takes a quick step so he can be past her, but he notices a curious thing—his right leg does not seem to want to respond the way he would like it to. At the moment he notices this, he feels a hot, searing pain in his thigh, and he looks down, and there is blood, lots of it. He looks back at the woman and catches what he did not see before—there seems to be a small gun in her right hand, lost in the folds of her *buba*.

She is still smiling. "I dressed like this," she says, "so you would know." Then she fires again.

It might have been a small consolation to Akuchi to see red blossoms erupt from the woman as Cayman, Halim, and even X-Prime fire on her, killing her on the spot. Except he cannot see this, he cannot see anything, because the second shot from the Yoruban woman took him in the forehead, and he is falling to the ground, and will not see anything ever again.

CHAPTER TWENTY-FIVE

THREE HOURS BEFORE THE BRIDGE

Groovetooth had heard stories of the old days, stories of when cyberdecks were large and cumbersome instead of sleek and light, when deckers were bound by cords and plugs and sometimes were left to do their own thing while the people they were working with did theirs.

She had some familiarity with that period—she had some memories of hardwired Matrix connections, and Lagos was a primitive enough place that some people still jacked in—but all in all, it was history to her, and she was happy to leave it behind.

Yet there she was, in Festac Town, sitting at a table in an Matrix café, watching the progress of the other members of her team while they were out doing stuff. But with people spread out across the sprawl, someone needed to be the central communication and monitoring hub, and that was the job she was built for.

The burden of her job was made considerably lighter by the fact that the action she was following was quite entertaining. X-Prime and Cayman were rummaging through dumpsters in Ikeja, Agbele Oku and Akuchi were on the road to Alimosho for some sort of rendezvous with the sort of people who schedule meetings in Alimosho, and Halim was running over people not far away in the slums of Ajengule.

He was the most fun to keep track of, though it would have been considerably better if he were doing his business in a part of town that was better endowed with security cameras. For the most part, she was limited to monitoring his actions through his own equipment, and Halim was either not set up to send her a visual feed, or he simply didn't feel like doing it. But every comm had a microphone, and so she could usually hear what was going on when she turned her attention to it, and she could even ask questions, and maybe one out of three things she asked was actually answered.

But the microphone on Halim's comm had decent quality, and her imagination was good enough to fill in some of the blanks left by her not being able to see what was happening. She had learned to tell the difference between a punch to the gut, a smack to the head, a kick to the crotch, and a sword slash across the torso. That last one, it was fairly easy to tell from the others. She even thought, sometimes, that she heard the ringing impact of sword on bone as Halim cut into a ribcage.

There was one of those cuts—a strong *thunk*, followed by a ringing that took nearly a full minute to fade, that was followed by a kind of quiet as the sounds near the microphone faded and left only the background noises of people walking and talking and doing their business, sensible people whose noises were not loud in the microphone because they kept their distance from Halim.

"That sounds like it's it," Groovetooth said.

"For now," Halim said.

"These ones have the box?"

"Yes."

She exhaled. Progress—taking one step closer to payday—was good.

"I guess you need to head northeast now."

"Yes. There might be more of them chasing me. Whoever they are."

"I'll watch when I can," she said. "It'll be easier once you're out of the slums."

"I'm already moving."

She returned her attention to the window that showed a map of Lagos. It was the result of a complex series of activities and reports from programs and agents, but like any truly worthwhile complex activity, the end result was simple. Five points on a map—one white, one tan (those two were the *oyibos*), one black (Halim), one blue (Akuchi), one red (Agbele Oku). The dots did not stay visible all the time—dead zones were inevitable, or her agents lost the others as they hopped from one makeshift network of nodes to another. But for the most part, she had them pinned, and she could watch their dots make their way around the city.

And there was another set of dots. They were gray. There were very few people in the sprawl who could track those dots. There were codes and keys that Groovetooth had that allowed her to track these particular individuals, and those codes were given to very few people. There was a point when Groovetooth had done five jobs for Tamanous, and she'd sent all sorts of agents digging Into whatever nodes she had access to, and she still didn't have the codes. It was only when they put her on retainer that she got the higher-level access. They had only given her limited access, of course, but she used that crack to open the door wider for herself, of course. She figured they must have known she would get more. She was a decker, that was what she did—taking a kilometer when she was given a millimeter was part of the job description. So she had a few sets of codes, and while some of them had been discontinued, she had enough to log in to some of their networks.

Which wasn't, in the end, all that useful most of the time. Perhaps Tamanous wouldn't worry so much about secrecy if they realized how few people who were not organleggers cared about what organleggers were up to. But if you are in the information business—and who is not?—you hold on to any bits of data you have, and wait for the right time to use them.

Most of the Tamanous activities going on out there were not of a concern to her. They were doing what they do, and she was grateful that the things they do no longer have considerable overlap with the things she does. But there was one group that she was keeping her eye on, for several reasons. It is a group of hitters.

Tamanous, like every other organization in the known world, has reason to occasionally hire people to do work that their regular staff could not perform, or was unwilling to perform, or should not, for various reasons, including deniability, perform. But they also had work that demanded they keep a certain amount of hitters on staff, because when you do the sort of work in which Tamanous is regularly involved, you often find yourself in need of having to convince people to leave you alone and let you do your business without interference. And so there are the hitters.

Groovetooth knew most of the Tamanous hitters in Lagos, since she found that they were very useful people to know. There was one team she had her eyes on, and that was Capstone's team.

Capstone is an ork, though not the most imposing specimen of his kind. In fact, there are several hitters on the Tamanous payroll who are more physically intimidating than Capstone, but none of them have his tracking ability. Capstone finds people. Whoever they are, wherever they are in the sprawl of Lagos, however fast and in whichever direction they are traveling, Capstone finds them. He always knows the right speed to travel, the correct angle to take to find who he is looking for. It is uncanny. If it were not for a lamentable stim habit and the unfortunate tendency to decide that there were some jobs that were just not worth his time, Capstone would be on the payroll of a much more powerful organization than Tamanous. But he was not, and this day he was out and on the prowl, and apparently had decided that whatever assignment he had been given was worth his time.

Groovetooth had this fear that Capstone's assignment and her job had an area of overlap, and that troubled her. The sources of her worry were vague, built on snippets of conversation with people who were very practiced in telling you only what they wanted you to know, giving you just a taste, so that you were left only with a nagging suspicion that there was something more you should know, but you could not quite piece together just what that something was.

One of these conversations happened with an ambulance driver Groovetooth had ridden with a couple of times, but who did not drive anymore because the amount of money he lost through crashes had started to exceed the amount of money he helped bring in through his driving. He no longer had a working vehicle to his name, and was in the process of drinking away what little cred he had left. If Groovetooth decided to ponder his future, she was fairly certain he would be on the streets within two months, then dead of malnutrition or gang violence in four. Or perhaps, once he started wandering the streets late at night, he would become an involuntary organ donor for the organization that had provided the money he was currently using to keep himself permanently intoxicated.

Though there might be other useful resources in his body, Groovetooth was certain his liver would be completely useless.

Despite his collapsing and drunken state, this rigger, who called himself Birdcage, had too long been in the habit of being careful with information to loosen his lips now. He could barely form coherent words, but when he did, those words did not betray a hint more information than he wanted them to.

They had been in a warehouse that had been abandoned so recently that the electricity had not been shut off yet. Soon the power would go, the wiring would be harvested, and the building would become one of a thousand squatter habitations spread across the sprawl. But for now, there was free juice, and deckers flocked to it to recharge and to use its relatively stable grid access.

Groovetooth was there to enjoy the luxury of a Matrix connection that did not come and go with the breeze. Birdcage was there because he knew that when deckers were in a good mood and absorbed in their work, they were often generous with whatever liquor they may have acquired.

Birdcage was, in the grand tradition of former work acquaintances who were no longer working, reminiscing about the past.

"Hearts," he said. "Hearts are the *worst*. I mean, everything, yeah, is rush, rush, rush, all the time, but hearts are the *worst*. Every time I had a heart, some jack-off was flashing AR messages at me the whole time. Looking for updates, telling me to hurry, on and on and on. It just, it just, you want to know what it makes me? It just makes me glad that they still don't know fuck-all about transplanting brains, right, because if we were shipping brains, how annoying would they be then? They'd be all up in my ass like a procoltolgis...a proloctogy...a...a...what's those things? Like an ass doctor, that's what they'd be like."

"You're right," Groovetooth said, partly because agreeing with a drunk is easier than arguing with him, and partly because he was, in fact, right. "I understand that is why Tosin does not work for them any more. Remember what happened?"

"Damn right I remember," Birdcage said. "He shot someone right in the heart."

Groovetooth laughed. "They had worked hard to find that one. That was a person with a rare blood type, *abi*? So they found a match, someone they thought no one would miss and who would have a decent heart, and they send in Tosin, and the guy fought back and surprised the hell out of Tosin, so he shot the guy. Shot him in the heart."

"They said it was a fifty thousand nuyen-bullet. What an idiot-hole."

"Hired goons," Groovetooth said. "If you hire someone off the street, you must remember that most of the time there was a reason why they were on the street to begin with."

"Yeah," Birdcage said, nodding, and then, somehow, his eyes seemed less red, and his gaze was more focused. "The good ones, they're on a payroll somewhere. Because they know what they're doing."

"Well, there's good ones on the street, too, I guess. You know, people who don't want to get tied down. It's just not always easy to sort out those ones from the posers and the—what was that you just said?—the idiot-holes."

"But the ones on a payroll, they know what they're doing," Birdcage said, almost repeating himself, but doing it with a certain emphasis on each word. "*Those* are the ones you have to watch out for." Is that what he said? Or was it "Those are the ones *you* have to watch out for."

"What? What do you mean?" Groovetooth said, but Birdcage had sipped the clear, extremely high-proof liquid in his glass, and that sip seemed to carry the weight of five shots, because his eyes became glassy again, and the red returned in full force, and the letters of the alphabet now seemed entirely unwilling to co-operate with Birdcage's tongue in the task of forming intelligible words.

That had been one conversation, and there had been others, and the cumulative impact of all of them was the unavoidable sensation that her old colleagues were after her. Or if not exactly after *her*, then looking to interfere with her work in some way. So when she saw Capstone was out, she kept an eye on him, and hoped her path would not intersect hers.

Though if it did, she hoped he would be on skates. He was really something to see on those skates.

But while she was watching her dots, she did not have time to focus on Capstone, because things were happening. Akuchi and Agbele Oku were meeting with some Daughters of Yemaja, and some of them had comms that Groovetooth's agents were working their way into. The information she was gathering did not have concrete evidence of approaching shedim, but she could feel them out there, as if their malevolence carried through the Matrix like an evil brand of resonance. So Agbele Oku and Akuchi have both shedim and Daughters to deal with. She sent them a brief message about this, with a lame *"let me know if there is anything I can do"* kicker as an attempt to be useful. They did not respond.

She did not see any other life forms around X-Prime and Cayman, but X-Prime had just sent her a two-word message—<*Devil rats!*>—that indicated they had their hands full. And Capstone's group had divided, and it looked like a few of them were on an intercept course toward Halim.

She sighed. The city was not being friendly, though this could not be considered news. She hoped all this was just coincidence. It had to be—since when did shedim, the Daughters, Tamanous, and devil rats plot together? It must be coincidence—and a bad day.

But they would be at the lagoon soon, and it would get better. The obstacles were all out here. The lagoon would be smooth sailing.

She sent a message to Halim, telling him to expect company soon, then got up to leave. If she could manage to have a safe trip across the sprawl, it would be fine. She made her way out of the relatively safe and welcoming confines of Festac Town, away from her haven of consistent Matrix access.

Once she was on the move, Groovetooth was back to her customary grid-hopping, agents always around her like feelers or tentacles looking for a new back door, being ready to switch to one grid if its access seemed clearer and stronger than the one she was currently on. It was a cumbersome way to work, but she was used to it.

There were advantages, though. Hopping around meant making connections with all kinds of hardware, and it is worth noting that you can make all the universal software standards you want, but different pieces of hardware and different pieces of software will work differently. When you are opening your nova-hot new nightclub with your spectacular New York City-in-the-1970s theme, with glitter balls and women in platform shoes and sleek plastic lines to every piece of furniture, you think that everyone who comes in will see it the same way you do. But everyone who has spent any amount of time with hardware knows that Renraku RazorSight goggles emphasize reds a little too much, while Evo's Hawkeye model is ultra-sharp—perhaps too sharp, giving AROs an edge that you could shave yourself with.

All this is to say that the reality around you can change based on the hardware that is displaying it. Or not displaying it, because even though there are AROs and other graphical representations all around us, it remains true that most of what happens deep in grids was never meant to be seen, as millions of lines of code have never been attached to any sort of icon. But there is still code. There is still something, and that something is handled differently by the different grids it might travel through. And if you are a skilled and somewhat paranoid hacker (and if you know hackers, you know that is what all the good ones are), you might have a program that looks at the transition between grids and devices, that looks to see if that transition makes something noticeable happen in the wireless network, and then looks to see if there are other pieces of code experiencing those same transitions from virtual place to virtual place as you travel along.

Groovetooth had just such a program, and it was designed to attach an icon to suspicious things that might not have an icon on their own. It is not a fancy icon, just a simple humanoid outline, designed to become darker and darker based on the program's analyzed certainty of whether there was in fact a piece of code following it or not. As she made her way through the streets of the city, Groovetooth noticed that she had a shadow on her tail. She did not know who it was or what it wanted—at the moment it was too early to tell if it was really someone following her or if it was just some innocuous code that happened to be traveling the same course as her.

But with Capstone out there and some Tamanous operatives tracking down Halim and the Daughters and the shedim and the devil rats, it made her think. How much was random, how much was being thrown at them on purpose?

It was a fun thought, but it was idle. Because she was a mouse on the road, and whether people were planning to step on her because they saw her, or they were about to accidentally step on her just because she happened to be where their feet were about to land, from her perspective it worked out the same—move quickly or get squished. The intentions of those doing the squishing are of little importance.

But still, she has some agents keep an eye on the shadow. She expects to be out of range of any decent grids soon, but when she is back in contact, it will be interesting to see what they have discovered.

CHAPTER TWENTY-SIX

They do not concern themselves with the proper disposition of Akuchi's remains, because almost no one in Lagos receives a proper burial. Or anything similar to it. He will soon be gathered up and likely dumped in the lagoon, which means he will be joining many people with whom he has run in the past, and that is as fitting and proper an ending as they can come up with in their present circumstances.

There was a flight instinct that kicked in immediately after Akuchi and his killer fell to the ground, and the team ran, but once their collective lizard brains settled and allowed logical connections to once again take place, they realized that what happened happened the way it did because Akuchi was supposed to die, and the woman who killed him was quite willing to die as well. There were two bodies lying on the street behind them because that was the way it was engineered to be. If there were more bad things the powers that be wanted to happen to them, they likely would have happened already. So, since they are still at large and continue to carry the packages they are supposed to have, they are now free to complete their mission.

But none of them want to.

Groovetooth and Agbele Oku have shielded the runners to the best of their considerable abilities, and they are walking with purposeful gaits while discussing how none of them want to arrive at the destination to which they are now traveling.

"All that stuff I've been saying I didn't want to know?" Cayman says. "I need to know it now."

X-Prime's mouth opens, and he has that expression on his face that he gets when he is about to start talking quickly in order to annoy Cayman as much as possible, but then he stops.

"Okay, what can I tell you?"

Cayman is surprised at his tone, but apparently the scene they had just left behind was enough to straighten the boy out, at least for a time.

"We've got a scalp, a heart, and a hand. Tamanous wants them, but that could just be because they're organs. The Daughters want them, and the Daughters might know who these parts belong to." Cayman pauses for air. "What else do we know?"

Everyone is quiet. Cayman looks at Groovetooth and waits for her to notice him, but she is walking ahead, eyes focused on the ground, not looking from side to side at all. He clears his throat, but that is not enough to get her attention.

"Mouse!" he finally barks, and that is enough to get her to look up. Her eyes are wide and her face has an undertone of ash.

"I said, 'what else do we know?'" Cayman says.

"About wha—oh," Groovetooth says, blinking. It seems she has just remembered who she is, what she does, and that she is currently surrounded by a good-good collection of wireless signals.

"Your agents," Cayman says. "What have they found out?"

Groovetooth nods, and her eyes start skittering here and there, looking at nothing that is tangible. It is disorienting, for a good decker at work with several AR windows open bears an uncanny resemblance to someone who is on both a manic high and a sugar binge.

Her eyes widen briefly, then widen even more, then narrow.

"Oh," she says.

Then she is silent for a time.

"*What?*" Cayman says, and in this he is joined by Halim and X-Prime.

She looks around at the red-tinged sky above and all the people rushing around.

"We should probably find a place," she says. "A place inside."

Like everything else in the world, distribution of security adheres very tightly to the exalted laws of supply and demand. That means that all you have to do to avoid security is to go someplace where most people do not want to be. And the quickest way to find a place where people do not want to be is to go someplace that smells bad.

In most of Lagos, that is an easy proposition, as the next bad smell is only a rotten egg toss away. But they are on Lagos Island, which is very careful to redistribute most of its unpleasant smells to other places. Still, as long as you are a place that is burdened with metahumans and their need to eat and defecate, you will have bad smells.

And so Groovetooth manages to find an online work order for the employee restroom of a grocery store where the toilet has been backed up. The work order has not yet been fulfilled. The runners do not exactly look like grocery store employees, nor do they look like plumbers, but what they do look like is people that should not be burdened by unnecessary questions, and so when they spread themselves out and make their way to the break room next to the offending bathroom, no one stops them, no one asks questions, and no one bothers to chase them out of the room that has been out of use for a good week due to the pervasive smell of human waste.

They sit at a single table, a once-tan table now brown with spilled soykaf and decades of absorbed tobacco smoke. They are on benches, so they cannot lean back, but it is of no matter because all of them would be leaning forward for this conversation, no matter what they were sitting on.

There is no preamble. When they are all seated, Groovetooth speaks.

"I lost a lot of good agents on this mission," she says. "Most of the ones I sent out didn't come back."

"I'm sorry for your loss, but they're computer programs," Cayman says. "I'm sure you'll learn to love again."

"I didn't tell you that for sympathy, jackass," Groovetooth says. "I said it so that you'd know there are people out there who look like they're against us, who know their shit. I wasn't just sending cheap alleyware bots after them. These were good agents. And most of them were wiped clean."

There are no more cutting remarks. The others nod.

"The fingerprint was pretty easy," Groovetooth says. "That work has been done for me—any time some corp puts together a biometric database, someone, or a lot of someones, is usually on top of it, trying to hack in. And most of the time they get something. So there's plenty of hacker havens where you can find a lot of matches, especially if it's someone who has been with a corporation a while." She takes a breath. "This person was a lifer."

"And she was?" Agbele Oku asks.

"Lydia al-Shammar."

And there is silence. The name even holds some meaning for the *oyibos*, though it still does not hit them with the same impact as the Lagosians. Global Sandstorm has a major presence in Lagos, with the struggle over the control of the oil pipeline continuing to generate conflict and profits. And at the head of Global Sandstorm sits the al-Shammar family.

Agbele Oku's mouth is slightly open, and she is blinking rapidly. Groovetooth is sitting up straight, enjoying the impact of her news. Halim, though—he is impassive, of course.

"The thing that cost me my agents was sending them to track a bit of code that I thought was following me. I'm still not sure what it was, program or human or what, but it was definitely following me, keeping tabs on me. I wanted to know who sent it.

"I don't know much about it, but I do know this—as it was jumping from node to node, sometimes it would clear a passage for itself by using a certain set of access codes. Codes that are used by the Council."

Again, there is silence. It is finally broken by X-Prime.

"So we got someone tied to the Council involving us in the murder of an al-Shammar family member," he says. "We should ask for a raise."

He smiles. No one else does.

"You all are boring," X-Prime says. "Okay, look. The al-Shammars. What tribe are they?"

"Yoruba," Halim says.

"There you go," X-Prime says. "I was right all along. This is a tribal thing."

"You said it was a Asamando thing!" Cayman says.

"That was only a theory I was toying with," X-Prime says calmly. "I discarded it. A tribal thing seemed more likely."

"Funny you didn't mention that until now," Cayman says.

"Despite what you think, not every idea that comes to my head goes out my mouth. So, I figured it was a tribal thing, and that whoever's behind it would be near the top of the tribal structure. We're not getting retirement money here, but it's certainly more than most people in the city could pay. And Groovetooth's information about the Council access codes just clinches it." He turns to Halim. "Who's the Yoruba representative on the Council?"

"Olabode Lekan."

"Would he want Lydia al-Shammar dead?"

"I don't know. I have never concerned myself much with the alliances and feuds of the rich and powerful."

"Would he want Akuchi dead?"

Something that might be the distant relative of a smile made a motion on Halim's lips. "Any Yoruba with any power wanted Akuchi dead."

A thought strikes Cayman, and he breaks into the conversation with it. "Does Lekan want you dead?"

Halim shrugs. "Perhaps. I don't know. It doesn't matter if he wants it or not. He won't get it."

"He doesn't have to," Groovetooth says. "He already has what he wants."

"Which is?" Cayman says.

"If Lekan is behind this, he knows what's in the packages," she says. "That's why he sent us after them, because he knows what's in them. There were cameras all around the gate, cameras everywhere, and we got through the gate, but they still must have taken some close shots of us. Shots of Halim carrying pieces of Lydia al-Shammar's body onto Lagos Island. That sort of thing could be very interesting to the right people."

There is a pause.

"They think they can blackmail me?" Halim finally says.

"It looks like it," Groovetooth says. "Lean on you a little to get your sword on their side. Nothing personal, but they probably think your loyalty to any particular employer may not be as strong as your desire not to spend time in jail."

Halim considers that for a moment. "They are probably right."

X-Prime is smiling, enthusiastic, with no apparent negative effects from the recent death of one of his partners in crime. The puzzle he is putting together is apparently a healing balm for him, assuming he was feeling much of a wound in the first place.

"So, Akuchi was hired so he could be killed, Halim was hired so he could be blackmailed." He points to the mouse. "And she was hired because where there are body parts, there's Tamanous, and she'd be well equipped to help us avoid them or deal with them somehow. So that's three out of six."

He looks toward Agbele Oku, who looks older than her years, possibly because the smell in the room tends to make one screw one's face up in an unappealing fashion. "Then there's you. Why you?"

She knows the answer, but she wishes she didn't. "Because of the Daughters," Agbele Oku says. "Whoever hired us, Lekan or whoever, knew we'd cross their paths, especially once they found out what it was we were transporting. They knew how I'd react to the Daughters. They thought I'd be able to deal with them. To hold them off." She sounds both flattered and appalled at the assumption.

"And me and Cayman ..." X-Prime begins.

"... are hired guns along for the ride," Cayman finishes. "We're perfect for the job. We'd come in, finish it, then disappear."

Again, there is silence. They have very little proof for all of the things they have just said, yet there is not one person in the group who feels like disputing the truth of it. And besides, there is another question on all of their minds, and it is a question that is looking at the future, planning what is going to happen next rather than pondering things that have already happened.

So rather than ponder the past any more, they plunge into the near future. There are things that need to happen when there is a job to finish, and one of your companions has been killed, so the runners set about planning them.

CHAPTER TWENTY-SEVEN

There is an axiom that is occasionally false, but is accurate often enough to have achieved axiomatic status, and it states that when something is going wrong for one person or group of people, there is another person or group of people for whom things are going right in approximately the same proportion. And so, in an office not far from where the runners are, there is a man who is quite pleased because things are going well. The Tamanous interference he had worried about since day one of the mission had been dealt with, the packages were still in the hands that were supposed to have them, and he had honored his entire tribe by eliminating the pest known as Akuchi. There had been many discussions among the tribal elders about whether Akuchi should be killed or should be positioned for extortion in a method similar to what they had planned for Halim. In the end, the elders had agreed that Akuchi's crimes were too numerous to be ignored. And since the Igbo had to pay for their actions in the matter of the Piri Reis Map—the debt was slow in being repaid, but that only meant significant interest had accrued—Akuchi was deemed to be the price (the elders decided that making the Igbo lose both Akuchi *and* Halim would perhaps be more than their rival tribe would be willing to bear, and so that action was not warranted).

And so this man, whom I have been calling Sir for the bulk of this story but who is, of course, Olabode Lekan, is happy.

Or at least as happy as he can be in the mess he has been in since his reputation started taking a downward slide a few years back. It had started with that damn auction, which was supposed to bring in a nice sum of nuyen. The auction had gone well at first, and got even better when the area boys sent by the Igbo to retrieve the map failed in rather spectacular fashion. It should perhaps have ended there, with the Igbo viewing their failure as a just punishment for their hubris, but it did not. Reprisals came from the Igbo, and they were more effective this time around. They struck some Yoruba mining operations, and then when the unfortunate VITAS variant came through town they struck Yoruba health clinics, greatly harming Lekan's tribe's ability to deal with the health peril. Pressure grew on Lekan to take firm action, and twice he acted to strike at Igbo leadership, but both times he acted on bad intelligence, and the missions came up with nothing. Whispers were spreading around town that he was weak, that he had lost his edge, that perhaps someone more effective should be put in his place. Then, to top it all off, Lydia al-Shammar disappeared.

Lekan, if he was pressed to admit it, would say he was not likely to miss Lydia al-Shammar much as a person. She had been forced into Global Sandstorm work in the same way that millions of children had been pushed into the business of their parents, and like so many of them she had shown scant enthusiasm for it, doing little actual work while happily spending the token salary that came with her job. While the income from the oil pipeline left a fair amount of room for waste in Global Sandstorm, Lekan had no desire to see the company become flabby.

Though Lekan might not have put much value on Lydia as a person, as a symbol she was of a fair amount of importance to the Yoruba tribe, and so the run that was unfolding in the city below him was devised as a desperate attempt to show how effective he could be. The main purpose had been to confirm that the thing the Igbos had been bragging about had, in fact, happened. If Lekan believed every rumor about a prominent Yoruba falling to the Igbo, he would have believed that a third of the tribe had been wiped out by now, and he himself had been killed a half-dozen times. So naturally confirmation was necessary, but when he put feelers out to learn how such confirmation may be obtained, he discovered it would be complicated indeed, as it seemed that the Igbo had not been gentle with Lydia's corpse. The operation had required considerable planning, and yet, despite its complications, it was working well, even despite the sad destruction of the runners' boat hours ago. Lekan had been hesitant to order it, knowing it would make the mission take significantly longer, but there were still things that needed to happen to keep all the plates Lekan had in motion spinning, and that would not have happened without the foot trip across the bridge.

He had not, of course, counted on that wave, whose origins were unclear. Lekan had his suspicions about it, but whoever had generated it had started it far enough offshore that the astral signatures of the magic involved were far distant. Those signatures would likely linger for a time, though, so if Lekan had a deep and abiding interest in just who it was that was making his work more difficult, he could look into it. As it turned out, the wave had not resulted in any losses of anything besides time, and at this point things are going so well that he is inclined to just let it go. He normally did not let people who crossed him go unpunished, but there was only so much vengeance he could dish out in a given time.

There is a blinking light, a soothing light blue, in the right of Lekan's vision. He allows it to grow into its own window so he may read the message he has just been sent.

<Targets have gone off the grid. Last seen in a grocery store 3.2 km from final destination.>

Lekan nods to himself. It is not unexpected—the runners had lost one of their own, and so they were going to throw a bit of a tantrum about it. He knows the abilities of the decker he had hired, and he was quite confident that she was capable of hiding from electronic surveillance if she felt like it. She had done remarkably well with the tail he had put on her earlier in the day—he knows that most of the hackers he has on his own staff wouldn't have detected it, much less made some tentative stabs at identifying its source. So, if she had done that—and she had—then it was quite possible for her to hide her group if that is what she wanted.

But you can only hide those parts of you that you know to be exposed. Olabode Lekan has a fair number of children, and he visits them when he can, and he enjoys making them laugh. He has watched many children grow up, and there are newer children of his who are still young, and the common element he has noticed is that all of them enjoy hiding. They will pull a blanket or pillow over themselves and wait for this man who has just introduced himself as their father to find them. They believe they have made the task difficult, because they have covered their eyes, so to themselves, they have vanished. But there are invariably legs or feet sticking out, since they have not yet grown fully aware of their feet and do not think to hide them.

So it is with the now-angry runners out there. There are some parts of them that they will not hide because they are not aware of them.

Lekan sends a message in reply.

<Activate the backup tracking system.>

The follow-up message to his is nearly instantaneous.

<Backup activated. Signal received. Oyibos being tracked.>

The wonderful thing about Mohammed International Airport, Lekan thinks, *is that it only* looks *out of control.* That is not to say that the chaos isn't genuine—it is. There is no strong, overriding authority, and so there is a certain ebb and flow of activity that comes when no one is in charge. The beauty of it is, the lack of central authority leads to a chaotic surface, and that appearance leads visitors to believe that surely nothing of consequence is happening there other than the continuing struggles for power.

That impression would be wrong. Lekan, and others in the area as well, have small networks of people who know how to work smoothly amid the airport chaos, and make the things happen that need to happen.

When the two *oyibos* arrived, they were greeted by the customary bedlam of the airport, and they, like so many others before them, focused solely on navigating the wilds of the place, hoping only to get out with their belongings intact. When they entered into negotiations with an ork with a gun, they were focused on saying the right things, getting a bribe down, and getting out. Other things, such a tiny drone crawling lightly up their leg and injecting even tinier stealth RFID tags into their ankles, were ignored. If they felt anything, they probably attributed it to the insects that took shelter in the airport's shaded areas.

The tags had remained inert bits of electronics that were quite hard to detect, especially to people who did not know to look for them. Now that the runners believed that they were safe under the shelter of whatever security umbrella Groovetooth had erected, the tags could be activated and used to keep an eye on them.

There was another softly blinking blue light. Lekan sighs. He works hard to be a hands-off leader, the kind of person who delegates responsibility, and then lets his people do whatever it is he has asked them to do. But he has found this to be difficult when his people refuse to operate on their own.

He looks at the new message.

<Sir, we think it would be best if you joined us in the situation room.>

Lekan finds the vagueness of the request to be an extreme irritant. He sends back a simple word.

<Why?>
The reply is rapid.
<There is a development we think you should see.>
Lekan rolls his eyes. Technology can evolve as fast as the techs of the world can push it forward, but it will always be hindered by those people who cannot, for whatever reason, find it within themselves to use it to its full potential. He fires off another message.
<Send me a link! I can monitor everything from here if you would just press the right buttons!>
He realizes, as he sends the message, that his wording about buttons is even more antiquated than the attitude he is fighting, but the message is sent, so it is too late. But the words will get the point across, which is enough.
There is no return message. The people with whom he is communicating know an order when they see it, and they know orders are to be obeyed. A new AR window opens up in front of Lekan, and he sees what it is that his technical people want him to see.
He observes. Then he sends them a message.
<I'll be right there.>

By the time he has arrived in the situation room, things have become worse. The room is in chaos, which is rather underwhelming because what Lekan calls his situation room is only two people with an array of electronics. There is not an oversize map, or a giant video screen, or anything that the old movies Lekan has seen has led him to believe should be in a proper situation room. But there is a considerable amount of gear, and that gear does a fine job in presenting information about a variety of situations, which in the end is all that a situation room need do.
Max Baer, born Maxwell Baer Prohaska, is running the situation room today, an efficient man who had arrived in Lagos many years ago from Russia while running from the Vory. Baer had made several hopeful inquiries in the intervening years, but he still had not reached the point where he believed it was safe for him to return to the motherland. He had a brown mustache that overflowed the corners of his mouth and ran down his chin, the two ends spreading away from each other as they

approached his jaw. The mustache makes him look like he is always frowning. Also making him look that way is the fact that he is always frowning.

Baer does not say anything when Lekan walks in. He stands straight, looks at Lekan, and waits. It is very possible that Baer believes that anything he says at this moment will be met with a wrathful response, and it is very possible that he is completely correct. And so he is probably acting wisely, but that does not reduce Lekan's annoyance at the whole situation.

"Baer!" he snaps. "What the hell!"

Baer points, though it is unclear to what it is he is pointing. "There are more of them," he says.

"I can see that!" Lekan snaps. When he first looked at the AR link sent by Baer, it showed that the two RFID signals marking the *oyibos'* location had been joined by two identical signals approximately two kilometers east of the first ones. Then, as Lekan was walking to the situation room, three more sets of signals had appeared. That meant that at the moment, it looked as if there were five sets of the *oyibos* planted at various locations on Lagos Island. "How did they detect those tags?"

Baer says nothing and only scowls. Or perhaps he does not scowl, and it is only his mustache forming the expression for him.

Lekan's mind moves rapidly. "Perhaps they detected the signals once the tags were activated," he says. "Then they worked quickly to mirror them, send out these doubles and triples and so forth." As he speaks, another set of signals shows up in the AR window. There are now, according to the window, six sets of *oyibos.* "That would mean that the first set of signals, the ones *here*, are the real ones." Unlike Baer, he does not physically point at anything, but rather calls up an arrow in the AR window that points to the relevant set of signals. A similar arrow should be appearing in Baer's display.

"Perhaps they are still coming to deliver the packages," Baer says. "The multiple signals are only meant to confuse us about the time of their arrival." A seventh set of *oyibos* has appeared.

"Why not just hide them, then? If they know the signals are there, just squelch them? No, they multiplied them for a reason." Lekan rubs his generous chin, and his jowls wobble lightly. "They want us to come after them."

"Then we probably shouldn't," Baer says.

Lekan jerks his head sharply. "Because we are scared of them? Never! They have what we want. They are waiting for us. Nothing they do to us is more powerful than what we can—what we *will*—do to them. We can spare seven"—he looks at the screen—"*eight* teams to chase after some ghosts and find which ones are real. Then we can finish the job."

CHAPTER TWENTY-EIGHT

"Is this part of being a professional?" X-Prime asks. He is sitting cross-legged, leaning back against a hard wall.

The room is dark, with only a hint of natural light edging its way past a closed door. Somewhere nearby, plastic sheeting is rustling in the wind, but whatever breeze is moving the plastic is not having any sort of impact on the dark room. The air is still, it is humid, and there is occasionally the sound of water dropping on concrete. That may be drops of sweat rolling to the floor.

"Yes," Cayman says. "Everything I do is part of being a professional."

"How convenient for you."

They sit quietly. Cayman thinks of many things—especially the many things that can go wrong. There will be things going wrong. How could there not be? It was supposed to be a boat ride, a simple twelve-kilometer boat ride, then a small drive through a decent part of town, then pay day. Instead, there had been the gangs and the ammits and the wave and Tamanous on skates, and all of that happened before Akuchi had been killed. It would be unreasonable to believe that everything would now be fixed.

But there is a difference, one thing that Cayman hoped would make what was happening now different from everything happened before. He is following his own script.

Eventually, as Cayman knew would be the case, the silence becomes too much for X-Prime, and he speaks.

"We have chips in our ankles."

"Yes," Cayman says.

"I've got implants. You've got implants. But they're sitting there, not bothering me, but my ankle feels like it's terribly itchy, and I think that if I started scratching it I'd scratch it bloody until the implant was gone. Why is that?"

"There's a lot of difference between the foreign object you invite into yourself and the one that's thrust upon you."

"Yeah. Makes me feel like I've been violated," X-Prime says. "Maybe I should talk to Agbele Oku about this."

"Do that," Cayman says. "I'm sure having a little chip in your ankle gives you a whole new insight into the female psyche. She'll be thrilled to talk about it with you."

That leads to another period of silence. Again, when the time has arrived for the silence to end, it is X-Prime who ends it.

"Okay, let's say we're being professional. That the things we're doing are the things we have to be doing, and are the kind of things that will make people think well of us and want to hire us."

"There's more to it than that," Cayman says. "It's not just about getting hired. It's about getting hired by people who will be reluctant to screw with us."

"That's a good thing," X-Prime says. He shifts, and there is a brief shower of sweat on the floor. "But are we being ..."

"What?"

"Are we being a little too theatrical? Is everything we're doing necessary?"

Cayman leans his head back quickly, accidentally hitting the wall much harder than he intended with the back of his skull. It makes a dull *thud*, and he is very hopeful that it is not noticed by X-Prime.

"There's four things in life we do that are necessary," he says. "Eat, drink, breathe, shit. The rest is just...different degrees of theatrics."

X-Prime is silent for a moment. Then he speaks.

"I'm not sure if that's cynical or...kind of fun."

"Why can't it be both?"

"Okay," X-Prime says.

There is quiet again, but Cayman feels he has not quite said everything that needs to be said, so he speaks again.

"There's a right way to do things and a wrong way to do things. What Lekan did—if he's the one doing it—made it so we have to respond. And do it right."

X-Prime does not have a response to this, and they are left again with the sound of plastic sheeting and dripping sweat.

Olabode Lekan spent as much time as he could stand in the situation room, then he moved the operation upstairs to his larger office once Baer had assured him that the information he wanted could get to him there quickly and securely. They had to leave someone behind to man the machines, but that person was not Lekan—rather, it was a person who was accustomed to spending large portions of his life in that room, and so should not be bothered staying there. That person was left behind, and Lekan is now in a spot where he belongs. There is no point, he believes, to constructing castles in the air if you never spend time in the wonders you have made for yourself.

He has told the eight teams spreading out across Lagos Island to proceed carefully. The eight sets of RFID tags displayed on his AR map have not moved since the moment they appeared. He knows that the runners know about the tags, and they must know that he has seen them. So, they know that people are coming for them, and they are waiting. That means that the real *oyibos*, wherever they are, are prepared.

At some point, Lekan has grown so impatient for progress that he has zoomed in on a particular team, putting the map on a scale in which one block equals one meter, so he can see how they are moving. The image of progress brings him some comfort, but not as much comfort as the words he longs to hear: "We have the packages."

He switches back and forth, from one team to another, waiting to see which one will be the first to its destination, and then he settles on a squad moving into the twelfth floor of an office building that is eight blocks away. He nods to Baer, and due to the fact that Baer has long experience interpreting Lekan's orders, Baer correctly understands that this means Lekan would like to listen in on this team's communications.

"—are sealed. Elevators are shut down," one of the team members says. "If they move anywhere, they're moving up."

"Repeating one more time—there is to be no weapons fire until we have conclusively identified the presence or absence of one of the packages," another voice, one that Lekan recognizes as Olaniyi Adenoke, a man competent enough to have been labeled as a captain by Lekan, even though Lekan is technically not a military commander, and does not have the ability to give out ranks. But really, he has men with guns to whom he gives orders, and is that not enough to make him a military commander? Can he not then give out ranks as he sees fit?

The other members of the squadron indicate that they have heard and understood this order, and Captain Adenoke gives the order to proceed forward. Lekan watches them, sees their black icons creep toward the red icons of the *oyibos*. He listens carefully for gunfire, but he knows that a trooper who is firing his weapon is not likely to be activating his comm at the same time, so he will not receive any further information about the situation until one of the squadron members deigns to give it to him.

The schematic loaded into Lekan's ARO shows two entrances into the room where this set of icons resides. The squadron has divided, four at one door, two at the other. The two will stay quiet for a time, there mainly to prevent the runners from making a getaway should they decide retreat is their best option.

Then two of the icons representing Lekan's troops burst forward, entering the room. Lekan leans forward, straining to hear something, anything that might tell him what is going on, until he hears the word he did not really want to hear but was fairly convinced he would.

"Clear," one of the troopers say. The other one in the room echoes him. "Clear."

"It's empty," Captain Adenoke says. "There is no one in here."

The red icons sit in the middle of the room, unmoving. Lekan cannot help himself from asking the question that next comes out of his mouth.

"Are you sure they are not on the ceiling or something?"

Captain Adenoke's answer, Lekan can tell, is delivered through gritted teeth. "They are not on the ceiling. Or the walls. Or the floor. There is no one in this room. No life forms nearby."

And then, just like that, the red icons in the room disappear.

"Councilor!" Baer says. "Our hackers are having some success against the false codes their hacker put into the system. We're getting some of them eliminated."

Lekan zooms his city map out. Sure enough, there are now only five sets of red icons. Three have been cut out.

"Send the teams who were going after those fakes to back up some of the other teams," he says.

"Sir, it's still possible that the *oyibos* are hiding at one of those locations and simply managed to mask the signal."

"No," Lekan says. "That's not how they're doing this."

"Sir?"

"They're leading us on," he says, staring at the map as another set of icons disappears. "They set this up. They're trying to show us where to go."

"That's an awfully roundabout way to—"

"Of course it is!" Lekan snaps. "They're pissed at us, which is what happens to most groups of people when you kill one of them. So, they're going to play their little game, but the point of it isn't to get them away from us. If it was, they would just leave. Blank out their signal and leave. No, they want us to find them, but in their way."

"Why in their way?"

"How the hell do I know? To exert some control again. It doesn't matter. They're fucking around, and I don't enjoy being fucked with, even if they eventually plan to give me what I want."

"But if they're going to lead us to them, how will we know—"

Baer is interrupted by reports from another team that has reached a set of red icons. The same annoying word is said by them. "Clear," they say. "Clear." And the red icons they had been hunting disappear.

Then the others follow suit, and they are all gone. His hackers have chased away all the phantom images, leaving nothing more for anyone to chase.

Until another set of red icons appears, glowing bright red, almost throbbing. Lekan jumps from his feet and points.

"There!" he says. "That's what they want us to see." It's another office building, and it's four blocks away. A mere four blocks.

He stands. "Get all the teams over there. Everyone at that building." He glances again at the map. "Except squadron six. Have them meet me in the lobby."

"The lobby?" Baer says.

"If that's what they want us to see, then I'm going to see it," he says. "Squadron six is the one closest to me. They can escort me."

Baer, as he has been trained, nods and works to make the order happen.

The bottom ten floors of the building are functional. They are financial offices, mostly, spaces where people sit in small rooms for hours on end and figure out how to make money for other people so they can take a percentage of that money for themselves. There are those in his tribe, Lekan knows, who sneer at such work because it produces nothing tangible, it involves nothing that you can hold in your hand. But to Lekan, it is a kind of miracle, that there are ways to move up into some of the higher reaches of society simply by knowing how to shuffle around the world's resources in the proper fashion.

It is even more of a miracle that some of those people are willing to pay significant bribes and offer other services to him to curry his favor, and it is through these kinds of connections that he is able to walk into the upper, unfinished floors of the building without hindrance.

He would like to simply charge right up to the sixteenth floor, where the RFID tags seem to be, find out what is there and deal with it himself. That is how he became what he is, and he sometimes believes that it was strange that he should abandon the skills and techniques that got him to where he was once he had arrived there. But people had impressed on him how willing they would be to sacrifice themselves for him, and he had become at least partially convinced that allowing them the opportunity to make this sacrifice was fair, and even noble on his part.

So he waits on the fourteenth floor while others move ahead, and those others are pretty numerous by now, having gathered here after conducting their other wild-goose chases on other parts of the Island. If the runners really are here, they will be overwhelmed by sheer numbers. They have no chance of getting away.

Lekan has no doubt that they are not here. He believes *something* is here. Just not them.

He listens again to the communications as the team moves in, slowly approaching, taking all due cautions. The mages are watching the astral plane intently. As it has been before, in all the other places where signals were supposed to be, they are not seeing any signs of life.

They approach the signals. Lekan watches his AR, waiting for the signals to disappear again. The longer this nonsense goes on, the more pain these runners are earning themselves. He is a man of honor—he will pay them, as long as they have the boxes. They will receive everything they have coming to them, and then they may use those proceeds to pay for nice funerals for themselves.

Except for Halim. Halim will live. All Halim is doing is guaranteeing a deeper level of servitude to the Yoruba tribe.

The signals have not disappeared yet, and it is enough to make Lekan wonder if something different is happening this time. And then, as it happens, something different does in fact happen.

"There's something here," Captain Adenoke says. "We don't see anyone, there are no signs of life, but there's something on the floor."

Lekan steps forward despite the fact that there is no justifiable reason to do so. "What's on the floor? Is it packages?"

"Yes, sir," Adenoke says. "Three of them."

Lekan is already running. "Is the floor clear?"

"We believe so, sir. We'll have final confirmation in a moment."

Lekan believes it would be a good thing if that confirmation came before he made it to the sixteenth floor, but it is not a crucial matter, as he will arrive at the floor in moments regardless of what anyone says to him.

CHAPTER TWENTY-NINE

Lekan bursts out of the stairwell onto the sixteenth floor, followed by security personnel who repeatedly and vainly insist that it would be more appropriate for them to be in front of him. He is all motion and fury until his foot hits the concrete floor with a slap and he sees the three packages in front of him. Three wonderful packages, the evidence that will be the basis of the vengeance he plans to enact on the Igbo over the next months.

As he draws closer to the packages, he sees there is something else on the floor next to them. Two things, two small things that he might not have noticed except for the bright red tinge they have. Since they are unexpected, they get his attention. He bends down, looks closer. They are very small. He squints and tries to see just what they are, and if he should care about them. Then he understands, and he stands up straight and takes a step backward. He looks at his AR window showing the RFID tags. He zooms in close. He knows what he is seeing. There are two runners somewhere besides here, and they both now have unpleasant wounds in their ankle where they dug out chunks of their own flesh. He wonders why their hacker did not just cancel the tags or mask their signals or something, but he has to agree this is more dramatic, and to the runners, that might have been reason enough.

Now for the packages. He looks at them carefully, as he knows what they contain, and he also knows that they have been through a lot in the course of the past few days. He does not really need them intact—he is not Tamanous, or some sort of ghoul—but the less decayed the objects are, the better. His quick scan indicates that the objects appear to be what they are supposed to be and they are as intact as they need to be. It is, of course, possible that the runners pulled some subterfuge and substituted someone else's body parts for the ones they are supposed to be, but while these runners have shown their theatrical side, he does not think they will have gone that far around the bend. But it is easy enough to get a scan of a fingerprint and check it against his databases. It takes seconds, and he discovers that the finger, at least, is legitimate.

He looks away from the packages and smiles.

"We're taking these away from here," he says. "Some of you will carry them, but they are never to be more than twenty meters away from me. Anyone carrying one any farther from me will be shot."

The men understand him so well that they do not even nod. They just stand ready.

Lekan turns back to the boxes and he gets a shock, for there is suddenly someone there. Someone not in the uniform of his security people, or in Yoruba tribal wear, or in any sort of garment he trusts. He has well-honed reactions for this situation, and they kick in, and there is a blue ball that shoots out of his hand and rockets toward the newcomer. It hits the newcomer. Then passes through him. The newcomer does not react.

Lekan looks closer at the image. If he remembers correctly, this is one of the *oyibos*. The larger one. He forgets his name. Bermuda? Jamaica?

He turns to his people and points at a mage. "Dispel that," he says, but then a sound comes from the image, so Lekan holds up his hand, and the mage does not cast anything.

The sound is a voice coming from the image. "Here's what you're going to do," the voice says. "There are three packages. They're out there, in the city. You're going to find them and take them to Lagos Island. That's all."

The words sound familiar to Lekan, and it does not take long for him to place them. When the mission began, he had listened in on the meeting of Mr. Johnson with Halim and Akuchi, to make sure all went as it should, and that was what he was hearing now—words the Johnson had said then. Halim has a good amount of cyberware, and people such as him often make recordings of any business dealings, as that sort of thing is generally useful to have. For circumstances like this one.

The voice covers a few specifics of the deal, and then it is quiet for a moment. Thankfully, run agreements are not full of legalese, and so the recounting does not take long. The pause is brief. Then the voice talks again, and this time it seems to be reciting its own words.

"We did the job," is what it says. "We brought the boxes here. You have them. You killed one of us, but we did the job. If you decide to tell anyone about us—and I think there's a chance you will—remember that no matter what else you can say about us, we did the job. We finished it. We're goddamned professionals."

Lekan is looking at his packages. He supposes what the *oyibos* is saying is true. They played their little game, but they did the job, and he cannot reasonably ask for more than that. He may not have to have all the runners except Halim killed after all.

Then the image is gone. Lekan hopes the illusion made the runners feel better about themselves. He knows the packages in front of him have certainly made him feel better about his day. He picks all three of them up and cradles them like a cherished set of small triplets. He walks slowly forward, and his people know to fall in around him. Their job now is to make sure he gets those packages somewhere safe.

He is somewhere near the elevator doors when his right arm starts to grow warm. He thinks it might just be from the packages leaning against it, perhaps they are hitting a nerve wrong, but he shifts that package slightly and the warming only increases. And then there is smoke.

His arms reflexively jerk open, and the packages fall to the floor. One of them cracks open, and flames shoot out from the inside.

"Put it out!" he screams at his mages. "Put it *out*!"

The mages respond quickly. The fire shrinks, then becomes a wisp of smoke, then is gone.

Lekan is down on his knees without thinking about it, his hands are stretching forward, pawing through the now-cold ashes inside the open box. He cannot see anything useable. The bastards must have set it to burn from the inside out. The body part—if his memory of the inspection he conducted a few moments ago is correct, the package he is holding had contained the scalp—is ash. He knows it will be the same for the others. The heart will be completely gone. The hand, at least, will have left behind some traces of bone.

All thoughts of mercy for the runners are now gone. He is not even sure he will keep Halim alive long enough to use him. If they were in front of him now, he would cheerfully order the execution of all five of them, and he would hope that their demise would be bloody.

"The spell," he says, looking furiously here and there at the rather befuddled security force that surrounds him. "The image they send here. Trace it. Find who cast it. They can't be far away." His head moves faster, looking back and forth at all of them. "Find them. And do not let them leave this island."

He walks quickly toward the elevator, stooping to pick up the box that has the now-cooling bones of the hand. The other packages, these he kicks as he goes by them.

CHAPTER THIRTY

There is a wonderful thing about the world that people can be engaged in the latest, cutting-edge activities, but in the end their livelihood might depend on something as primitive as running. They may take advantage of the latest breakthroughs in magical research to befuddle and bemuse whatever opposition they may face, they may have access to bleeding-edge technology that allows them to sneak into places where they have no business being, they may be surrounded by gizmos and powers and all sorts of things, but they still may be reduced to something as simple as churning their legs as fast as they can, pounding the hard ground with their feet, breathing rapidly, keeping it up long enough to build up a sweat, and they may use the opportunity to make a connection to their ancestors, who long ago managed to be the ones in their group who stayed alive because they were fast enough to outrun the lions or cheetahs of the savannah—or, to be accurate, they were fast enough to find a small crevice or a tall tree where they could go and the lion or cheetah could not, and they could get there before they were harmed. The effort of the two legs are something that unite all generations of humans over the centuries, and running for your life should be considered a noble occupation that connects you to many of your greatest ancestors.

Cayman and Agbele Oku, they have the chance to make this connection as they are tearing down some stairs and running through a lobby and charging into the streets of Lagos. They know they would have a brief moment for a head start, but they also know that brief would be the operative word, and that they should take as much advantage of the moment as they can.

They run by the security guards, and those guards do nothing but look at them and smile slightly, because these guards are often amused at the way people hurry through this lobby as though they were on world-shaking business when in fact they were caught up in something that maybe five people in the world cared about, all five of whom were in this building. The guards found this inflated importance to be pathetic, and they watched people run through their lobby with a growing sense of superiority. Now, it is true that the two people running through the lobby were grubbier and better armed than most who were on the premises, but the guards were under no orders to stop people simply because they looked odd and were in a hurry. So they watched them go and smirked.

Cayman and Agbele Oku heard the alarms and the noise and subsequent tumult indicating the guards had been informed that they should, in fact, be concerned about the two people who had just passed through their lobby, but by that point it was too late, as the two of them were on the sidewalk, running toward a small, white car and jumping inside. The engine of the car revved, and it leaped heedlessly into traffic, assuming that other cars would move out of the way if only because that was the way things typically worked. X-Prime sat in the back, Halim was in the front, and Groovetooth drove, for it was Groovetooth who had found the car, and Groovetooth who had the programs that were helping the car move smoothly through traffic. The car was a final gift from Akuchi, who had sent the vehicle ahead and had it wait on the Island in case it was needed. All of them in the vehicle give a silent tribute to Akuchi, and they are unified in the belief that the best tribute to Akuchi would be to put the car to some kind of dramatic use—a use that, ideally, would anger the Yoruba tribe. Groovetooth accelerates, and they are gone.

The streets of Lagos Island, unlike those of the mainland, are drivable. Pedestrians agreeably stay on the sidewalks and do not stride into the street at random times, and drivers drive with the calm assurance that they do not need to hurry too much because wherever they are going, things will wait for them. Groovetooth moves to a speed that is faster than the pace of the cars around her but not overly so, because she is firm in the belief that you do not call attention to yourself unless it is absolutely necessary. She passes cars on the left, she passes them on the right, she moves gently ahead, while AROs measure gaps for her, telling when it is safe to move and when it is not, and she trusts their data completely.

There is a brief moment where the drive even seems pleasant, where it seems as though they will be able to cross the streets without difficulty and the lights will never tell them they need to stop, and they will make their way to the First Mainland Bridge—the First! The short span, the quick trip to the mainland!—and they will cross it and they will disappear into the mass of humanity where they will not be sought because the effort to find things in the mainland is entirely out of proportion to the returns people are usually able to generate. Though it is widely thought of as one of the most dangerous places in the world, the surviving runners sprint toward the mainland because it will make them safer.

Then there are lights. They flash red and blue, and it is quite a relief to Groovetooth that Lagos is not a GridGuide city, because at this point GridGuide would have totally locked them down, and Groovetooth was paying a great deal of attention to driving and she did not want to take on the additional task of convincing an automated traffic system that she should, in fact, be allowed to proceed. It is not a good thing when a security vehicle has pulled sideways in the street ahead of you to prevent you from proceeding, but it is at least a better thing than having an entire city grid plotting against you.

It is a four-lane street, and it is too wide for a single car to block, but there are other cars who stopped out of instinct as soon as they saw the security vehicle, and they are enough to make the current street impassable, and so Groovetooth makes a very tight turn with a skid that almost sends the rear of her vehicle into the side of another, but does not. Then she is accelerating, moving through the middle of a stopped line of cars, making a left as soon as a left turn is available, and it is a turn that takes her down an alley, and if a security vehicle beats her to the other end of the alley she is in trouble, they are all in trouble, so she flies through it, and there are high curbs in this alley, almost as high as the car windows, leading to a very walled-in feeling and a moment of panic when there is a dumpster ahead of them and though the AROs in front of Groovetooth insist that there is enough room for her to pass she cannot find herself believing it but she also does not have any choice to keep going, and there is a moment where she rushes up toward the green and rusty dumpster and squints and squints and then closes her eyes until she remembers that is a terrible idea so she opens them wide and then she sees that she is through. She takes a quick look at the others, and none of them even seem that worked up about it. She is not certain if that is because of their confidence in her or their general weariness.

She makes a right at the alley because she sees security cars coming from the left, and then the time is completely past for any degree of caution. The vehicle they are riding in, it is a Tata Raj, and it normally would be skidding all over the road at the speed Groovetooth has now obtained, but Akuchi had done his work on this vehicle and while not handling like a dream, it at least was not especially nightmarish, and Groovetooth is generally able to go where she wants and dodge or feint with a light touch on the steering wheel, and she is staying in motion and not yet letting anything stop her.

Halim has two weapons out, a pistol in his hand and a shotgun in his lap. He is on the right side of the car, and Cayman, in the back, is on the left, and his guns are ready, so each side of the car will be protected to a degree, and the two of them wonder if they will be enough, but they forget they are not the only protection the car has.

There is another security car ahead of them, and it does the same thing the other car did, pulling itself sideways to make the start of a roadblock and then letting all of the other cars in traffic finish the job. Again Groovetooth sees that there is no path through, and again she prepares to make a fast turnaround, but this time, before she can start the motion, she is stopped by the voice of Agbele Oku.

"Keep moving straight ahead," she says. "Full speed."

Groovetooth does not know that she has developed any sort of trust in Agbele Oku, but it seems she has, because she does not turn, she does not slow down, she only charges ahead. Halim and Cayman are leaning out of the window, firing occasionally, not hoping to accomplish much besides keeping the security grunts from getting off a clean shot at them. They wait to see what Agbele Oku is going to do.

Then they see it. They see it after they feel it, the shake in the air that feels as if the void that surrounds everything has suddenly decided to no longer tolerate petty forces such as gravity and that the meager bit of air that has been permitted to stay around the earth will be broken up and hurled into cold space. But then the shaking stops, as if the void had a second inexplicable change of heart. After the shaking of the air there is movement, and that movement is the front of the security car lurching into the air, the back of it grinding and screeching against the ground, the officers inside dropping their weapons as the car they are in bucked up and back, and the car is nearly vertical when Akuchi's vehicle passes through the space that had until recently been occupied by the front of the vehicle, then the forces holding the security car let go, and the front of it comes crashing back to the ground with a bone-rattling *thump*, and neither the vehicle nor the officers inside are in a condition to make any more movement.

Agbele Oku grunted. "If they serious, they should send something besides mundanes to come get me."

"Patience," Halim says. "They will."

They are driving fast now, very fast, and at every intersection the light is red because that is how Lekan's hackers are programming them, so that unwitting drivers who do not know what is happening pass through and form at least a partial blockade, which makes each intersection a challenge to Groovetooth, but they are challenges she meets with aplomb and, more importantly, with success. The gaps in traffic are all but invisible until Groovetooth's passage through them proves that they do in fact exist. At each intersection, Halim and Cayman look to the vehicle's flanks and see security cars racing to intercept them, leaving the mouse little choice but to move forward, which she does.

"We're going the wrong way," Halim says. "We are getting farther from the bridge."

"I don't have much choice," Groovetooth says. "They're not giving me much."

"Do not wait for them to give you an option," Halim says. "Just take it."

Groovetooth nods, a single motion, short and stiff. Then she turns left.

There is a security car just ahead of them, of course there is, because that is what the entire Island is now, it is security cars who are after them. Halim's arm is out the window, and it makes a throwing motion, and a small, dark object flies out of his hand. By reflex the driver of the security car dodges, a slight bobble to his left, and Groovetooth is there, shooting the car through a barely open gap, while Halim sprays handgun fire on the car they are passing. He hopes that if any occupants of the security car are still living once he has passed them by, they are able to discover that their driver swerved to avoid a wadded-up ball of black tape.

There is another left turn, then they are back on track, headed toward the First Mainland Bridge. There is security ahead, security behind, but they are closer to the First Bridge than they were before. Cayman finds that he wants that bridge like he wants food, water, and sex, it's an instinct in his gut. He just wants to be there, even though he can't be sure getting there will help anything.

Then X-Prime says the last words he wants to hear. "Uh-oh."

Cayman looks at him, then past him, since the boy is pointing at Agbele Oku. She has stiffened in her seat, her eyes have rolled to the back of her head, and she is twitching slightly. He cannot be certain why this has happened to her, but he is fairly certain it is not because she is prone to seizures.

He looks ahead. Someone took their mage out for a reason, and he has a guess about what that reason is.

And then he sees it. A red sedan traveling at a nice, moderate speed up the road stops suddenly, slides slightly sideways, and crumples. It appears to have hit nothing, to be bouncing and sliding off nothing, and to have been wrecked by nothing.

Nothing clearly is a serious problem.

"Turn around!" Cayman says. "Turn around now!"

Groovetooth listens, because she has seen what Cayman has seen, and she does another skidding turn like she has done before, and the practice seems to be doing her good, because each turn is tighter than the last. But the car is still moving toward the nothing as it spins, it is drawing closer to the wrecked red car as it bumps sideways then backwards, then Groovetooth accelerates, hoping the wheels catch and pull them away from nothing, she can feel them gaining traction, she leans forward, as if that will change anything.

There is a *bump*. The rear of the car has hit nothing. It is a solid *bump*, but not a crumpling *bump*. In fact, it is a helpful *bump*, for it gives them a bit more acceleration in the direction they would like to travel. The wheels were catching hold, and the *bump* helps then, making Akuchi's car leap forward. They drive on. Nothing has failed to stop them.

Cayman turns and watches nothing as they drive away from it. It did not stop then, but it redirected them. Again, they are going away from the bridge.

Groovetooth makes another turn, and it seems to get them out of view of the mage who had used his juju on Agbele Oku, for she blinks and starts to look around and wonder what happened and why she has such a bad headache. Then she remembers, and she sits up straighter. They will need her.

That thought proves quite prescient.

When they put up the wall of nothing, they likely hoped that maybe it would be the end of the chase, but prepared for the likelihood that it would not. That preparation means that they placed cars, better armed cars, at places the Raj would be likely to go. That preparation means that there is a significant blockade in front of them now.

"Can you flip them?" Cayman asks immediately. "Like that one?"

Agbele Oku shakes her head wearily. "I couldn't do enough of them," she says.

Cayman turns to look at Halim, but the ork is not looking at him. He is leaning out the window, exposed to the bullets the occupants of the stationary cars are firing, and his arm is moving in a long, rapid sweep, and a grenade flies out of his hand, and with the speed of the car combined with the velocity of Halim's throw it is traveling at well over 80 kph, and maybe the security mages don't see it coming, or maybe there are not mages in these cars, but they do nothing to stop it, and it flies through and hits the front of one car, which erupts into orange and yellow and smoke, and that explosion carries to the front of another car, and both vehicles are shoved backward by the force of the explosion, and so there is an opening. Agbele Oku puts up as good of a shield as she can muster, and all the occupants of the now bullet-riddled car slump, hoping the thin metal of the car's doors provide more protection than the even thinner glass of the windows. Bullets fly into the vehicle as they run the gauntlet, there is no way Agbele Oku can hold them all off, and there is one that Cayman sees, it pushes its way through the car's shell, dragging sparks behind it like a fast and particularly aggressive fairy, and maybe it is his imagination, but he believes he can see the grooves and dents of its battered lead surface as it speeds toward his face, and he jerks his head back, which makes no sense because who can move faster than a bullet? But as he moves back he sees the bullet pass by him, just near his eyes, and it leaves him unscathed, because that bullet had many marks on it, but the one thing it apparently does not have is his name.

He is quite relieved to be alive, but then the boy next to him ruins it by speaking.

"How come we're not dead yet?" he says.

Cayman sits up in his seat, as the pounding rhythm of bullets on the car has slowed to almost nothing. "I don't know why you're alive," he says, "but I'm alive because I'm fucking *fast.*"

"No, I mean why haven't they really stopped us yet? Put up a serious blockade? That, back there, that was like four cars. Anyone out there believe that's really the best Lekan can do?"

No one has an immediate response. Then Groovetooth spins the car and accelerates to avoid yet another pursuing car, and they all are pushed to the left with the force of the turn.

"You really think we need to talk about that now?" Cayman says.

"Yes I do," X-Prime says. "I think it's important because I think I know what's happening. I think we are being herded."

"Herded where?" Cayman asks.

The answer to that is provided by Groovetooth. A new ARO appears in all of their visions, except Agbele Oku, who at the moment is burdened with seeing only through her own eyes. She is forced to look at a small display on the front dashboard between Groovetooth and Halim.

What they all see is a map. The car's nav system has dumped data onto the map in the form of a bright yellow trail showing them where they have just traveled. It is not detailed enough to show the explosions and wrecks they have caused, nor does it show the finer nuances of Groovetooth's driving—the slips, the swerves, the spins. What it does show is the general direction they have been traveling through the Island, and that direction, while not entirely consistent due to the various digressions and evasions, is unmistakable.

"Son of a bitch," Cayman says.

"They want us at the bridge," X-Prime says. For that is where they will end up, undoubtedly—at the south end of the Third Mainland Bridge.

"What the hell?" Cayman says. "Why make us go back there? He could kill us anywhere."

Halim shrugs. "Who knows?" he asks. "It could seem fitting to him, to bring us back to the crucible we have just passed and finish us there. Perhaps, in his mind, it would take away from us any merit or honor we might have earned from surviving that gauntlet. In the end, in Lekan's mind, it will be the bridge that will bring us down. I suppose he will see that as apt."

"What is that, some sort of Yoruba bullshit?" Cayman asks.

"It is Lekan," Halim says. "It is his own bullshit."

And as they talk, Groovetooth continues to bob and weave and avoid the security coming at then, and all the while they draw closer to the bridge that none of then has any desire to set foot upon again.

It is actually some small comfort, then, that they are fairly certain that Lekan intends to have them killed at the checkpoint.

CHAPTER THIRTY-ONE

Olabode Lekan knows that a proper balance sheet includes every relevant credit and debit. It is not enough for him to merely consider how much cost he is incurring by allowing this mad chase through the Island. There are broken cars and damaged buildings, and lost personnel that he will have to replace. If he were the type of man who only looked at those expenses, he might have considered this long chase to be a considerable waste. But there are credits to consider. There is personal satisfaction. After what the runners did to him, they should not be able to feel one iota of personal satisfaction or, heaven forbid, triumph. They could not be allowed to believe they had beaten the bridge, so they would be dragged to the bridge once more, and it would crush them.

That was also useful in the not-minor area of reputation. While it was true that the runners would shortly be dead, and thus not in any condition to be sharing their exploits with anyone, he knew too well that unfortunate information had a way of getting around. If he did not utterly crush them in dramatic, even flamboyant fashion, there might be others in the world who started to develop the belief that it was possible, even admirable, to fuck with Olabode Lekan. And that could not be borne. Stopping that, that was worth whatever price needed to be paid.

Lekan knew where he could get the best vantage point, as these runners would not be the first people he had assigned to meet a grisly fate at this location. He was not foolish enough to be anywhere near the gate, as that would likely be the target of any last-ditch offensive mounted by the runners. He doubted they would do any significant damage to the structure, but there was no point in exposing himself to stray gunfire or some wandering spell. He was, of course, at his office, as one of the perks of having money and resources at your disposal is that there are many ways for you to bring the world to you, rather than you having to go out to it. He knows the cameras that are available, he knows which ones will show him what he wants to see, and he has them loaded up in various AROs floating around him. In the middle is a lovely composite, a trideo image his computers have assembled from the various 2-D cameras, and it shows the broad plaza on the Island side of the gate. Even in the best of times there is not much outbound traffic through this plaza, as those who do business on the Island generally have the means by which they can avoid the Third Mainland Bridge. But since Lekan likes to occasionally feel that he is making a positive contribution to the people of this city, he has ordered the plaza cleared so as to prevent any injuries to bystanders. He does not believe the runners will be careful or precise with their fire when they arrive at the gate, and he has instructed his people to err on the side of thoroughness over precision. Should any bystanders decide to ignore his order to clear the area, they likely will not live long enough to regret their mistake.

One ARO, the one on his right and at the bottom of a column of images, keeps changing. He has instructed the system to lock on the small, white car holding the surviving runners, and so as they leave the range of one security camera and come into the range of another, the screen blinks and shows the next block they are entering. It is hypnotic, for the images are largely the same— the vehicle starts at the bottom of the screen, then moves to the top, then the scene flickers and it is back on the bottom again. Bottom, then top, bottom then top. Plenty of movement without any real indicator of progress.

He is frustrated by some of the detours and indirections they take, but he cannot expect them simply to go into the middle of his web without delay or interference. It is even possible that they have some idea what he is doing and what lies ahead for them, for their overly elaborate destruction of his packages shows that they possess a certain degree of cleverness. It does not matter, though, if they have figured it out or not. They are outmanned, outgunned, out-maged.

Another of his AROs is a map of the Island that shows the runners' progress so that he knows when they are getting close. And as he glimpses at this, he sees that they are almost there, and that the final small blockade he has set up is pushing them off Ring Road as they fly southeast, and they now only have one choice. They will hit the ramp, curve onto the gate, and then they will be his.

They whip around the ramp, skidding on most of it, seemingly on the verge of losing all grip on the road and sliding into a wall and making it too easy to kill them. It would be a shame for the hastily improvised set piece to end that way.

But they stay clear of the wall, they make it the entire length of the ramp, and for the first time they are visible on his trideo image, a small white dot coming at him. By his guess, they have just over three seconds before they are engulfed in bullets and flame and whatever else his people throw at them.

Except something is wrong. He leans forward so he can look closer at the trideo image. Those are not headlights he is seeing. They are doors. The car is sideways, and it is still moving.

He speaks immediately, and he is miked in so the entire security team can hear him.

"They're doing something," he says. "Move on them, now, now!"

He does not know what they are doing. There is nowhere to go, just an administrative building between the bridge and the lagoon.

There are bullets flying now, invisible except for the impacts they make, and some of them hit the car, but it does not seem to be slowing down. There must be magic out there, too, but Lekan has no way of seeing it, and it, too, does not seem to be doing anything to the car. Perhaps they did not have enough time to adjust to the car's unexpected trajectory, as it was a brief moment between when the car appeared and when it slammed through the double doors of the administrative building.

He would not have thought the doorway wide enough to admit a car, but he is unhappily wrong. The car is inside, and he had not bothered to patch into the administrative cameras.

"Get me a view inside that building!" he yells. "What's going on in there?"

It does not take long, but it is still almost too long, because when the new ARO appears in front of him it shows a white car on the other end of a plain lobby, approaching a glass wall. On the other side of the wall seems to be an employee break room. On the other side of that is a patio that overlooks the lagoon. Lekan cannot imagine that anyone ever uses the patio, for the normal scents of the lagoon do little to encourage the appetite.

It is over in a brief flurry of broken glass as the vehicle crashes through two glass walls. In the break room tables and chairs scatter, flying in all directions, some of them crushed as the car passes over them. Lekan believes that three, possibly all four of the car's tires are flat. The rims of the car will likely be no good after this, but Lekan does not believe that is a significant concern. The car, he now understands, has one last purpose, and then they will be done with it.

The railing that separates the patio from the lagoon is metal, and most of its rust is hidden by lumpy green paint. The railing is held up by concrete that rises up about a third of a meter. A part of Lekan's mind, the part that is not being consumed by rage, takes a moment to wonder just how the physics of the situation will work out. How much speed was the vehicle able to retain on its trip through the lobby?

He is not getting audio from the administration building security cameras, but he imagines he can hear the engine revving as the driver makes a final appeal to the vehicle. It looks to be gaining speed as it approaches the railing.

The front end of the car hits the wall. It is too low. If it had hit the railing, maybe they would have had a chance of carrying over the concrete. But they won't. The car will crumple, then stop, and they will be his.

And it hits, like he had anticipated, and the front end of the car starts to crumple, and Lekan is not sure because the part of the image he is watching most intently is blurry and dark, it is like trying to find your reflection in a muddy pool of water during an earthquake, but he thinks he can make out the metahuman forms in the car, and he thinks they are moving in the helpless manner of those who have not been adequately able to prepare for the impact they are experiencing. Perhaps the steering column has already crushed the driver's chest; perhaps one or more of them is already dead.

But then there is movement he does not expect. There is no reason for the back of the car, or any part of the car for that matter, to rise into the air, yet that is what the back of the car is doing. It is rising up, and it is still moving forward, so the car is flipping. It flies up, the whole car does, like the arm of a trebuchet, and it is launched, flipping over, clearing the railing—well, clearing the parts of the railing that it does not tear through. What matters to Lekan is that it is not stopped, but somehow the vehicle has found a way to keep moving, if only a bit farther. It is upside-down, but it is still rotating its slow roll, and Lekan wonders briefly if he is watching this happen live or if it is a replay, but then it hits the lagoon. It has made almost a complete turn, so that the back end hits with a *slap* that Lekan can almost hear, then the rest of the vehicle lands in the water and quickly goes under.

Lekan is watching closely, he is leaning forward, he is waiting to see if any doors or windows open or if there are signs of movement, but there isn't any, though the thorough murk of the lagoon means that there could be an entire tribal naming ceremony occurring under there and he wouldn't see it. But the runners, if any of them still survive, have to surface sometime. He will watch as much of water as he can until he can firmly believe that that are dead.

Then some security guards finally arrive on the patio, and Lekan praises their names, even though he does not know the particular names of people, or even the units, currently involved. They run toward the ruined railing and look into the water, and they only hesitate a moment before firing numerous bullets into the water where air bubbles are rising from the sinking car. Lekan hopes bodies will now rise to the surface, but it is possible that so much lead is hitting the runners that they are sinking down into a final resting place in the slimy deep. Though in truth, the lagoon seldom rises to a height of more than two meters, so their bodies must be content with resting in the slimy shallows.

The firing stops. There is nothing left to fire at. There is no sign of anything living. Also no sign of anything dead. Nothing but water.

Lekan considers dragging the lagoon, but that plan has several flaws—it would be expensive, it could cover much ground and still not find anything, and it could possibly disturb things on the bottom of the lagoon that are better left alone.

So the runners may be dead, or perhaps, if they are fortunate in ways seldom seen among the people of Lagos, they are not. Either way, Lekan is satisfied. He had intended to send a message that if you cross Olabode Lekan, you will end up dead. But what he might end up with is the message that if you cross Olabode Lekan, you will wind up either dead or floating in Lagos Lagoon, and he finds that to be a satisfactory outcome.

He sends out an order allowing most of his officers to return to their posts, and he shuts down most of his AROs. He will go and look out his window for a time and take in a view that is comfortingly solid. He will look at the lagoon, because from this height, even that water looks pretty and soothing.

The lagoon is shallow, but it is broad. There are shores of the lagoon that are far away, far enough that the line between land and water is mostly just a hint of color seen through the hovering dust. What happens on those shores is far out of sight of anyone in the city.

A disgruntled ammit patrols one of those shores. It has not had a good day. To humans, the lagoon is a hostile environment, but to the ammit it is a good home, full of stupid, slow, poorly armored prey. The waters are calm, allowing the ammit to float along at will and find whatever it needs to find.

The water has been unsettled today. There were waves in the water, and if the ammit's small-small brain had any desire to deal with matters of physics, it would know that the waves of the type it saw were impossible. It might even be curious about what, or who, caused those waves. But it is an ammit, and all it knows is that the disturbance that roiled its world was annoying.

But things have settled. The waters have calmed, and there is a hint of food in the water. It is a smell both familiar and strange, but the ammit has enough memory to know that when it has smelled this scent before, it has resulted in a good meal, one that came with few difficulties.

It approaches the smell carefully. In its brain it cannot recall things of this scent ever putting up much of a fight, but it has its way of doing things, and that has helped it survive to this point, so it sees no reason to deviate from it now.

From above, it is still, its broad back poking out of the water here and there, gliding without discernible effort. All the effort takes place under the water as it paddles its stubby legs through the murky water.

Its eyes poke above the water, giving it a limited look at its prey. Its vision is not good, but it can see enough to know that it will be a sizable meal. Had the creature known anything about home refrigeration, it would have known that that is what it would need to store the leftovers, for it would have more than it would need for a single feeding.

The thing with the scent is even more motionless than the ammit. It is not even gliding through the water. It is just floating there. It has perhaps been dead for a time, but its smell has not grown unappetizing, which is all that matters to the ammit.

The approach is slow, but the final lunge will be fast, and it is almost time for it. Just a handful of centimeters more, and it will strike. Then the distance is crossed, and the time is here. The ammit turns to scaly lightning and strikes.

It is perhaps charitable that the blow that strikes the ammit happens so fast that the beast does not have time to feel disappointed that it will not be getting its anticipated food. One moment it is lunging at its meal, the next it is becoming a limp mass due to the knife that has gone through the roof of its mouth and penetrated its brain. It is now still again, and it will stay that way forever.

The mass that was to have been its prey is moving, though. It has stuck its head above water so that we can say that it is not an "it" but rather a "he." In fact, we can say more than that, because as he stands in the shallow water and wades to shore, we can see that it is Cayman.

He comes to shore to find that the boy, the inescapable X-Prime, has made it to shore ahead of him. He is cleaning mud out of his ears. He is looking at the corpse of the ammit Cayman has slain.

"Is it edible?" he asks.

"How the hell would I know?" Cayman says.

"It's kind of like an alligator," X-Prime says. "Alligators are edible."

"You want to sit here, field-strip an ammit, build a fire, and cook it? Or do you want to find a way home?"

X-Prime stands. "Good point," he says.

They begin walking, even though neither knows where they should be going. They operate on instinct, which is nothing new.

They are walking, they are tired, and so of course X-Prime must talk.

"Halim made it away," he says. "I was crawling around the bottom of the lagoon like a lobster or something, and he was gliding along, skimming the bottom, like a manta ray." He pauses. "He's a lot more graceful than I am."

An entire host of dismissive rejoinders come to Cayman's mind, but he is too tired to actually say any of them. The fact that the boy's ego would remain unpunctured does not cheer him.

"But I don't know about the others," X-Prime says. "Agbele Oku and the mouse. I don't know what happened to them."

"They're fine," Cayman says.

"Really?" X-Prime says. "You saw them?"

"No."

"Then how do you know they're—"

"Agbele Oku was okay enough to do the spell that sent us over the railing," Cayman says.

"That's something," X-Prime says. "But not much. She could have died when we hit the water, or while the guards were firing all those bullets. So you don't know that she's okay, or that Groovetooth's okay."

"We're probably never coming back here," Cayman says. "We're never going to see them again. They could be alive, they could be dead, and it wouldn't affect our lives at all. So I'm going to assume they're alive, because I want them to be. And they deserve to be."

X-Prime thinks for a moment, then shrugs. "Okay," he says.

They walk for a time in silence. Cayman enjoys it, X-Prime does not. He finally speaks again.

"You know, I've been thinking. The objects we had—a scalp, a hand, a heart—those are all things a person could do without, if they had the right medical care. And a Global Sandstorm bigwig could certainly afford that sort of thing. So maybe we weren't helping prove Lydia al-Shammar's death—maybe we were just helping convince people that needed convincing."

This time, Cayman is able to summon the energy needed to speak.

"Shut the hell up."

ACKNOWLEDGEMENTS

Many years ago, after the six WizKids *Shadowrun* novels came out, I started poking around for ways the line might be able to continue beyond those books, or for other ways to get *Shadowrun* fiction out. I was very fortunate to find an enthusiastic co-conspirator in this effort in the form of John Helfers. Each year at Gen Con we held meetings to work on what we could do, and each year we inched closer to a solution. Now *Shadowrun* fiction is back, and I get to write some of it, and John gets to edit it and write some, too. I'm happy to have plotted with him all these years, even when it didn't seem like we were getting anywhere, and very pleased to have him as an editor.

Thanks also go out to the entire Catalyst crew who let me play in the *Shadowrun* sandbox and who make the things we try to do so much cooler. From management to the mighty freelancer corps, I get to work with intelligent, funny, interesting people, and I am incredibly lucky to do so.

I also am lucky to share living space with an intelligent, passionate, committed, creative, hard-working, beautiful woman, and I am grateful for her patience, her ideas, her good humor, and her company through it all.

ABOUT THE AUTHOR

Jason M. Hardy is in his thirtieth year of a continuous performance art piece wherein he plays the part of a mime who talks, does not wear makeup, and interacts with physical objects as one normally would. He hopes someone will eventually notice what he's up to, or he may be forced to spend a week standing in a refrigerator box just to make a point. He is also the *Shadowrun* line developer for Catalyst Game Labs and is the author of several previous novels, including the *Shadowrun* novel *Drops of Corruption* and the original fantasy *The Last Prophecies.* He also wrote a book called *Stranded on Earth: A Guide for Misplaced Aliens* for people unwittingly stuck on this planet, of whom there seem to be several.

He lives in Chicago with his wife, son, and daughter.

DARK RESONANCE
BY PHAEDRA WELDON • COMING SOON!

Some Secrets Can Kill You...

Kazuma Tetsu is a technomancer—one of the rare people who can manipulate the Matrix without technology, using only the power of their mind. But he's on a more personal mission—he's searching for his missing sister, Hitori. Following her trail leads him into a tangled web of corp execs, mercenaries, and double-crossing rogues—usually just another day in the Sixth World.

But as Kazuma digs deeper, he uncovers a plot that could bring about the end of the world. Upon seeing a simulation of the technomancer's Resonance Realms, an A.I. has declared it to be its final destination—where it will ascend to a higher plane of consciousness. Actually creating this realm in the Matrix was thought to be impossible—that is, until a gestalt of technomancer minds is formed to use dissonance to open a true gateway to heaven. But opening such a dissonant hole in the Matrix could trigger a new crash, and it's up to a shadowrun team, including a pair of shadowtalkers, the best of the best, to free those technomancers trapped inside the gestalt, and stop the Dark Resonance before it destroys the entire Matrix...

CHAPTER ONE
4 MONTHS AGO

Kazuma Tetsu gasped when the node around him revealed a ravaged world.

At first, he wasn't sure he was in the right place—it looked like a battlefield. There were no trees or grass under a hazy sky of gold and dark smoke. Jagged, silver tiers of once familiar buildings rose into the setting sky like broken bones sticking up through charred, blackened skin.

"Wow, chummer...nice pajamas."

He turned to see a standard, out-of-the-box avatar of a man with dark hair, squared jaw, scruffy chin, and long, dark coat. Yep, generic P.I. from a gaming box.

Kazuma smiled. "Dirk. Nice Dick Tracy motif." He stepped over a puddle of oily water to take the man's offered hand. "Interesting choice of node. This an art piece?"

Dirk shook his head. "Not really. This is a replica made from another node—one a bunch of technomancers nearly died in. They created this to show what almost killed them. But it's just a representation. If you were really on the node right now, you'd become deathly ill."

"Sick from a node?"

"A node totally corrupted, *omae.* I wanted to meet you here so you could see what's creeping along the periphery of your realms. Take a good look at this, Kaz, and don't ever get caught in it. The artists for this call it dark resonance. And that description isn't far off. Memorize, and know it's real." He stepped closer. "Your sister's missing again."

"Yes, I know," Kazuma answered, but he kept looking around at the node. "But I don't think she's submerging this time. I think she's in trouble."

"I think you're right." Dirk reached out and put his hand on Kazuma's arm. "There's not a lot more I can do for you. You're going to have to look for her on your own. But there are a few things I can advise you to do, and you should get quicker results."

He had Kazuma's full attention.

"Even after you let me know that Hitori had showed up a few weeks after the fun at Cup O' Sin, I kept doing research because a name kept coming up. Caliban."

"You mean like *The Tempest*?"

"Yeah. Like that. Do two things." He moved in close, so Kazuma could see every painted cell of the comic book icon. "I need you to change your online handle from Dancer to Soldat. Got that, *omae*?"

"Soldat?"

"It means soldier."

"Yeah, yeah."

"It's better than Dancer. That's a drek name. Then I want you to refine your searches to include the name Caliban. Just keep Hitori's name and add Caliban. Got it?"

"Yeah..."

"Good." Dirk stood back. "That's good. Do those two things and you should be reunited with her soon. Or if not, you'll definitely attract some interesting company."

CHAPTER TWO

GiTm0

Welcome back to GiTm0, *omae*; your last connection was 13 hours, 9 minutes, 22 seconds ago.

BOLOs

Just a reminder—this board's got less than six hours before it terminates in your comms. Send your sprites out twenty-four hours after that for the new link.

New Shadowrunner handles to look out for: Mangle, Blackwater, blessie89, and DongleSave. Full list available [Link][Guest], but don't read the list online. And don't forget, these runners are out for the nuyen, and they don't give a damn about us.

Remember, GOD is always watching.

NeW oNLiNE

* Twenty more known technomancers vanish from Novatech Arcology. No trace. Families won't even acknowledge they're missing. [Link]

* Saw in an early morning feed that Contagion Games' latest MMORPG, TechnoHack, crashed another node early this morning, toppling several regions of play and causing a semi-brownout with a Matrix Gateway near Seattle. CEO Ferdinand Bellex held a press conference apologizing for the downtime, and promptly blamed the failure on the resurgence of decking units not syncing with the Nodes. He also made a few odd comments about technomancers attacking their mainframe, and is in negotiations with Knight Errant for tighter security to prevent this type of breach again. Bellex also announced a new UV node opening within the week that should relieve traffic to their home node and prevent anymore grid inconveniences once Knight Errant's got their systems firmly in place. Anyone in here played this game? We need reasons why Bellex even brought us up. [Link][Review Posts]

* A breach in security at an Ares facility in Lower Los Angeles has the Pueblo CC buzzing around with hi-tech might—though the local corps spokesperson insists nothing was stolen or tampered

with. This is the fifth in a series of random glitches plaguing the company two days after an employee in the personnel department was fired. Coincidence? [Link]

  * In a similar thread, Cup O' Sin coffee house—whose name was in the news cycles a few years ago when it was attacked by hackers—is back in the news. One day after the firing of the above mentioned Ares employee, the shop experienced the same glitches with the establishment's PAN. When a Frappuccino machine exploded in an employee's face, she blamed it on one of the shop's regular customers—that customer was identified as the same employee fired from Ares the day before. When no commlink was found on him, the man was beaten to death. During his autopsy, they found an internal comm. Things are not happy out there for us, people. Always have a commlink or decking unit visible. If you got jacks, use 'em for show.

EYES OPEN
>>>>Open Thread/SubNode221.322.1
>>>>Thread Access Restrictions: <Yes/**No**>
>>>>Format: <**Open Post**/Comment Only/Read Only>
>>>>File Attachment: <Yes/**No**>
>>>>Thread Descriptor: **Denial**
>>>>Thread Posted By User: Shyammo

- Hey Shyammo! Thanks for finding that article on the missing Novatech Employees. I noticed there hasn't been any comment at all except a blip on a late night vid-squawk. In fact, when I saw the story carried only once, and then it wasn't carried over to the other networks—I started to wonder if I'd seen it at all.
- 404Flames

- Not sure they were all employees. Read the article. Says most were employees and the others were just members of employee families. What kind of harsh piece of drek do you have to be to deny your family member is missing?
- MoonShine

- We need to look deeper into joint ventures. Corporations working in tandem on projects involving technomancers. Look for tags like electronic magic, hacking research, dark waters or caliban.
- Soldat

- Hey Sol, where you been? It's been ages since you posted.
- HipOldGuy

- Did that bit of intel you were checking help, Soldat? Did you find her?
- 404Flames

- I didn't find her, but I found something that might help. Which is why I'm throwing the suggestion on those tags out there. We need to watch for the corps working together. Possibly forming hush-hush covenants when it comes to technomancers.
- Soldat

- What did you find, Soldat? You sound like you saw or read something.
- Netcat

- I'll get on that, Sol. I've already started looking into Contagion Games and their issues. I wasn't happy old Bellex felt the need to bring us into his problems. If the guy's team can't build a decent game, take responsibility. Don't go slinging mud. I'll see if anything pops up.
- HipOldGuy

- I don't want to say yet, Netcat. I've got Silk working on a few things. I'll post when there's more. It's just that…have any of you felt something weird? And I mean weird while in AR or the streams?
- Soldat

- Thanks ahead of time on that, Hip. I always like to make sure you guys know how much you're appreciated out there. I was happy I didn't have to report any of us missing this week. Last week's number took a toll.
- RoxJohn

❂ Hey Hip, been doing a little grade work for Contagion. I'll check out the game. Been a little curious myself. Might be a little more nuyen to be made if they keep breaking the Matrix like that.

❂ Venerator

❂ Sol, what do you mean weird? I'm asking because last time I submerged, I did run across something. It wasn't in the streams, but it was there waiting when I left. And I had the feeling I was being watched.

❂ Netcat

❂ Yeah...Ten gone in a matter of a week. Rox, did you find out anything more about their disappearance? Like did they all work for a corp, or were they even connected?

❂ EasterBunnyun

❂ That's close to what I felt, Netcat. Almost like something's on the edge in there, on the outside looking in. I'll make sure to get back when I know more.

❂ Soldat

❂ You know I can't give out that information on the board, Easter. But if you click this [Link] I can give it to you.

❂ RoxJohn

CHAPTER THREE

HORIZON ARCHIVE ANNEX
LOS ANGELES
RETIRED DS NODE
THURSDAY EVENING

Kazuma Tetsu's living persona, a red-headed ninja, stood within the drab, gray-walled Virtual Reality of the Horizon node, sword held in front of him. An antique desk with a worn, leather briefcase visible in the open lower drawer stood between him and his opponent. He raised his weapon as the blade reflected his opponent's icon.

The icon, a simple, snarling, drooling white wolf, looked like one of those out-of-the-box personas Kazuma had seen with the resurgence of decking units.

He didn't have time to linger inside the node and fight the persona of whoever this was. He needed to do a bit of technomancer hand-waving. A diversion—something with enough power and strength behind it to distract and detain this bastard long enough for him to grab the information and get out.

The use of his skin-linking echo was draining, but not enough to alarm him just yet. Kazuma hadn't planned on compiling, given that it would require a bit more of his stamina than he could afford. If he hadn't physically been next to the node and accessed it remotely, perhaps a fight would be justified. But not right now.

He moved his sword up and around and slowly re-sheathed it on his back. The white wolf roared and drooled as it showed its teeth and pushed its back end up as its front went down. Drek—it was going to attack within seconds. *Have to be a fast compile...*

With his hands now free, Kazuma held them out to his side, palms up and opened his senses to the whisper and buzz of the Matrix around him. The space between them abruptly swirled with wisps of incandescent smoke filled with 1s and 0s of data. With his arms held out he inhaled and drew those wisps to him, brought his imagination to bear, and thought into sharp focus as he spoke to the datasphere, gave it purpose, and asked it to stand in the enemy's way.

The Matrix answered him with action as the wisps formed ribbons of colors that spun and danced before him. The 1s and 0s wrote themselves into existence as he called forth its form...that of a Bengal tiger. Twice the size of the wolf hacker and for a brief time, far more clever. Because Kazuma liked to give his sprites the freedom of imagination. This decker might think he knew what he was up against, but he would be wrong.

Feeling the drain impact his physical body, Kazuma took a step back as his newly compiled Paladin Sprite roared in the face of the white wolf.

The white wolf answered with an attack. It vaulted upward, claws extended as the user's voice came through. *"I'm gonna take you down!"*

Kazuma's Paladin sprang forward and intercepted the wolf. Both beasts crashed into a side wall, then the tiger burst into a cloud of small, iridescent, yet iron-clad butterflies that flew into the wolf's face, knocking off chunks of it.

While the two programs tangled, Kazuma grabbed the briefcase, turned, and ran. The Paladin would fight long enough for him to disengage from the node, and its essence would return to the web-like whispers of the data-sphere.

Weaving his way through the endless maze of corridors, Kazuma used his katana to cut away the lingering ghosts of previous security protocols, now too weak to be useful. While slicing and dicing, he considered his options. Before big, ugly, and drooly showed up, he'd planned to open the briefcase and gather only the information he found that referred to his sister and the name Caliban. He hadn't counted on anyone else being in the node—much less wanting what looked like discarded files. But there wasn't time for that now, so he decided to get the briefcase as far from the node as possible. It would be simple to compile a courier sprite and have it squirrel the briefcase away to a secure location in the Matrix, where he could retrieve it later.

Unfortunately—this node wasn't connected to any grid.

No outside connections to the Matrix itself.

But there was a wireless signal nearby that allowed *him* access.

Boss!

Ponsu, Kazuma's registered sprite, appeared beside him as a large, golden origami swan. She was his first sprite—a creature born and nurtured within the Matrix. She contained information from both himself and from the resonance streams that pulsed like rivers around him. She—and he called her a *she* because she spoke to him in a soft, feminine voice (not the voice he'd purposely given her either)—had been with him for over two years, his constant companion within the Matrix.

Kazuma shoved the briefcase into her beak. The node itself wasn't connected to the Matrix—but Kazuma was. He'd never tried it before—but it stood to reason that *he* could be the conduit between the two. "Get this away from here—just hide it safely in the Matrix somewhere. I'll get it later."

You want me to leave you alone? I can't do that–have you noticed that big, ugly wolf back there?

"Yeah, that's kinda why I'm running." Kazuma glanced back, sensing the dissipation of the paladin. It hadn't lasted as long as he'd liked. The wolf might look generic, but its strength wasn't.

He looked back at Ponsu. "Just get it out of here. I've got this guy mad enough to follow me."

But the sprite was looking down the corridor behind them. *Let me take care of the fool. I can–*

"Ponsu! *Please!*"

She gave him a lingering look with iridescent eyes before vanishing.

"YOU GIVE ME THAT BACK, YOU ASSHOLE!" shouted the wolf as it charged into the hall.

Running along his escape route, Kazuma jumped out of VR and back into the disorienting world of reality. The wolf-hacker would have to leave by his own way in—most likely via a deck. Kazuma assumed they were close by. *Physically* close by. The wolf's user had to be *in* the annex and physically wired to the node in order to be inside—and they weren't a technomancer. That much Kazuma knew.

Before attempting this harebrained idea, Kazuma had disabled the two other terminals in the building that had been daisy-chained to the node he needed. But somehow the jackass had managed to fix the sabotage. Should have made sure they couldn't be fixed—but he hadn't wanted to draw attention to himself in case another tech took a look.

Hindsight. Twenty-twenty. All that. Dammit.

Coming out of VR hot was always a bit of a disaster for Kazuma—re-orientation took a few minutes as he stumbled blindly from where he'd propped his body in an office chair. Compiling that paladin had cost him a bit, not to mention Ponsu's escape to the Matrix. The dim room grew dimmer as he took his hand from the node's outer shell and took several deep, stabilizing breaths. He needed to get himself and his gear out of the annex before the idiot wolf hacker tripped a security wire he hadn't disabled.

The deck was still packed in the small bag, but he kept his commlink visible. His datajack was still prominently positioned on his temple, and he kept his hair pulled back to emphasize its presence. He wouldn't let anyone—especially his employer—know he was a technomancer. Not exactly an advertisable skill nowadays. More like a curse that could get him killed, or vanished.

Like so many others.

He carried a Fairlight headset, the very first commlink he'd bought. But if anyone took a hard look at it, they'd find the thing was factory-modeled. Just like the deck. No upgrades. Not even an app for the most mundane tasks of being a KE tech. His partner, Silk, called his bluff all the time—hammered home that he needed to at least pay for the upgrades and have them visible.

"If you're going to live the lie, then live it right," was her constant advice.

But he didn't need them. Which was a major plus when it came to expenses.

Kazuma had the commlink connection set in place on his wrist, but not turned on. He managed to stumble back into the chair in front of the desk when the door to the terminal room burst open.

He turned, genuinely startled, as an ork in a Horizon Security uniform came in, weapon drawn. Clearing his throat, he presented the guard with his best smile. "Sir—"

"Show me some I.D.!" the ork barked.

Kazuma nodded quickly, taking in the security officer's yellowed tusks protruding from his jaw over his upper lip. The ork's jaw was built forward, allowing for the added weight and space for the powerful teeth. His small, pointed ears twitched, and Kazuma could smell his fear. Something was wrong within the building itself. And whatever that was had this security guard spooked.

Damn that wolf-hacker.

Kazuma slowly reached into his suit jacket and retrieved the single fold wallet that held his SIN, offering it to the ork. The guard kept his weapon trained on Kazuma, but managed to shove the SIN into his wrist commlink. Though Kazuma could see the AR window in the guard's PAN, he already knew what it would show.

Morimoto Toshi, Human, Knight Errant Supervisor, Birthplace: Chiba, Japan. The image would be that of an older human. Kazuma had used nano-paste to change his face and hid the arching points of his ears beneath a bushy gray wig.

The ork appeared to be satisfied and handed his wallet back. "Sorry, Mr. Morimoto, but the silent alarm got tripped—over on the south side of the building. We suspect there's a hacker in the node. Luckily this is an off-grid system. We've got people looking around the building for them."

Damn it. The hacker *had* tripped the alarm. *Baka.* He nodded as he carefully made a show of unhooking his deck from the terminal. "That's quite all right, sir. Are you here to help an old man out of the building for safety?"

The ork was about to answer when the door opened and a human dressed in the same uniform as the ork stepped inside. "Brigg," the smaller man said with a narrowing glance at Kazuma. "Got anything?"

"No," the ork named Brigg said. "This is Mr. Morimoto—he was here working on the security system for KE." He leaned in close to give a hoarse but audible whisper. "I think he was in the system when the alarm got tripped. He doesn't look so good."

The human moved past Brigg and glared harder at what he perceived to be an elderly Asian man. "You need a crashcart, old man?"

"No, no." Kazuma shook his head. "It's just—your friend is right. I wasn't prepared for the tertiary failing of subsidiary drives, causing a cascading failure that—"

The human guard put up his hand. "I got it, I got it."

Kazuma smiled inwardly. It was always better to blind them with bullshit. The key was to know *who* and *when* to bullshit. Coming off as a tech-head security flunkie could be disarming enough.

"I am sorry to be so much trouble." He smiled as he continued packing his gear into his bag and stood.

Ponsu was back, hovering just inside of Kazuma's peripheral vision within his own AR. She gave him a nod to let him know the briefcase was hidden. Nothing to see here—and nothing to find in his deck or his commlink.

The human nodded at the terminal. "You finished? 'Cause we think the auto dial's already contacted your people's security unit—that happens in a time like this. You want to wait for them?"

No, he did not want to meet them at all. Fooling these two had been easy—but fooling a Knight Errant officer? Or worse, GOD, in case Ponsu had triggered the attention of the Grid Overwatch Division spiders. Kazuma wasn't ready to test his skills at disguise just yet. "Yes—I would very much like to be here when they arrive. May I gather my things and meet them at the front—"

But as he spoke, the room fell into total darkness. Though the node itself wasn't on the grid, the annex's security system was. Kazuma unconsciously tapped into the faint wireless signal, asking Ponsu to check on the blackout. Within seconds the swan appeared in a new AR window to his left.

Boss—all the power's still on—otherwise the network wouldn't be viable. The lights are still in operation.

He cursed under his breath. It was dark, but the power was still on. In theory, the lights were on as well—only none of them could see. That meant the blindness was *magically* induced. And there was no telling how far the range went, or if the hacker himself was immune. But Kazuma was sure the wolf-hacker was still in the building, waiting on him.

A single shot echoed outside the small room's darkness. Kazuma didn't need sight to know *both* guards had drawn their weapons.

"They've cut the power," the ork said. There was a *click*. "Mullens, this is Brigg. We heard gunfire."

Another pause, then static before, "Yeah, we're in the dark here—you?"

"Yeah, us too. We're in the center basement. Mr. Morimoto is here from KE doing work—we're gonna try and find the shooter."

"Copy. We'll advance along the south ring. You go north."

"Roger."

Kazuma winced at the exchange. They'd used *open* communication—voice activated. Any hacker worth his cybereyes would have already had taps on bus to bus. Basically, they'd just given out their plan to the shooter. Unless it was code for something else. But he didn't really believe that.

A small light appeared in the ork's palm, illuminating the room in a greenish glow. Whether the ork knew he was countering magic with magic was uncertain—but it was enough. Kazuma could see their faces—prints in shadows and emerald ocher. "That's about as big as I can make it, Chief."

"That's good," said Chief, the human. "Mr. Morimoto, I need you to stay here. This room has a steel door. Once Briggs and I step out, I want you to lock it and just stay calm. I'm sure the KE cops will be here in a few seconds. Can you do that?"

"*So-ka,*" he said.

"Do you have a weapon?" Briggs asked.

"*Ee-ae,*" he lied. "I'll be fine."

Once the two were outside, Kazuma touched his watch. He could see the glow in the dark. The magic had only affected the environment, which meant it had vulnerabilities. Like the ork's light and the illumination from an electronic device. Using the watch as a flashlight, he found a utility drawer, and in it a small, battery-powered light.

He pulled up a minimized window with a chewing gum-smacking blonde inside it. **>You get all that?**

>*Yeah*, she said as her persona blinked. Her gaze looked to be tracking something Kazuma couldn't see. >*Wolf dude pulled the fire alarm in the south side.*

Fire alarm? Kazuma moaned. **>So KE isn't coming?**

>*Oh, they're coming all right. I'm just making sure a few red lights stay red long enough. Your car's where you parked it. I found a rigger nearby–she's a few tables over from me. Seems I picked the right place.*

>She with this wolf-hacker?

>*That's my guess. I'll draw their attention away. Ponsu's got the strategy. Take care, and remember the GODs are watching.* Her window disappeared.

After surveying the area one more time to make sure he hadn't left anything visible that could be traced back to him, Kazuma opened the door carefully, wincing when it made a *click* that resounded throughout the darkened corridor. Hooking his bag around his shoulder, he decided the flashlight would bring too much attention. Since the blackout was magic, then a camera should see just fine.

Mentally reaching out to the closest data-sphere whisper, he opened the back door of the building's security network—which he'd helped install, of course. A new window appeared in his AR—giving him a fully lit corridor on both sides. The angle was going to throw him off, since he was going to see himself coming down a hallway instead of what was directly in front of him. "Ponsu—you got the strategy?"

Right, Boss.

A grid of the building's corridors, rooms, and exits appeared in a window to his left. He noted the flashing red dot telling him where he was. The basement. One level up to street side. There were three possible exits out of the annex—but he didn't see any vehicles nearby that might belong to the wolf-hacker. Unfortunately, he hadn't made a contingency plan—never considered anyone else would want the information. Another fact Silk was going to yell at him for.